D0981235

Other Books by John Scarne

Scarne's Guide to Casino Gambling
The Mafia Conspiracy
Scarne's New Complete Guide to Gambling
Scarne's Encyclopedia of Games
Scarney Dice—40 New Kinds of Dice Games
The Woman's Guide to Gambling
The Odds Against Me
Scarney—25 New Kinds of Skill Games
The Amazing World of John Scarne
Skarney—30 New Card Games
Scarne on Teeko
Scarne on Magic Tricks
Scarne on Card Tricks
Scarne on Cards
Scarne on Dice
Three Card Monte

by John Scarne

WORLD'S FOREMOST
GAMBLING AUTHORITY

Scarne's Guide to Modern Poker

by
John Scarne
World's Foremost Gambling Authority

A FIRESIDE BOOK
Published by Simon & Schuster, Inc.
NEW YORK

First Fireside Edition, 1984
Published by Simon & Schuster, Inc.
Simon & Schuster Building
Rockefeller Center
1230 Avenue of the Americas
New York, New York 10020

Designed by Irving Perkins

Manufactured in the United States of America

Printed by The Murray Printing Company
Bound by The Book Press, Inc.

10 9 8 7 6 5 4 3 2 1
10 9 8 7 6 5 4 3 Pbk.

Library of Congress Cataloging in Publication Data
Scarne, John.
Scarne's Guide to modern poker.

Includes index.
1. Poker. I. Title. II. Title: Guide to modern poker.
GV1251.S25 1979 794.4'12 79-19651

ISBN: 0-671-24796-4
ISBN: 0-671-53076-3 Pbk.

DEDICATION

In memory of my beloved father, who taught me my first card trick and with whom I played my first Poker game

Contents

Introduction

In his other classic books that are universally recognized as the most definitive and informative volumes about games and gambling, the Introductions invariably carry a line to the effect that "only John Scarne could have written this book." Once again, that claim is true, for here, in turning his talents and expertise to the most popular of all card games—America's 65 million Poker players compile the astronomical sum of $100 billion a year in the amounts wagered—Scarne has gone far beyond anything ever previously published on the subject. This book will become a necessity for every Poker club, or for regular less-organized sessions for that matter, because it includes everything required to settle arguments that inevitably arise during play. Once games were played "According to Hoyle," but now smart-money players throughout the world know that the modern rules of all gambling are "According to Scarne." And the game of Poker, never static, has evolved and changed so much over the years that the countless so-called Hoyle authors would probably barely recognize it.

Scarne's goal in this book is to give the Poker player the most scientifically reliable information and the best possible playing strategy for each of the more than one hundred most popular and commercialized Poker games extant. He presents a host of highly guarded Poker secrets which, if used intelligently, will make the average player as Poker wise as the top professionals in Las Vegas and other gambling havens. He teaches the reader how to protect himself, or herself (more than half of the Poker players in this country are women), against the Poker cheat, who isn't necessarily only the professional cheat but might well be someone you invite into your regular friendly Friday night game.

The famed magazine writer and editor Sidney Carroll aptly wrote, "To call Scarne an outstanding expert on games of skill and chance is to praise him with a faint damn. He is by all odds the world's greatest." And the late John Lardner wrote, "Scarne is to games what Einstein is to physics." John Scarne's previous books on gambling have proven the validity of such statements, and have become the standard works on such topics as casino gambling, cards, dice games and magic. (Scarne is no less a magician than he is a gambling authority. John Northern Hilliard, manager of Thurston the Magician, said of Scarne when he was only nineteen, "I have yet to see anyone who surpasses him in originality and sheer skill of hand; his skill is unbelievable.") John Scarne is a man of such outstanding talents and knowledge in such varied fields that it would be well to stop quoting what others have said about him, and put down what he himself says about this new Poker book. Quite simply it is: "This is the best and most practical book for a games player that I have ever written."

SIMON AND SCHUSTER

Scarne's Guide to Modern Poker

1

Poker: America's Biggest Gambling Game

AMERICA'S $100 BILLION GAMBLING HANDLE

Poker is without a doubt the most popular international card game in history. The major reason for this worldwide popularity is due to the countless Poker variations that suit the temperaments of card players of all nations. In addition, Poker fits any card-game situation, whether it is a serious money game among topnotch gamblers in New York or Las Vegas or a penny ante game for the entertainment of family and friends in the United States, Italy, England, Hong Kong, and the world over. Poker, for sure, is by far the most popular gambling game in America today and is as characteristically American as baseball, hot dogs and apple pie. In fact, many of our most famous Presidents were Poker enthusiasts.

My 1978 nationwide survey of Poker gambling in the United States shows that it is the leading private and commercialized gambling game in the nation both in the number of participants and the amount of money involved, despite all the federal, state and local restrictions against it. Poker's betting handle is about double the combined total money volume of all the legalized gambling casinos situated in Nevada, Atlantic City, Puerto Rico, Aruba, Curaçao, St. Maartens, the Bahamas, Haiti and elsewhere in the Caribbean Islands. Today about 65 million adult Americans, of whom 37 million are women and 28 million are men, are gambling the astronomical sum of $100 billion annually at Poker.

Before 1930 or thereabouts Poker was exclusively a man's game.

Today the weaker sex, with its 37 million Poker adherents, outnumbers male Poker players by 9 million. Every day millions of women now gamble with one another in thousands of private homes and at card clubs, and more millions gamble with men every day in the tens of thousands of mixed Poker games. My survey reveals that the reason for the 9 million more female than male Poker players in America lies in the continuous police raids (federal, state and local) on clubs and private homes where men are suspected of illegal card playing. Most law enforcement agencies think twice before raiding an all-women's Poker, Rummy or Bridge game. As far as I can ascertain, in the past twenty years only ten illegally operated all-women's card games were raided by police in the United States. When we compare this to the hundreds of police raids conducted weekly all over the country on various card or Poker clubs patronized by men only, we can readily understand why more women than men play Poker. Although women Poker players outnumber male players by 9 million, the yearly total betting handle for women is $30 billion as compared to $70 billion for men.

SCARNE AND THE LAS VEGAS WORLD SERIES OF POKER

Today's most celebrated and biggest money Poker tournament is the annual Las Vegas World Series of Poker. The top winner of this Poker extravaganza takes home a few hundred thousand dollars in prize money plus achieving the glory of being hailed everywhere as the World's Poker Champion for the year. The publicity given this tournament by the national and international press and television has not only made an obscure Texas Poker game named "Hold Em" (see pages 212–16) popular throughout the globe, but it has stimulated Poker playing the world over by making millions of new players.

In late December 1975, I appeared as a guest star on the Merv Griffin national television show, which devoted its entire ninety minutes to big-time Poker games and the annual Las Vegas World Series of Poker. Other guests on the show included Benny Binion, Johnny Moss, Jack Strauss, and Poker player and television star Jack Klugman.

Benny Binion and his son, Jack, are the owners of the highly publicized Horseshoe Casino, situated in Glitter Gulch in downtown Las Vegas, where once a year they host the World Series of Poker. Johnny Moss, dean of the Las Vegas big-time Poker players, has won more than $8 million during his Poker-playing career—and has lost it at the Las Vegas dice tables. Moss was the first to win the World Series of

Poker tournament more than once. The other big-time gambler to appear on the Griffin show was the big six-foot seven-inch Texas Poker whiz Jack Strauss, a man who throughout his life has bet on most anything that moves including a cockroach race. He once bet $250,000 on a pair of hidden nines in a Seven Card Stud game and was called by Benny Binion with a pair of hidden jacks.

The last half hour of the *Merv Griffin Show* was devoted to John Scarne and his card miracles. Griffin had had a Poker table with cards and chips set up on stage. The four television cameras were several feet away, ready to spot every finger movement I made from four different sides. "This will be fun," I thought to myself, "with four television cameras on top of me and three of the world's top Poker players seated at the same table with me to try and spot any flaws in my card manipulations."

Seated at the table at my left was Benny Binion, followed by Johnny Moss, Jack Strauss and Jack Klugman, with Merv Griffin seated at my extreme right. My performance began when Griffin picked up the deck from the table, opened and shuffled the deck several times, then handed the cards to me and remarked, "Scarne, you're on."

I looked at each of my Poker-playing adversaries and said, "Gentlemen, I shall begin my manipulative demonstration by performing a card trick that I have had the pleasure of performing at the White House in Washington, D.C., for Presidents Franklin D. Roosevelt, Harry S. Truman, Dwight D. Eisenhower and their guests." I then handed Binion the deck and had him select a card, mark it for identification and tear a corner off the selected card, return it to the deck, shuffle it, and hand the shuffled deck to me. After receiving the deck, I immediately spread the deck face up ribbon fashion across the table with my right hand, and with my left hand produced my wallet from my inside coat pocket and placed it on the table alongside the spread-out deck. The wallet was completely enclosed on its four sides by twelve tight-fitting different-colored rubber bands. I slowly removed the rubber bands from the wallet and out came Binion's selected marked card minus the corner. Griffin quickly matched the torn corner and remarked, "It fits perfectly."

However, as expected, it was a Poker-dealing trick that most impressed the three big-time Poker players (Binion, Moss, Strauss) and it went as follows: As dealer, I shuffled the deck several times, then had the deck cut by Griffin and Binion. I picked up the cut deck and dealt everyone a five-card Poker hand, including myself. When the Poker hands were exposed, they each revealed four of a kind—but naturally, I held the four aces.

Upon completion of this Poker feat, Griffin turned to Benny Binion and asked, "Mr. Binion, do you permit John Scarne to gamble at your Horseshoe Casino?"

Binion, wearing his characteristic smile, replied, *"I would not let John Scarne gamble at the Horseshoe Casino even if he wore boxing gloves!"*

The World Series of Poker is usually played in May of each year in a roped-off corner of the Horseshoe Casino, where the Black Jack tables have been temporarily replaced by a number of oval-shaped green felt-topped Poker tables. Adjacent to this roped-off area in horseshoe-shaped glass-enclosed case is $1 million, in one hundred $10,000 bills.

The idea of running a championship Poker tournament was first brought to Benny Binion's attention in 1968 by Tom Moore, a Reno gambler and casino owner. The Horseshoe Casino hosted the first World Series of Poker Tournament in 1970. Most of Las Vegas' high-roller gamblers participated. The games played were California Draw Poker, California Lowball, Seven Card High, Seven Card Low (Razz), Seven Card High-Low Split, Five Card Stud, and a little-known Texas variation of Seven Card Stud called Hold Em. The winner of each division was named World Champion. The news media paid little or no attention to this tournament.

After the dismal publicity showing of the 1970 World Series of Poker Tournament, Binion knew that to be successful his format needed improvement. In the 1971 World Series of Poker Tournament a few rule changes were made, as follows: The chip buy-in for the Hold Em segment of the tournament was increased to $5,000 per player and the game was to be played table stakes freeze-out fashion until one player had won the players' total chip buy-in. In the 1971 World Series Hold Em Tournament, six players were involved, each having purchased a $5,000 chip buy-in. Johnny Moss emerged the World Hold Em Champion and collected the $30,000 in prize money.

By the time the 1972 World Series of Poker Tournament rolled around, Benny Binion had decided to feature just one Poker game, and that game was Hold Em. In my opinion, this was the perfect Poker game to choose, for the obvious reason that Hold Em, unlike all other card games, is a great spectator sport. This is because the five community cards resting in the center of the table can be seen and studied by everyone present, and, most important, can be seen by television viewers. This spectator feature, coupled with Hold Em's table-stakes freeze-out arrangement where each contestant has to ante up a $10,000 chip buy-in and cannot quit playing until he either loses his $10,000 or wins the total chip buy-in of all the contestants, has made the World Series Hold Em Poker Championship Tournament an instantaneous smash hit. This is proven by the vast publicity given each yearly tournament by the national and international press and television.

The World Series Hold Em Poker Championship Tournament held in 1972 featured eight top professional Poker players, each of whom bought in $10,000, making a total prize award of $80,000—which incidentally was won by that colorful Texas gambler "Amarillo Slim" Preston.

The many variations of Poker described above as played during the 1970 World Series of Poker are still part of the annual Series. Today, however, they are only preliminaries to the main event—the World Series Hold Em Poker Championship.

Since the contenders in the various divisional Poker championships pay a small house charge of $15 to $50 for table time and dealer services for the duration of the tournament (which runs about three weeks), it could not possibly have been the money to be made on the tournament that prompted Benny and Jack Binion to develop the World Series of Poker for their Horseshoe Casino. Their angle, I'm sure, was to promote the Horseshoe Casino's table games of Black Jack, Roulette, and especially Craps, with its free double-odds bets to big-time gamblers throughout the country. Benny Binion became famous in Nevada for his big betting limits at the Horseshoe Casino. Binion's betting-limit policy is to allow the big-time gambler to bet 10% of his cash chip buy-in at any one time—that is, if a high roller buys in $100,000 in chips, his maximum single bet is $10,000. The biggest craps-player win in Nevada's legalized casino history was $400,000, paid out by Benny Binion to Nat Jacobson, casino owner and professional gambler who founded Caesars Palace hotel casino on the Las Vegas Strip.

Each World Series Poker Tournament is a table stakes freeze-out Hold Em game in which contestants battle each other for eight hours a day. Players draw cards for tables and table position. Nine, ten, or eleven players are usually seated at each table. The tournament starts with each player anteing $10, and there's a $50 blind opening bet and a $100 blind raise. At each table during the play of the tournament, betting limits and antes are raised according to a predetermined time schedule, and as players are eliminated, tables will be systematically combined until it's down to the final two players and each player must blind-bet $1,000 and blind-raise it for $2,000. These two blind bets may increase to $3,000 and $6,000 or more according to the discretion of the tournament director.

For the first eight years of this Hold Em Tournament, the winner took everything. Doyle Brunson, winner of the 1976 and 1977 World Hold Em Tournaments, took home a total of $560,000 in new crisp $100 bills for winning both events. However, in the ninth annual World Series of Poker, held in May 1978, with 42 entrants and $420,000 going to the winners, the prize money distribution rules were changed, giving Bobby Baldwin, the winner, half or $210,000; the remaining $210,000 was divided among the four runner-ups—20% or $84,000 to the second longest-lasting player, 15% or $63,000 to the third, 10% or $42,000 to the fourth, and 5% or $21,000 to the fifth longest-lasting player. Having five finalists rather than one share in the tournament prize money will no doubt increase the number of contestants entered in the World Series of Poker each year.

Generally speaking, the tournament is a knock-down drag-out table stakes elimination contest between some of America's best Poker players, where luck is most important. But the human trait that wins the World Series of Poker year in and year out is betting courage.

NEVADA'S POKER ROOMS

Nevada, the gambling mecca of the world, harbors some one hundred-odd licensed Poker rooms, which are situated mostly in Nevada's hotel casinos. There are some thirty Poker rooms found in major hotel casinos in Las Vegas, including the Las Vegas Hilton, the M-G-M Grand, Caesars Palace, the Dunes, the Aladdin, the Stardust, the Silver Bird, the Golden Nugget, Holiday Inn and others. Strange but true, the Horseshoe Casino, home of the annual World Series of Poker Tournament, does not harbor a Poker room and permits Poker playing only during the month of May when this tournament takes place.

Most of the major casinos situated in downtown Las Vegas do a good business in their Poker rooms which operate twenty four hours a day. These include the Golden Nugget, the Union Plaza, the Freemont and the Mint. Most of the Nevada casinos operate their own Poker rooms, but a few rent their rooms to independent operators.

The usual Las Vegas Poker room contains from eight to ten Poker tables. The Stardust Casino, however, operates fifteen Poker tables, the greatest number found in any one Las Vegas Poker room.

The five most played Poker games in Nevada, in order of their popularity, are: 1. Seven Card Stud High; 2. Hold Em (a Texas variation of Seven Card Stud); 3. Seven Card Stud Low, known as Razz; 4. Lowball; and 5. Five Card Draw.

The Poker rooms are public and you can participate simply by asking the floorman. He will see to it that you are seated at the first opportunity.

In Nevada Poker rooms, only the house dealer shuffles, cuts, and deals the game. Players are not permitted to cut the deck. A button (a chip marked "button") is moved around from player to player in clockwise sequence to identify the imaginary dealer in all games. In Draw games, the button bets and acts last, while in Stud games it is merely used to determine who gets the first card dealt. After each betting interval and before the next card or cards are dealt for the following betting interval, the house dealer burns the top card of the deck. The betting limits, rules of play, percentage of rake-off (amount extracted from a pot by the house dealer) and irregularities and penalties extracted differ only slightly in most Nevada casinos.

A player needs a minimum sum of money to sit in any game, and this is in the form of a buy-in. The usual minimum chip buy-in amount, the ante and the betting limits in most Nevada casinos are as follows:

1. At a $1 to $3 betting limit game—the minimum buy-in is $10, the ante 5 cents, and the house charge, known as the cut or rake, is 10% on all pots up to $30; maximum rake $3 per pot.

2. At a $3 to $6 betting limit game—the chip buy-in is $20, the ante 25 cents, the rake 5% on all pots up to $40; maximum rake $2 per pot.

3. At a $5 to $10 betting limit game—the chip buy-in is $50, the ante is $1, the rake 5% on all pots up to $30; add 50 cents when pot reaches $70 or more; maximum rake $2 per pot.

The above described buy-ins, antes and percentage rakes apply only to the low-limit games played in Nevada. At the Dunes Hotel Casino Poker room, which is leased out to Johnny Moss, the hourly house charge is $75 for a full table at the $100 and $200 limit Razz game, and every 20 minutes the dealer removes a $25 chip from the pot in progress. The same house charge holds true for the $300 and $600 limit game. The maximum number of raises permitted in most Nevada Poker rooms is *three,* and in a few, *four.* However, when there are two active players remaining in the pot, the number of raises is unlimited.

The above are basically the general rules that make Nevada Poker playing different from that in clubs situated elsewhere.

The general house rule concerning the rake, or house cut, in Nevada casinos is, for obvious reasons: The smaller the game limits, the bigger the house rake. This factor can be borne out by visiting some Las Vegas downtown casinos which, in addition to their big money games, also deal a 50 cent and $1 game in which the posted sign reads, "House rake 1 to 25%."

I don't care if you are the best Stud player in Las Vegas—if you buck a low-limit game with rank suckers and the house takes a 5, 10 or 25% straight rake of the pot from a winner, you must go broke if you play often enough. However, when I consider the valuable casino space required by these Poker rooms and compare the per foot profits to those of such rival table games as Craps, Black Jack, Roulette and Baccarat, I learn that the Poker room earnings are only a small fraction of those of each of the table games. I must then wonder if these Poker rooms could survive with a smaller house rake. My recent Poker survey reveals that the yearly average gross revenue for a Las Vegas Poker table is $145,000.

CALIFORNIA POKER CLUBS

California permits commercialized Poker playing only at Five Card Draw and Five Card Lowball (ace to five). The reason for this is that the California law considers Closed or Draw Poker to be a game of skill and Stud or Open Poker a game of chance. Towns in California may, by local option, issue licenses for Draw Poker to Poker clubs which rent tables at an hourly rate and supervise the honesty of play.

I agree with the California law that Draw Poker is a game of skill and am glad that at least one state recognizes it officially as such. I suggest that all other forty-nine states should do the same. I must, however, disagree that Stud Poker is a game of chance. Actually it requires more skill than Draw Poker.

There are over 400 licensed and legalized Draw Poker card clubs throughout California, including Sacramento, the state capital. Some of these clubs have been operating since 1936. A number of these clubs have added Pan (a Rummy-type game), only recently legalized.

To illustrate the rules and games, I've selected the town of Gardena, situated in Los Angeles County, California. After scouting Poker clubs here and abroad, I've concluded that Gardena is rightfully the Draw Poker capital of the world. Gardena possesses six multimillion-dollar Poker palaces: the Monterey, Rainbow, Horseshow, Gardena, Eldorado, and Normandy, all of which have the thirty-five Poker tables legally permitted by the city council.

Unlike most Nevada Poker rooms, the Gardena Poker palaces have strict rules regarding play and player behavior, and these rules, in booklet form, may be obtained by a player upon request. These Poker palaces employ floormen and security guards to see that the games are run honestly and efficiently.

The fact that each Poker palace possesses exactly thirty-five tables brings up some other features about Poker playing in Gardena. Playing rules and hourly charge for playing in all six palaces are standardized by local council. All players must pay a fee per half hour of play, since there is no house rake. In the $1–$2 game, the house charge is $1 per half hour; in the $2–$4 game, $1.25; in the $3–$6 game, $1.50; in the $5–$10 game, $2; in the $10–$20 game, $3; in the $15–$20 California Blind game, $4. And don't expect free drinks, as is customary in Nevada Poker rooms. Gaming incentives of this kind are illegal in Gardena.

Following is a quote reprinted from Gardena's standardized rule book:

> *Facts About Poker in General:* Poker is America's favorite card game. 70 million adults play cards and about 47 million Americans prefer poker. Poker is as American as baseball and hot dogs. Many of our most famous Presidents were poker enthusiasts. Poker contains a greater element of skill than bridge, or any other card game, according to authority John Scarne.

I made these statements concerning Poker in *Scarne's Complete Guide to Gambling* (1961) and am pleased that the Poker palaces of Gardena have included them and John Scarne in their rule book. However, a slight change in Gardena's "Facts About Poker in General" is now in order. Today 85 million adults play cards, and about 65 million prefer Poker.

A condensed version of the principal general Poker rules found in each of Gardena's six clubs follows:

1. The chip buy-in is ten times the minimum bet. In the $1 and $2 Draw, $10; in the $5 and $10 Draw, $50; in the $20 and $40 Draw, $200. Antes run from a quarter in the $1 and $2 Draw to $5 in the $20 and $40 Draw.
2. Players take turns dealing each player five cards one at a time.
3. The dealer must burn the top card of the deck before dealing active players the requested number of cards on the draw.
4. Players can draw as many as five cards.
5. Check and raise (sandbagging) is permissible and there is no limit on the number of raises.
6. Verbal raising or calling is not binding.
7. Chips in the pot denote action.

8. The joker in a 53-card deck is used only as an ace and as a wild card to complete a straight or a flush.
9. There is no such thing as a "double ace flush."
10. You must protect your hand at all times—more or less than five cards on the showdown constitutes a dead hand.

The above are basically the general Poker rules of play that make Gardena different from Nevada.

After studying Gardena's standardized rules of play, the internal control operation, and the anti-cheating measures taken by management to protect their player clients against possible card cheats, I unhesitatingly go on record: Gardena, the Draw Poker capital of the world, has the finest card clubs both for service rendered and for player protection that I have ever visited both here and abroad.

However, I don't mean to imply that Gardena's six Poker palaces with their hundreds of players seated at the 210 Poker tables are free of player cheats. This can never happen. Like Nevada casinos, the Gardena Poker palaces must be constantly on guard against player thievery. It's an impossibility for Gardena or any big Poker club elsewhere to operate Poker games where there isn't some sort of thievery or attempted thievery taking place at one time or another. This, coupled with the presence of teams of Poker professionals and card hustlers who earn their living playing Poker angles, is a tribute to Gardena's six Poker palaces for the small amount of thievery that takes place at their tables.

That Poker can be played commercially in only two states, and that private Poker is not permitted by law in any one of our fifty states, is an example of how unrealistic and outdated our gambling laws are. Illegal though it may be, 65 million Americans do gamble at Poker in private clubs and homes in every city and town from the Atlantic to the Pacific and from the Canadian to the Mexican borders, and in Alaska and Hawaii as well.

There are hundreds of variations of Poker played today but they can all be placed in two large classes: Closed (or Draw) Poker, in which each player's cards are hidden from the other players until the showdown or the completion of the hand; and Open (or Stud) Poker, in which some cards in each player's hand are exposed to all the players as the betting progresses, all the active players' cards being exposed at the showdown.

To most Americans, Draw Poker means the game of Five Card Draw—Jacks or Better, and its popular variations: Lowball, Draw Poker—Blind Openers, High-Low Poker, etc. Stud Poker usually means Five Card Stud and its variations: Seven Card Stud, Hold Em, Six Card Stud, Low Stud, High-Low Stud Poker, etc. These variations and many others are played in various combinations: Table Stakes, Freeze-out, Pot Limit, Deuces Wild, Joker Wild, Dealer's Choice, Jackpots, etc.

In all these variations two factors remain constant:

1. The value or rank of each Poker hand.
2. At the showdown the hand cannot consist of more than five cards, even though more cards are used in many other Poker variations.

Poker has achieved its outstanding popularity for the following reasons.

1. It can be played by rich and poor alike. The stakes may vary from big to penny ante, just as long as the minimum and maximum betting limits are agreed upon before the game begins.
2. It is easy to learn.
3. It may be played in a great many different ways.
4. Any number of players from two to eight or more may play, although four, five, or six makes the best game.
5. It is strictly a gambling card game, whether it be Draw Poker penny ante style or Five Card Stud table stakes. Without the gambling factor it would be one of America's least-played games.
6. Each player, on his own, battles all the others. There is no partnership play.
7. It combines both chance and skill, and is the only game in which a player can win only one hand all evening and still come out a winner, or win many more than the average number of hands and still lose to the game's action.

If there is any more engrossing gambling card game for a group of reasonably congenial friends of fairly equal playing ability than Poker, I have yet to learn about it. The longest Poker session always seems too short.

THE HISTORY OF POKER

It is impossible to say that any specific earlier card game is the direct ancestor of Poker; it seems to have borrowed elements from many games. The basic principle of Poker is such an obvious one that its use must be very old. I once gave my three-year-old son John (Teeko) twenty shuffled cards, all the aces, kings, queens, jacks and tens, and without any prompting on my part he separated them into those five groups. The first Poker in this country was played with just such a deck, and one could say that Teeko had discovered its basic principle.

The first reference in print to Poker which I have found is one by

Jonathan H. Green published in 1834. He gives the rules for what he calls a "cheating game" which was then being played on the Mississippi riverboats. He stated that this was the first time the rules had been published, he noted that the *American Hoyle* then current did not mention the game, and he called it Poker. The game he described was played with twenty cards—aces, kings, queens, jacks and tens. Two, three or four players could play, and each was dealt five cards.

By the time Green wrote this, Poker had become the number one cheating game on the Mississippi boats. It received even more action than Three-Card Monte. After losing heavily at Monte only the dumbest chumps would later fail to realize that they had been swindled; but twenty-card Poker seemed to be a legitimate game, and they would come back for more. In my opinion Poker, like Three-Card Monte, was developed by the card sharps.

Most dictionaries and game historians say that the word "Poker" comes from an early eighteenth-century French game, Poque. Others say it is derived from an old German game, Pochspiel, in which the element of bluffing played a part and the players indicated whether they would pass or open by rapping the table and saying, "*Iche poche!*" Someone has tried to trace the word to *poche*, the French word for pocket, and I have even heard it argued that Poker derives from the Hindu *pukka*.

I doubt all these theories, and I have my own. I believe it was originally underworld slang and came from the pickpocket's term for pocketbook or wallet: *poke*.

The card sharps who evolved the twenty-card game as a cheating device to relieve the sucker of his poke may even have called it that among themselves, disguising it slightly by adding the *r* to make it "Poker" when using the term in front of their victims, some of whom might have been hep to underworld slang.

To go even further back, the work "poke" probably came from the hocus-pocus of the magician. In the Middle Ages, before pockets came into fashion money was carried in a bag which hung from the belt, and the first pickpockets were called cutpurses because they lifted the purse by cutting it free. Many of the fifteenth-century paintings and engravings of magicians performing show cutpurses busily at work in the crowd; some of these cutpurses may have paid the conjurer a percentage for working in his audience just as pickpockets once did in this country when they traveled with circuses. Like the magician, they also used misdirection and sleight of hand and were, in their own way, hocus-pocus men.

The Mississippi River sharpers who first called the game Poker may have got their original inspiration in New Orleans from sailors who played a very old Persian game called Âs-Nâs, whose basic structure is the same. Twenty cards are used, five are dealt to each player, pairs and such combinations and sequences as form the melds at Rummy are winning combinations, and bluffing is an important factor.

Âs-Nâs may also have been the father of the Italian game of Primero and the French Gilet, which, during the reign of Charles IX (1550–74), became Brelan and later fathered its variants Bouillotte and Ambigu. In *le Poker Américain* as the French play it today *brelancarré* means four of a kind. The early published Poker rules in this country also hint at French antecedents: the 32-card Piquet pack was used, it was cut to the left, the cards were dealt from the bottom of the deck, and certain combinations of cards bore French names. The draw feature of Poker is found in Ambigu, and the blind, straddles, raise, table stakes and freeze-out in the pre-Revolutionary Bouillotte. Bluffing and the use of wild cards were important features in the English game of Brag. In all these European games, however, a hand consisted of only three cards. The credit for the use of a five-card hand and also the bluff must go to the Persian Âs-Nâs, from which our word "ace" may also have come.

In 1845 an early American edition of Hoyle included Twenty-Card Poker and also "Poker or Bluff." Twenty years later *The American Hoyle* added the game, calling it simply "Bluff." Perhaps a few players who may have confused it with the the English Brag also called it that, but most players have always called it Poker. Game-book editors who do their research in previous game books sometimes still call it "Poker (Bluff)" although no player has used the latter term for nearly a century.

POKER NOT ACCORDING TO HOYLE

"How do you play?" they would inquire cautiously drawing up their chairs in Guadalcanal, Bizerte, Fort Benning, Okinawa, or Los Alamos, sizing each other up, trying to guess whether the guy in khaki across the table had been a bank teller, a parking-lot attendant, an actor or a sharecropper farmer.

"How," the Second World War's GIs would ask, "do you play Poker?" And, "According to Hoyle," was the answer up to the time I was named gambling consultant to the United States Armed Forces and my Poker articles began getting published in *Yank: The Army Weekly* and other worldwide military and private publications. From then on, Poker throughout the world began being played "According to Scarne."

On March 2, 1974, the prestigious London *Times* ran a six-column feature article on John Scarne by Richard C. Moon which read in part, "Edmund Hoyle passed away in 1769. He left us with a rich legacy of games and game rules. I think he would have been proud to see his mantle passed to John Scarne. According to Hoyle—not anymore. Now it is according to Scarne."

Ever since Americans decided Poker was their own, their native game, unsuspecting players have believed in Hoyle as the ultimate authority on the play. I'm no iconoclast and I don't believe in making it tough for any man to make a living; but we'd better at the outset face the facts about this venerable myth. You can't play Poker according to Hoyle simply because Hoyle (a) never played Poker, (b) never uttered a ruling on Poker, and (c) never even heard of the game of Poker. Edmund Hoyle was an English barrister who wrote a book on three card games—Piquet, Whist and Quadrille—the first two of which are now virtual museum curios and the third of which was just recently dropped from the functional game books. Poker was not heard of until years, decades, after Hoyle's death in 1769. But—for reasons which have so far escaped me—it is the custom of modern writers on card games to call their books "Poker According to Hoyle" or "The Up-to-Date Hoyle" or "The Revised Hoyle" or some comparable nonsense. It seems to me about as intelligent as some research engineer's publishing a monograph titled "Fulton on Diesel Engines" or "Richard the Lion-hearted on Atomic Energy." With this exception: the writers on Poker who have put on the mantle of Hoyle and handed down their own private prejudices about the game have simply reduced Poker rules to utter confusion. Poker players, confronted by a shelf of Hoyles who don't know what they're talking about, have been compelled to formulate and live by their own regional, village or house rules. This confusion has created a not-too-healthy atmosphere in which to play for money.

POKER HAS ENRICHED OUR LANGUAGE

Talk around the Poker table has introduced many colorful phrases into the American language. Used in many contexts are "chip in," "fourflusher," "joker" (one not to be taken seriously), "two-bit hustler," "poker face," "stand pat," "pass the buck," "pass me," "ace in the hole," "call your bluff," "penny ante chiseler," "showdown," "aces," "close to the vest," "cold deck," and many other pokerisms too numerous to mention.

SIX KINDS OF POKER PLAYERS—WHICH ONE ARE YOU?

Sixty-five million men and women are spending more of their leisure time gambling at Poker than at any other form of gambling. These 65 million Poker players are made up of six different kinds. Which category are you in?

1. *The occasional Poker player,* who knows little or nothing about the hard mathematical facts and subtleties of the form of Poker on which he now and then wagers some money. About 40% of America's Poker-playing fraternity fall into this class, and it is their yearly losses at Poker that contribute nearly 80% of all yearly moneys lost at all forms of Poker.

2. *The habitual Poker player,* who visits a Poker game at any opportunity he gets. He knows a little more about the artifices of Poker playing than the occasional Poker player, but is not smart enough to know that he can't beat the house charge nor the skullduggery that takes place in high-stakes games.

3. *The Poker chiseler,* who knows considerably more about Poker than the occasional and habitual Poker player and looks on both with elaborate contempt. As often as not, the Poker chiseler proves to be a grifter with morals at low tide. He is a champ at stealing chips, failing to put his ante into the pot—and when reminded swears on a stack of Bibles that someone else was the culprit. The Poker chiseler steals from the occasional and habitual players but is barred by Poker players who can't stand chiselers.

4. *The professional Poker operator,* who earns his living (or most of it) by operating a Poker room. He usually gambles to start the game. Basically, he is a businessman who understands his trade, who runs a Poker game for direct hourly levies or a fixed percentage on each Poker pot for defraying his overhead and giving gamblers a place to play Poker.

I have a grudging respect for the professionals of Las Vegas and Gardena, and those that operate illegal Poker rooms throughout the country. These professionals charge what the traffic will stand; but they provide a service, and since they operate Poker rooms, they are known as gamblers.

5. *The Poker professional,* also known as a Poker hustler, is a gambler who above everything else continuously talks, dreams and plays

Poker. Due to his many years of Poker-playing experience and knowledge, he earns all or part of his livelihood by playing Poker—mostly with nonprofessionals. A Poker professional will travel hundreds of miles to sit at a Poker table, especially if it happens to be a high-limit noncommercial game.

The code of a professional states that friendships and sympathy don't belong at the Poker table, and a pro may do anything to try and get his opponent's money as long as he does not actually cheat. However, I'm not so sure that the majority of pros would not cheat if they knew how to do so without being detected.

Today the dream of almost every Poker professional in the United States and abroad is someday to win the annual World Series of Poker with its glory and the hundreds of thousands of dollars in prize money.

6. *The crook, the cheat,* whose gamble is not in winning or losing but rather in getting away with it or getting caught. To the average Poker player, the man who makes his living by cheating at Poker is a crook, cheat, sharper, sharp or shark, but to card hustlers and to seasoned gamblers and house men, he is known as a card mechanic or hand mucker. Card mechanics and hand muckers are the magicians of the underworld—they deal cards from the bottom of the deck, switch Poker hands, and at times the entire deck. To protect yourself against the professional card cheat, see Chapter 14.

2

The Science and Skill of Poker

CAN LUCK BEAT SKILL?

Whether you'd rather be lucky than skillful or skillful than lucky or just can't make up your mind . . .

You've argued from time to time—haven't you?—the immemorial question "Can the more skillful player beat his opponents who are luckier?"

Hundreds of earnest, honest, sincere Poker players have asked me that.

And there's an earnest, honest answer.

But before I write it out, let's try to define our terms; let's see what we're talking about.

A game of skill is a game where the element of chance has been utterly eliminated. Examples are Chess, Checkers, and Teeko, a skill game which I invented myself. (If you happen to like skill games, you should love Teeko.) In these games the skilled player will invariably win against an unskilled opponent, and the skilled player's winning percentage will be an exact reflection of the relation between his ability and that of a less skillful opponent.

A game of chance is a game from which the element of skill has been eliminated (unless you assert that cheating is a form of skill!). Games of chance number thousands. Examples are Roulette, wheels of fortune, and most of the dice games such as Private and Casino Craps.

But most Poker variations, like hundreds of other games played with cards, combine the elements of skill and chance.

Now, what's chance? How does it work?

You'll forgive me if I sound a little pedantic about this. But it brings up a subject which I think should be taught along with the three R's in every elementary school. If it were so taught, gambling would be reduced from a national problem to a sporadic eccentricity, and gambling casinos would close. With a very few dangerous exceptions, the average educated citizen has no knowledge of the subject and no interest in it, and this high-mindedness costs average educated citizens of the United States many billions of dollars a year.

I'm talking about a branch of mathematics called the theory of probability. It is called by gamblers—erroneously—the law of averages.

As far as we're concerned, the theory of probability affords a method of calculating what can be expected to happen in a situation in which some of the factors are not at hand or, being at hand, are too complex to be easily broken down, assimilated and used.

When you double the insurance on your car you are both gambling and making use of the theory of probability. The whole gigantic life-insurance business is based on the actuarial mortality tables, which are just a list of probabilities. Any businessman drafting a budget or schedule or sales program is applying a theory of probabilities.

The theory holds rigorously true for all Poker games. Each player, the theory goes, will in the long run be dealt an approximately equal number of good and bad cards, good and bad hands.

"Malarkey, Scarne," you say, "there are times when for hours on end I can't get a decent hand dealt me; and even when I draw a fairish hand I can't improve it by drawing cards to it."

You're right. But it's not "malarkey, Scarne"; it's the theory of probability. Like dice or coins, cards don't and mustn't be expected to behave *exactly* according to the probabilities. But they'll come awfully close.

Toss a coin. It may fall heads up ten times in a row. Then it may fall tails up ten times in a row. And there are gamblers who, after heads have been turned on several successive tosses, will bet heavily that it will be tails up next. They think the odds, the probabilities, favor tails. Likewise most card players operate on the belief that, after they have been dealt four or five successive bad hands, the probabilities abruptly shift to favor their being dealt a good hand. Thereupon they raise the stakes from 25 cents to 50 cents or from $2 to $4 on the next hand, and are shocked and saddened when they lose.

This notion, that luck has a cumulative tendency to change, is known academically as the doctrine of the maturity of chances. Mathematicians have for years referred to it as "the gambler's fallacy." But gamblers—many of them brilliantly educated persons—go right on believing in it and losing their money on it.

The theory of probability is not that a player will be dealt a run of good hands after a run of bad hands. It is that in the long run the cards will be just as good as anybody else's, which is something very different.

"Very well, then," I think you may be saying, "my opponent can indeed be luckier than I am, hand for hand, game for game, night in and night out. Now what?"

You have raised the question: "What is luck?"

Well, my dictionary defines luck as "that which happens to a person as if by chance; a person's apparent tendency to be fortunate or unfortunate."

The key word in that formula is "apparent."

Any card player who really can believe that an opponent is luckier than he just ought to give up the game. He belongs in gypsy shoppes, getting his tea leaves read.

When your Poker opponent to your right is dealt three terrific pat hands in five deals and you don't even catch a pair, you appear to yourself—*appear*—the unluckiest Poker player in the world, and as far as you're concerned that closes the subject.

As a matter of fact it is just the threshold of the subject, for the odds have been, are, and will remain exactly even that you will be dealt a hand as good as or better than your opponent's! Over a number of deals sufficient to let the probabilities get their teeth into the statistics, say 10,000 or 100,000 deals, the distribution of the cards will be just about exactly even.

It's true in theory; it's true in the practice of many experimenters; and it's the truth on which casino operators grow rich, since their income is based on the inexorable certainty that the percentages never fail over the long run.

I recently watched a rank novice win $10,000 in an hour-long Poker session at the Dunes Hotel Casino in Las Vegas from five men who are considered to be among the twenty best Poker players in Las Vegas. That was chance, luck, a momentary aberration in the probabilities. They are inevitable in any gambling game. If it weren't for them—and the long-odds winning they make possible—gambling would be barren of what makes it gambling. Certainly luck operates, to this limited extent, within the theory of probability. All that the theory guarantees is that ultimately each player will have been dealt an approximately equal number of opportunities to win, an approximately equal number of good, bad and indifferent hands.

Five or more players, equally skilled, playing Poker once a week for a year will probably have won and lost an equal number of big and small pots.

So much for probability. So much for luck.

You understand me now.

In any game involving skill to any appreciable extent, the more skilled player will outdistance the less skilled in games won, over a long period.

The more pronounced his advantage in skill, the shorter the period required in which the difference will show in money won.

In the long run, then, the element of chance is canceled out, leveled off, reduced to zero.

I'm not going to try calculating the exact percentage of influence exerted by chance and skill in any single-deal Poker-game situation because:

1. Just for instance, there are 2,598,960 possible five-card hands in standard Poker.

2. No two to eight Poker players will play the same kind of game consistently, and the probabilities that the same players are dealt the same exact hands run into one in trillions.

But I can assure you of this: In any Poker game, be it Stud or Draw Poker or any of their countless variations that combine skill and chance, the more skillful player will win the money in the long run.

Does that settle your argument? Or are you going to keep squandering your money on that fickle, blind, perverse and cold-bloodedly fair old baggage, Lady Luck?

POKER, AMERICA'S MOST SCIENTIFIC GAMBLING CARD GAME

Poker contains a greater skill element than any other card game including Contract Bridge, Pinochle and Gin Rummy. Poker is the one and only game where a skilled player may hold bad cards for hours and still win the money. "How come?" you may ask. Because Poker is a game of money management in addition to card management. It is a game where there is a correct technical play in every situation. It is a game where the best possible Poker hand need not win the pot, due to a bluff. Furthermore, anyone who is not dealt a good hand has the option of throwing in his hand before the first round of betting.

I believe that there are more science and skill in Poker than in Bridge for the reasons that follow.

My observations of Poker games over the past 60 years have convinced me that if a Poker expert played three average players for 52 sessions, each lasting six hours, the expert player would emerge the winner 51 times. The odds against any such result at Contract Bridge under similar conditions are high.

Contract Bridge is a partnership game, and, as in all such games, one partner is usually more skilled than the other. Their combined ability is therefore less than that of the better player. In Poker, with each player on his own, a skilled player is not handicapped by a less able partner; his skill potential is not reduced.

Contract Bridge is basically a game of strategy plus partnership signals (bidding). Poker is a game of strategy, deception, mathematics and psychology, with a considerable amount of courage thrown in. Judgment of one's opponent's psychological traits or habits plays little part in Bridge strategy, whereas a top Poker player must be a master of Poker psychology in order to analyze properly and simultaneously the playing traits of as many as ten opponents. Deception is much more used in Poker than Bridge, and a knowledge of the game's mathematics is much more important in Poker than in Bridge. Money management is important in Poker and not in bridge.

The probability is that in any card game each player will in the long run receive an equal number of good, bad and indifferent hands, and most Bridge experts agree that a skilled partnership will, in the long run, score more points than a less skilled partnership. This means that skill rather than chance is the deciding factor in Bridge. But Bridge partners, no matter how skilled, must always play a series of bad hands out to a finish and take their beating. This is not true of Poker.

In most forms of Poker the game is pure chance only until the players looks at the cards dealt him. From then on, unlike in Bridge and most other card games, chance plays a lesser role, because the players need not play bad hands out to a finish. The player can throw a bad hand in and take a small loss, or perhaps none, or he can continue to play a bad hand and sometimes win by bluffing. In Stud and its variants this decision can be made by the player each time another card is dealt until the showdown.

The skilled Poker player will play fewer bad hands than the unskilled player and thus increase his winning chances in a way that an equally skilled Bridge player cannot do.

WHAT POKER SKILL CAN'T BEAT

If you play cards in any commercial Poker game, whether in a licensed Poker room in Nevada or California, or in a swank home on

Park Avenue that caters to both women and men, or with the boys in the dingy back room of Joe's barbershop, you must pay for your Poker seat. How much you pay depends upon who operates the game, and the kind of game you pick is up to you.

I must warn you at the outset, however, that even if you absorb all the Poker skill described in this book, it won't help you a bit and you must wind up a loser if the house charge known as a "rake" or "cut" is too exorbitant to overcome. Therefore, I suggest that you read this section several times before continuing to read further.

In the licensed Poker rooms of Nevada there is a sign hanging at the entrance of each Poker room that reads, in part, "Rake 0 to 10%. Maximum Rake $3 per pot." In short, this means the house dealer may take nothing or the maximum 10% out of a pot. In this 0 to 10% house cut atmosphere it's difficult to know exactly what the house cut actually is. So, in order to find out, I suggest that the player clock the cut moneys collected from the pot by the dealer for one hour, then divide this total by the number of game participants. This final result will give you an approximation of your hourly house charge. If this result equals 25% of your initial chip buy-in, I recommend that you seek another Poker game in town.

In the licensed Poker clubs of California the operators charge a fee for playing on an hourly basis which usually averages about $5 per person. This pays the operator's overhead, salaries, taxes, etc., and earns him a profit. Since Poker gets a lot of play it is sometimes quite a lot of profit: one of the California Poker palaces nets more than $3 million a year—which is not peanuts.

Since in California's Poker rooms you know the hourly house charge you are bucking, you'll have to make up your mind if the pleasure you derive from Poker is worth the price you are paying.

But if you are one of the millions of average Poker players who patronize an illegal limit Poker game in your community, and the operator takes a 5% house cut of the total moneys in each pot, you are paying a lot more than you may think.

For every licensed Poker game in America there are thousands and thousands of illegal games. Many are friendly weekly games that rotate from one player's home to another. Others are club games run as a business. In many house and club games the operator's take (his charge for furnishing the gaming facilities) is a 5% cut taken from each pot.

If this doesn't sound like much of a charge, would it surprise you to learn that even the world's best Poker player, playing against rank suckers in a small-limit game, would eventually go broke bucking that small 5% cut? The operator calls it 5%, but it is actually much greater, often as much as 10%. In most games the operators get a percentage or cut of the players' winnings, but Poker is one of the few games in which a charge is also taken from the winning player's bet.

An example: Four Stud players play an entire hand to the showdown, the pot totals $20, and the house takes a 5% cut, or $1, out of the pot. The winner of the pot has paid a cut not only on his winnings but also on the $5 he put into the pot. The house is really taking a cut of 6⅔% on that player's $15 winnings.

Or suppose two players play a hand to the showdown. The pot totals $20. The 5% cut gets the operator $1, as in the four-handed game, but from the winning player's standpoint this is 10% of the $10 he won.

I recently clocked twenty different Stud games for a period of two months. The maximum betting limits ranged from a low $2 to a high of $600. When I averaged my figures I found that:

1. It takes about 1½ minutes to play an average hand.
2. In a fast Stud game approximately forty hands are dealt per hour.
3. The average pot in an eight-handed $4-limit game contains about $30 on the showdown.

Now let's see how strong the 5% cut can be in this average game. Forty $30 pots per hour means that the operator's 5% cut gets him $60 per hour. In a session lasting six hours the operator takes a total of $360.

Let's assume that each player began with $100 and that he received the number of good, bad and indifferent hands that probability says he can expect in the long run. The total money the players had at the game's start was $800. The total cut is $360, leaving only $440 in the game. Each player has paid the operator $45 of his original hundred. That small 5% cut has accumulated to 45%.

Suppose the game continues and lasts for ten hours, as many Stud games do. If, by that time, six players have gone broke, leaving only two, these two will have only $200 between them. The operator has taken a charge of $600 out of the original $800. That deceptively small 5% cut has taken out 75% of the total amount the players brought into the game!

Never having stopped to dope this out, there are millions of Stud players who try to win under these conditions. Many of them play two or three nights a week without the slightest realization of the enormous price they are paying for the privilege of letting the operator get most of the money.

And, believe it or not, many operators aren't satisfied with the way that 5% cut earns them money. They often steal extra amounts from the pot. This is usually done when making change or taking out the cut. The player who wins the pot is so pleased at winning that he seldom notices that the cut has been taken, let alone spotting the theft.

It is difficult to understand the logic, if any, of illegal Poker-game operators. If they charged a reasonable house percentage (cut or rake) as dictated under Scarne's General Rules for Commercialized Poker (pages 60–63) they would have a Poker game most of the time. As it is, they break most of the players in a few weeks and then wonder why they no longer have a game.

The operator's alibi, if you object that the 5% charge is too high, is that the ice he must pay for protection is high. It is. He has to pay quite a bit even to run a $1 limit Poker game. But it isn't so high that he has to take all the players to the cleaner's.

Many Poker players who have gone broke stay away for a while as they try to figure out why. Most lay it to bad luck. Some think they were cheated, which is possible. But more often it's the 5% cut that did the trick. Not knowing the real reason, these losers eventually come back and try again to buck the impossible.

If you play in such a game after reading this analysis of the 5% cut and still think you can hope to come out ahead, don't read any further. Any advice I can give you won't do you any good.

Some operators charge a 2% or 3% cut per pot, which eats up your bankroll just as the 5% charge does, except that it takes about twice as long before you go broke.

Another thing the player should learn is how to protect his money from cheaters. Otherwise, he should stop playing the game for fair or big stakes right now. The best Poker skill in the world means nothing against a cold deck. Study carefully the information and detection methods explained in Chapter 14, because all the moves and gimmicks described there are used by the cheat in Poker. A sharper at work in a fair- or big-limit Poker game can break you for that session and plenty of others.

Keep your eye on the discards; an unskilled cheater will often reach for a valuable card for use in his hand. When you spot him, he is kidding; when you don't, he takes your money.

If the game is honest and the cut or playing charge is small or nonexistent and you still lose consistently, what is the cure? It's a simple one, and I've already mentioned it, but it bears repeating. Here's the way I put it in one of my World War II lectures at Fort Benning when a soldier said, "I have been a consistent loser at Poker since the first day I arrived in camp. Is there any advice you can give me to help me win at my next Poker session?"

"Yes," I told him. "There is one big secret, a Poker policy which, if put to use, will not only make you a winner at your next session but at most of them. It's a policy that is practiced religiously by the country's best Poker hustlers. It is the only surefire rule that wins the money.

"It's a simple rule: *Don't sit in a Poker game with superior players.* If you have been losing consistently in the camp's pay-day Poker games, it's a cinch the boys you've been playing with are better players. Find another game. Find one in which the players are *softies* (poor players). Poker is the world's greatest skill game and an inexperienced player who knows too little about it hasn't the ghost of a chance against seasoned players or hustlers."

I gave him that advice thirty-four years ago. It is just as true today. You may object that Poker is not as much fun when playing against poor players. I agree. An even better policy is to study the game and improve your Poker skill so that you can win even among good players. In short, don't just read and forget the Poker strategy that follows here: study it, remember it and put it into practice.

3

General Rules for Poker

POKER ACCORDING TO SCARNE

The Poker rules that appeared in *Scarne on Cards* on its first publication in 1949 have been regarded by millions of Poker players throughout the United States and abroad as the prime Poker authority. At the time, these rules went far beyond the so-called Hoyle books and replaced them as the outstanding authority on Poker.

It is thirty years since my Poker rules first appeared in *Scarne on Cards*. In that time they have been revised numerous times and have provided guidance to millions of Poker players throughout the world. But with many more millions of Americans playing Poker today, it was inevitable that many new Poker games would be invented, and many changes in the popularity of different Poker games would occur; also that many rule changes would take place. Because today these changes are substantial and most important, I am revising and updating my Poker rules—hence this book.

The Poker rules set forth here are not according to the countless so-called Hoyle books, but according to Scarne. They are based on modern conventions and conditions of play. They have been devised for players who like to gamble and love Poker. They are based on exhaustive studies of current Poker rules here and abroad. They have been tested in private games and clubs throughout the country—and they have stood the test of time. They are mathematically sound, they recognize the realities of Poker play, and they are authoritative. I firmly believe that the rules set forth in this book will in due time be accepted as the first and only standardized Poker rules for home, clubs and Poker rooms the world over for the obvious reason that they are the best possible.

GENERAL RULES FOR POKER

Although Poker is played in countless forms, it is only necessary to understand its two basic principles: the values of Poker hands and the principles of betting, such as the ante, opening bet, check, raise, reraise and fold (dropout). A player familiar with these can easily adjust himself to play in any style of Poker game.

Object of the Game

In Poker everyone plays for himself. There is no such thing as partnership play. The object of the game is to win the pot. The pot is the accumulation of bets (chips or cash) made by all the players in any one hand or deal. All the chips or cash a player puts into the pot indicate that he is betting that he holds, or will hold, the highest-valued Poker hand around the table. After the betting is over, each player exposes his five-card hand (called the showdown), and the highest- or lowest-valued hand wins the pot. A second way a pot can be won is by being the lone remaining active player in the pot when all other players for various reasons have folded or dropped out of the pot.

In case of a tie, tied players share equally in the pot. If a pot is not equally divisible by the number of winners, the odd sum left after division—breakage, as horse bettors call it—goes to the player who was called. In High-Low Poker, the indivisible odd amount goes to the winner of the high hand.

Players

Two to nine or more players, depending upon the style of Poker game being played.

The Pack of Cards

The Poker deck consists of four thirteen-card suits: spades, hearts, diamonds, and clubs. The suits have no relative superiority to each other. The ace is the highest-ranking card, and in order of descending value the rest of the cards are the king, queen, jack, 10, 9, 8, 7, 6, 5, 4, 3, and 2 or deuce. But the ace may be used at either end of the suit, as the highest card in a straight or royal flush and as the lowest card in a straight or straight flush. Thus in the straight flush A-K-Q-J-10 the ace is high; in the straight flush 5-4-3-2-A the ace is low.

Playing Poker with Two Packs of Cards

I recommend the use of two packs of cards having backs of sharply contrasting design or color. This is to enable a change of packs at the request of any player. In two-pack play a contestant can ask for a change at any time, and the change takes place immediately after the showdown of the current hand.

Standard Rank of Poker Hands with a 52-Card Deck

It must be specified for clarity's sake that in the following list of Poker hands in ten categories, called ranks, any hand listed in a superior rank beats any hand listed in an inferior rank. The royal flush, listed in Rank 1, beats any hand listed in Rank 2. Any hand listed in Rank 6 beats any hand in Rank 7, 8, 9, or 10, and loses to any hand in Rank 5, 4, 3, 2, or 1.

RANK 1 (THE SUPREME RANK)

The Royal Flush: the five highest cards, namely A-K-Q-J-10, of any one of the four suits. The suits have equal rank. Royal flushes tie for winner.

RANK 2

The Straight Flush: any five cards of the same suit in numerical sequence, such as the 10-9-8-7-6 of spades. This flush is called a *ten high*. If there are two or more straight flushes in competition for the pot, that one wins whose top card is of the highest denomination; a *ten high* beats a *nine high*, etc.; if two or more players hold a straight flush whose top card is of the same denomination, the hand is a tie.

RANK 3

Four of a Kind: any four cards of the same denomination (A-A-A-A-2). The odd card is irrelevant and does not affect the rank of the hand.

RANK 4

The Full House: three of one kind and two of another (3-3-3-2-2). In evaluating two or more competing full houses, the hand with the highest three-of-a-kind wins, regardless of the rank of the pair. *Example:* A full house including three aces regardless of the pair beats a full house including three kings regardless of the pair.

RANK 5

The Flush: any five cards of the same suit but not in sequence (10-7-5-4-3 of spades). In evaluating two or more flushes, the winner is determined by the rank of the highest card in the hand. If the highest cards in contesting hands are of the same rank, then the next highest cards determine the winner. And if these are of the same rank, then the winning hand is determined by the third highest cards. Et cetera! If all the cards of the players are equal, then the hands are tied.

RANK 6

The Straight: five cards in consecutive sequence but not of the same suit (3-4-5-6-7). In evaluating more than one straight, the winner is decided by the rank of his highest card. Straights of the same denomination are equal, and tie.

RANK 7

Three of a Kind: three cards of the same numerical value plus two different and irrelevant cards that are not paired (K-K-K-5-4). In evaluating two or more such hands, the hand having the highest three of a kind wins regardless of the value of the unmatched cards.

RANK 8

Two Pairs: two different pairs of cards plus one odd card (10-10-5-5-4. This example is called *tens up*). In evaluating two or more two-pair hands the winner is the player holding the highest pair. If the highest pairs are tied, the rank of the second pair in the hands determines the winner; if the second pair also are tied, then the highest odd card determines the winner. If all cards of the competing hands are of matching value, the hands are tied.

RANK 9

One Pair: two cards of the same denomination plus three indifferent (unmatched) cards (10-10-9-7-3). In evaluating two or more hands each including a pair, the player who holds the highest pair wins. If the pairs are of equal value, the hand with the highest indifferent card wins. If these are of equal value, the next card is the determinant, etc. If all the cards in the competing hands match, the hands tie and the winnings are divided.

RANK 10

High Card: a hand which contains five indifferent cards not of the same suit, not in sequence, and falling into none of the above combinations (A-10-7-5-3 not of the same suit). The example cited would be called an *ace high* hand. If the highest card of two such hands is the same, the next highest card determines the winner; if these tie, the determinant is the next, then the next, etc. If all cards in more than one hand are of matching value, the hands tie, and the pot is divided.

THE STANDARD RANK OF POKER HANDS WITH A 52-CARD DECK IN ORDER OF VALUE, RANK 1 BEING HIGHEST AND RANK 10 BEING LOWEST

1. Royal flush
2. Straight flush
3. Four of a kind
4. Full house
5. Flush
6. Straight
7. Three of a kind
8. Two pairs
9. One pair
10. High card

Wild Cards

By mutual prior agreement (and often!) certain cards are designated as being wild. The wild card can be used to represent any card of any suit and any denomination, even as a duplicate of a card already held by the player. Here are some wild-card combinations.

1. The joker, which when added to a standard pack makes it a 53-card deck. Often more than one joker is introduced into the play. If no joker is handy, any 53rd card can be added to the deck, as wild.

2. Deuces wild, the most popular wild cards next to the joker. Any one of the deuces, or the two black deuces, or the two red, or all four deuces may by mutual consent be declared wild.

3. In combination with one or both of the above variations, threes are occasionally declared wild cards.

4. It is not unusual for players to declare wild the low card of a five-card hand, the one-eyed jacks, the jacks with mustaches, the black sevens, or the profile kings. For that matter, any card or group of cards may be arbitrarily designated as wild.

The table on page 43 gives the rank of Poker hands with one or more wild cards (in order of their value, Rank 1 being the highest and Rank 12 lowest).

Stripped Decks

In a game where there are only a few players (2, 3 or 4) or where faster action is desired without the use of "wild cards," it may be decided to strip a deck, i.e., to remove certain low cards and play without them. Generally the twos, threes and fours are stripped, making a 40-card deck. If the players so desire, twos, threes, fours, fives and sixes can be removed from the deck, making a 32-card deck. In England's gaming clubs, Five Card Stud with a 32-card stripped deck is widely played, and for big stakes I might add.

RANK OF POKER HANDS WITH ONE OR MORE WILD CARDS

1. Five of a kind	7. Flush
2. Royal flush	8. Straight
3. Straight flush	9. Three of a kind
4. Four of a kind	10. Two pairs
5. Full house	11. One pair
6. Double-ace flush	12. High card

Rank 12 (High Card) can occur only when none of active players has a wild card.

Rank of Low Hands in Poker

Low or High-Low Poker differs from other forms of the game in that either low or both high and low hands bid for the pot. This one variation in Poker rules has such a great effect on the play of a hand and provides so many unusual and interesting situations and strategies that it has replaced many other forms of Poker. The rank or value of high hands is the same as in any Poker game; however, low hands are the reverse. The Scarne rule that follows is to count aces as high and low. Therefore, the cinch, or perfect, low is six, four, three, two, and ace of mixed suits. If they are all of the same suit it counts as a flush and in effect becomes a disaster when playing for low. Similarly, straights including ace-two-three-four-five are considered high and disastrous for the low player. Treating the aces as either high or low adds extra zip and skill to both Low Poker and High-Low Poker.

The low hand is evaluated by the rank of its highest card; if there is a tie between highest cards, by the rank of its second card, etc. The value of the lowest card is irrelevant to the hand's value except when on the showdown the four higher cards are exactly matched by another player's. Example: A mixed-suit hand such as nine, seven, six, five and three, being a nine low, would beat a mixed-suit nine low with nine, eight, six, five and three. To repeat, the lowest-ranking perfect low hand, known as a cinch hand, is the six, four, three, two, and ace in mixed suits.

In the following table are listed the best twenty low hands in Poker. These are mixed suits, of course. And any hand in a superior rank beats any hand listed below it.

RANK OF LOW HANDS IN POKER

1. 6-4-3-2-A (Cinch Hand)	11. 7-6-3-2-A
2. 6-5-3-2-A	12. 7-6-4-2-A
3. 6-5-4-2-A	13. 7-6-4-3-A
4. 6-5-4-3-A	14. 7-6-4-3-2
5. 6-5-4-3-2	15. 7-6-5-2-A
6. 7-4-3-2-A	16. 7-6-5-3-A
7. 7-5-3-2-A	17. 7-6-5-3-2
8. 7-5-4-2-A	18. 7-6-5-4-A
9. 7-5-4-3-A	19. 7-6-5-4-2
10. 7-5-4-3-2	20. 8-5-4-3-2, and so on.

The ranks of the low hands in Poker as stated above hold true for all Low and High-Low Poker games found in this book unless specified to the contrary in the game being described. Examples: Lowball where a "bicycle" (5-4-3-2-A) is the best low hand, and at Seven to Deuce Low Poker where 7-5-4-3-2 is the unbeatable hand.

Rank of Low Hands Explained

Being diametrically opposite in value to the hands of standard Poker, the worth of the Low hands can best be explained by comparing each to the closest equivalent hand found in standard Poker. The following comparisons do not reflect exact mathematical equivalents —nonetheless they do give the Low or High-Low players an easy method to gauge the strength of their hands. Following, for the first time in print, is the best possible comparison of Low hands to those of standard Poker.

1. The 6-4-3-2-A, also known as a sixty-four or a six, approximates a royal flush and cannot be beaten. 2. The 6-5-3-2-A, known as a sixty-five or a six, approximates any straight flush. 3. The 6-5-4-X-X, also known as a sixty-five or a six, approximates any four of a kind. 4. The 7-4-3-2-A and 7-5-4-X-X, known as a seventy-four, seventy-five or a seven, approximates any full house. 5. The 7-6-3-2-A and 7-6-4-X-X, known as a seventy-six or a seven, approximates any flush. 6. The 7-6-5-X-X, known as a seventy-six or a seven, approximates a straight. 7. The 8-4-3-2-A and 8-5-X-X-X, known as an eighty-four, eighty-five or an eight, approximates any three of a kind. 8. The 8-6-X-X-X

and 8-7-X-X-X, known as an eighty-six, eighty-seven or an eight, approximates any two pairs. 9. The 9-X-X-X-X, known as a nine, approximates any pair. 10. The 10-X-X-X-X, J-X-X-X-X, Q-X-X-X-X, and K-X-X-X-X, known as a ten, jack, queen, and king, approximates no pair. X's shown represent lower-valued cards (except fillers for straights and flushes) than the cards that precede the X's.

So that the reader can see at a glance the comparison of Low hands to the closest equivalent hands found in standard Poker, here they are, for the first time in print, placed together in the following table. Rank 1 is the highest-ranking Low and standard Poker hand. Rank 10 is the lowest-ranking Low and standard Poker hand.

LOW HANDS COMPARED TO STANDARD HANDS

Rank	Low Poker Hands	Standard Poker Hands
1	6-4-3-2-A	Royal flush
2	6-5-3-2-A	Straight flush
3	6-5-4-X-X	Four of a kind
4	7-4-3-2-A and	
	7-5-4-X-X	Full house
5	7-6-3-2-A and	
	7-6-4-X-X	Flush
6	7-6-5-X-X	Straight
7	8-4-3-2-A and	
	8-5-X-X-X	Three of a kind
8	8-6-X-X-X and	
	8-7-X-X-X	Two pairs
9	9-X-X-X-X	One pair
10	10-X-X-X-X, J-X-X-X-X	
	Q-X-X-X-X and K-X-X-X-X	No pair

As mentioned earlier, the above table reflects an approximate equivalent of low-rank Poker hands to those of standard Poker. However, it provides an invaluable comparison for the Low or High-Low Poker player to help him determine the importance of each five-card Low hand.

X's shown above represent all possible cards of lower value than the cards that precede the X's in the low-rank hands shown above.

How to Declare in High-Low Poker

There are two basic methods of declaring (announcing) high or low, or both high and low, before the showdown in all High-Low Poker games. They are: (1) simultaneous declaration, which is recommended for high-limit games; and (2) consecutive declaration, which is recommended for low-limit games.

The Simultaneous Declaration. Prior to the showdown, each player takes two chips and moves both hands under the table. He returns one clenched fist to the center of the table. Now, when all the active players have their hands above the table, the dealer calls "Open." All players must open their hands immediately. The absence of a chip indicates a low call, the presence of one chip indicates a high call. The presence of two chips indicates the player is going for both high and low. If chips are not available, coins can be used.

The Consecutive Declaration (which I do not recommend). Prior to the showdown in all High-Low games, the player who made the last aggressive move (raised or bet first on the final betting round) declares first. If everyone checked on the final round, the high hand showing must declare first. Declarations then proceed in clockwise rotation from one active player to another. In all the High-Low Draw Poker games, should all players check on the last round, the last aggressive player in the preceding round or rounds must declare first.

It is a sad but true fact that this consecutive method spoils the entire game. It is a great advantage to call last, or near the end of the declaration, because very often a player with good position is able to win half of the pot with a very weak hand because all others have declared in one direction. Such a position is called being *in the driver's seat.*

How Winners Are Determined in High-Low Poker

A winner in High-Low Poker games is determined as follows:

1. When playing High-Low Poker variations, the player holding the highest-ranking hand, provided he has declared for high, and the player holding the lowest-ranking hand, provided he has declared for low, share the pot equally.

2. If a player declares his hand incorrectly, he may correct the error if no other player after him has declared as yet; otherwise the declaration stands.

3. The rank of a low hand is inverse to the rank of a high hand. If the hand contains less than a pair its determinant is its highest-ranking card; if two players are tied as to highest-ranking card, the next highest-ranking card decides the winner, etc.

4. When a player announces for low, he no longer has any interest in high.

5. When a player announces for high, he no longer has any interest in low.

6. When a player announces high and low both, he must win both high and low to collect the pot. Should he lose either way or tie for either high or low, he loses the entire pot.

7. If the high-low declarant loses or ties in one direction but wins in the other, the player defeating him is awarded the entire pot.

8. If two or more players are tied for low, half the pot is equally divided among the winners tied for low. The other half of the pot goes to the winner, or winners, with the high hand. If there is an indivisible amount left over and a lone player has bid either high or low, he gets it. Otherwise, it goes into the next pot.

9. If there are two or more players in at the showdown and they all declare high, the highest of the hands takes the entire pot. If they all declare low, the lowest of the hands takes the pot.

10. If there are two or more high-low declarants at the showdown and each of the high-low declarants loses or ties in one direction, but neither high or low is won or tied by a one-way declarant, the pot is divided by the high-low declarants as in Cards Speak, which follows.

Cards Speak

Cards Speak, also referred to as Cards Speak for Themselves or Cards Show, is a third method of determining the showdown at High-Low Poker. In this version of High-Low showdown, players do not declare their intentions—they simply lay down their hands and the best high- and the best low-ranking hands split the pot.

This form of High-Low Poker is the showdown version of the game that's played in the public Poker rooms in the Nevada casinos, where it is known as High-Low Split.

The main reason why High-Low is played without a showdown declaration in Nevada casinos and in many private and commercial Poker clubs throughout the country is that it would be difficult for the game dealers to keep track of each player's declaration and settle arguments arising from such declarations. Furthermore, partner collusion and cheating is more prevalent in a High-Low game with showdown declarations than in Cards Speak.

Preparation for the Play: The Banker and his Duties

One of the players is selected by mutual or majority consent to be the banker for that session of play. If cash is to be used in the betting, the banker must make change and see that players bet or ante properly. As a rule it is the banker who takes the cut out of certain pots (which pots and how much cut are determined by the players) and puts that cash into a kitty—used to buy cards, food, drinks, or to help pay the rent. Under the common usages, all other players help the banker with these chores during the play. If chips are used the banker keeps the supply, sells them to the players, and redeems them to settle accounts at the end of the game.

Professional Poker, or the House Game

In a house or casino game, the management

1. Supplies all the essentials for Poker playing, namely, the casino, a special kind of Poker table, the chips, the cards, and a dealer and lookout man;
2. In return for these goods and services, takes a cut or an hourly charge.

The amount of the cut is just exactly what the traffic will bear then and there, in that ward of the city, in that month of the year.

Value of the Chips

Nationwide, this is the most common evaluation of Poker chips:

White—one unit.

Red—five units.

Blue—ten units.

Yellow—twenty-five units.

The value in cash of the units is entirely up to the players. It may range from 1¢, as in the classic penny-ante game, to $10—or $100, or $500, as in the Las Vegas World Series of Poker.

Optional Rules Better Discussed Before the Start of the Game

1. Before the game starts there must be common agreement on the kind of game to be played. Local conventions on such things as royalties and bonuses must be talked over before the game and clarified further by writing them on a pad. These conventions or rulings must be thoroughly understood by all players.
2. Although any player has the right to quit whenever he wants to, a time limit ending the game must be decided on before the start of the game.
3. Before play starts, there must be common agreement as to the amount of the ante if any, the minimum and maximum amount of money or chips that can be bet at any one time, and the maximum number of raises at any betting interval. As a rule a limit is rarely put

on the number of raises permitted at any betting interval—but see sections on Draw or Stud Poker for details on betting.

Number of Raises Permitted: The rule I recommend on the number of raises permitted is the one used in most Nevada casinos' public Poker rooms, which is: The maximum number of raises permitted at any betting round or interval is *three*. However, when there are only two active players remaining in the pot, the number of raises is unlimited, since either player can put an end to the raises by simply calling the bet.

Freezing a Raise or Possible Raises à la Scarne

The following rule is recommended to big-money Poker players who do not want restrictions on their raises but at the same time desire some protection against whipsawing. How often have you been sandwiched between two players who are raising and reraising each other with no consideration for you, and you had to cough up enough money to match their raises just to stay in till the decision? You had made up your mind to stay to the bitter end, even if you lost all your money, and there were times when you did exactly that. One night I counted thirty raises between two reckless high rollers in one round of Draw Poker, and one player who never raised had to match the thirty raises to stay in the pot. Then and there I decided something must be done to protect a player from being whipsawed between two confederates, two cheaters, or two reckless players with no regard for the other men in the game. I give all Poker players a rule that eliminates this hazard from Poker without putting a limit on the number of raises permitted. Here it is—a freezer.

A *raise freezer* is a special call bet that can be made by any active player at any time after three raises. That puts an end to all raises for that particular betting round or interval. Whenever three or more raises have taken place on any betting round, any active player, at his turn of play, after placing an amount equal to the last player's bet into the pot, calls "Freeze," and puts an end to any further raises for that particular betting round.

Check and Raise

Check and Raise, also known as "sandbagging," is permitted. It's part of the skill of Poker and is permitted in all styles of Poker with the possible exception of Private or Social Poker.

Royalties or Bonuses

Some players elect to pay a royalty to any player holding an exceptionally high-ranking hand, such as a royal flush, a straight flush, or four of a kind. This is not incorporated in my rules, and is optional with players. I mention it just to make this chapter definitive and complete. Royalties and bonuses on a royal flush or any other bonus hand are optional with the players, but as a rule are from three to five times the amount of the maximum permitted bet. Each player, whether active or not, must pay the player holding the bonus hand the amount agreed on at the start of the game.

Seating Positions

As a rule at the start of the game players may sit wherever they like. A new player may take any vacant seat he chooses unless the game is Dealer's Edge or Ante, in which case he must wait until it becomes his turn to deal before he can have cards.

Just to avoid any possible dispute about seating positions, the start of the game, the seating of new players and the selection of the dealer, I think it might be well to incorporate the following rules into the game:

SELECTING THE DEALER AND ESTABLISHING SEATING POSITIONS AT THE TABLE

1. Any player shall by mutual or majority consent shuffle the cards, and the player to his right shall cut the deck.
2. The player acting as dealer shall deal one card to each player face up, starting with the player at his left, dealing clockwise around the table, and ending with himself.
3. The player dealt the highest card shall become the first dealer and select any seat he wants.
4. The player with the next highest card selects any remaining seat, the player with the third highest any remaining seat, etc.
5. In case of ties, each of the tied players shall be dealt a new card face up until the tie is broken.
6. At the completion of each hand the deal shall pass to the player at the immediate left of the player who dealt that round.

The Shuffle

The dealer shuffles the cards. Any player may call for a shuffle at any time before the cut, although the dealer has the privilege of shuffling the cards last.

The Cut

1. After the cards have been shuffled, the dealer presents the pack to the player at his right to be cut. If he refuses to cut the cards, the player to that player's right has the privilege of cutting, etc. If all other players refuse to cut, the dealer must cut. *It is mandatory.*

2. At least ten cards must be in each of the cut packets should a player use a regular cut. Should he desire, a player may use the "Scarne Cut" (see page 257) or cut the deck more than once. After the cut, the cut portions must be squared or reunited and dealt as a complete pack. It is not permissible to pick up one cut portion of the pack and start dealing with it.

Asking for a New Cut

If a player does not like the way the cards have been cut before the start of the deal because he doubts the legitimacy of the cut, or for any other reason, he may call for another cut; and any player other than the player calling for the new cut may cut the cards.

The Deal

The dealer deals one card at a time to each player, starting with the leader (player to the dealer's left) and continuing clockwise until each player in the game has the required number of cards. The cards are dealt face up or face down or both according to the rules of the game being played. The dealer must make certain that the players place their bets or antes, if any, into the pot at their proper turn of play, and check each player's bet to make sure it is correct. He must gather in all player discards as they are made and place them face down to one side out of play forming a discard pile. In Stud Poker games, the dealer must call the high hand in every round and instruct the high hand that he must act first.

Dealing from Part of the Deck

A dealer is not permitted to deal from a cut portion of the pack. The cut portions must be united, and the dealer must deal from the entire pack.

Cutting the Pack During the Deal

No player is permitted to cut the cards after the cards have been dealt or the betting has started unless some overt crookedness has been observed and proved.

Misdeal

In case of a misdeal, there must be a new shuffle and cut. The same dealer deals again.

Pot, Ante, Bets, and Their Functions

The betting features of Poker are the pot, the ante, the check, the bet, the raise, the reraise, the call and the fold. Each possesses its own specific function. A general explanation of these functions, which apply at any betting interval, be it at Draw or Stud Poker or their variants, follows.

1. *The Pot:* an imaginary area somewhere near the center of the table where the ante and bets (cash or chips) of the players are placed. The winner or winners of the hand take the contents of the pot.

2. *The Ante:* a compulsory amount of chips or cash placed in the pot before each deal begins. Practice varies, but in Draw Poker and its variants, the ante I recommend is one fourth, or 25%, of the minimum bet allowed. Stud Poker and its variants, with four or more betting intervals, produce far bigger pots than Draw Poker, with its two betting intervals; therefore Stud Poker is often played minus the ante. However, when an ante is used, I recommend that the ante amount be 25% of the minimum bet.

The practice of pot ante prior to the deal was introduced to give the players "something to go for," to prevent too many tight players from drawing cards without paying for them, and to force these tight players to loosen up a bit.

3. *The Check or Pass:* refusal to bet at the time, but retaining the option to reenter the betting should another player bet later.

4. *The Bet:* the first bet of each betting interval, which may be either compulsory or voluntary.

5. *The Call, See, or Play:* putting into the pot an amount equal to the last active player's bet.

6. *The Raise:* the increase of the amount of the last active player's bet.

7. *The Reraise:* the increase of the size of the last active player's raise.

8. *The Fold or Drop-out:* throwing in one's hand and quitting that round of play; this may occur during any betting interval.

The Showdown

In any form of Poker, when two or more active players remain in the pot after the conclusion of the final betting interval (round) and the equalization of all the remaining active player bets has taken place, each of the remaining active players must expose and spread out his competing hand in its entirety for everyone to see.

The main purpose of the showdown is to determine the winning hand (highest valued) by the face value of its cards regardless of any verbal value given to the hand. It is a basic rule in Poker that the cards shown speak for themselves. However, should a player's hand after the showdown reveal a winning hand and he has called a lesser-valued or losing hand, and should he or his opponent or opponents have failed to correct the verbal error and the pot been collected, the error stands. Players are not obliged to correct opponent's verbal errors on the showdown. If prior to the showdown only one active player remains in the hand he wins the pot.

Time Limit

Before the play begins, players should agree on a quitting time at which the game session will end and stick to it. Violation of this time limit may eventually turn pleasant sessions into unpleasant ones.

Coffeehousing

A weekly Poker game session is more often than not a get-together to play cards and talk about life's latest events. Table talk at these once-a-week games is as much a part of Poker as the card playing and money wagered; yet there are times when the talk around the table can be boisterous and annoying, especially when a big money pot is at stake.

In money games, small or big, this kind of table talk is called "coffeehousing" and should not be tolerated. Coffeehousing is the practice of trying to confuse and mislead the opponents through excessive talk and expressions concerning the round of play. Although coffeehousing may at times serve as a relief from tension, it also can be used to try to befuddle opponents and gain a psychological advantage over other players.

During my national Poker survey I watched many a Poker game and observed just what coffeehousing is tolerated. Most social weekly games made up of women only that I scouted permitted a player to say anything she liked, even lying about the strength of her hand.

Coffeehousing, permissable or not, is also used discreetly in big-time Poker games including the annual Las Vegas World Series of Poker, when and where the stakes totaled $420,000 in 1978. There are, however, Poker games in Nevada casinos and in private clubs where coffeehousing is prohibited and players who persist in its use are told to take their card playing elsewhere.

The range of coffeehousing may include such heartbroken complaints as, "What lousy cards," or "One more hand like this and I'll find myself a new game"; or when the pot is raised, the coffeehouser may exclaim, "You're nuts to try and bluff me. I'll raise you, and I know you don't have the guts to reraise me." Or, the more subtle remark heard in big-money Poker games when in Stud a card is about to be dealt and the coffeehouser shouts, "Come Ace," when in reality he is wishing for a nine spot. Or a remark such as, "Throw your hand in, I don't want your money."

Coffeehousing, when used too freely and too incautiously, may become a disadvantage to the perpetrator because the smart intended sucker realizes that the coffeehouser has more strength in his mouth than cards in his hand.

The Scarne Rules for Poker prohibit coffeehousing when the talk is directed to the play of the hand in progress. As to the penalty for coffeehousing, that must be left to the management or the players.

Miscalling a Hand

A player cannot overcall his hand. (If his opponent throws his hand away when the player says, "Kings up," the player must produce kings up or better. Otherwise his opponent wins.) This rule doesn't apply until the last person has acted after the draw. Before that, overcalling a hand is just "table talk."

Discard Before Drawing

In any form of Draw Poker, before receiving cards the player must discard the same number of cards he is drawing, insuring that his hand consists of five cards at all times.

Verbal Announcement

Verbal raising or calling is not binding. Chips in the pot denote action.

Clocking the Opponent's Chips

In a Table Stakes game each contestant has the right to know how much money in chips every other player has on the table. Therefore it is the duty of each player to keep his chips stacked neatly so that an opponent can approximate the money value by observation. Furthermore, should a player ask another player the total money value of his chips resting on the table, that player must comply.

Calling Time

A player must call time if he is not prepared to act at his turn of play. If one or more players have acted after a player has failed to act or to call time, he has forfeited his right to play and his hand is dead.

Passing the Deal

A dealer cannot pass his turn to deal unless he is incompetent to deal the cards. When an incompetent player passes the deal, the player to the player's right becomes the substitute dealer. However, the substitute dealer must deal himself the first card and the incompetent player receives the last dealt card of that hand. In addition, the substitute dealer must speak first should he be required. Immediately after the substitute dealer's round of play has ended, the substitute dealer takes his proper turn as dealer.

Illegal Cutting of Cards

Under no circumstances may a player ask to cut the cards after a bet has been made. I must stress particularly that cards cannot be cut after the deal has started, or for that matter at any other time except before the start of the deal, unless some crookedness has been suspected.

Two-Minute Time Period for a Play

If an active player has called time and is taking too much time to decide how to play his hand, any other active player may call time, and if the hesitant player fails to complete his play within two minutes after time is called his hand is dead: he is forced to drop out. *Note:* This situation happens often in a high-limit game; I have seen players take a half hour or more to decide on a play.

Changing Positions at the Table

At the completion of any hour of play, players may demand a new deal for a change in their seating positions. The procedure is the same as in establishing places at the table at the start of a game. The player whose turn it is to deal (1) deals for seating positions and (2) deals the next hand in play.

Tapping Out

When a player has put all his money into the pot and no longer can bet, this is called a tap-out. That player is permitted to play for the size of the pot up until the time he no longer has money. If the other players keep betting, they put their bets to one side, as the tapping-out player has no legal interest in that side pot. The tapping-out player receives cards until the hand is completed, and should he have the highest-ranking hand on the showdown, he wins only the original pot, not the side pot. That is won by the player having the highest-ranking cards among the remaining bettors. Except in Table Stakes and Freeze-out, when a player taps out and loses, he is out of the game. However, if he wins on the tap-out and therefore has money, he may continue to play as before. A player is permitted only one tap-out during a Poker session.

When tapping out, a player may raise only if he still possesses an amount equal to the maximum limit so that in case of a reraise he can call the bet. A player cannot tap out with money on the table.

Going Through the Discards

In no circumstances is a player permitted to look at the discards before or after the showdown. Nor is a player permitted to look at another player's hand even though he is out of the pot. Looking through the undealt cards or another player's hand are forbidden. These rules should be strictly enforced.

Lending Money or Chips

Under no circumstances is a player allowed to borrow money or chips from another player during the play. If a player desires to borrow money from another player, it must be done before the cards are dealt. Passing money or chips from one player to another during the play is not permitted.

Betting for Another Player

Under no circumstances is a player permitted to ante or bet for another player.

Angling

Angling is positively prohibited. For example, discussing among two or more players to split the pot regardless of the winner, or to give back part of the money, or to ask for a free ride or call is prohibited.

Overs in the Pot

No money or chips may be taken out of the pot except when the stakes are cash, under which circumstances a player may take out his proper change after placing a bet at his turn of play. The players must observe that the proper change is taken.

Should a player ante or put into the pot an amount larger than required, and thereafter should another player make a bet, the overage cannot be taken out of the pot.

Exposed Hands on Showdown

All players, active or nonactive, are entitled to see all active players' hands on the showdown, provided a bet has been called. Therefore, on the showdown all the players in their proper turn must spread their cards face up on the table.

Removing Money from the Table

Money and chips cannot be removed from the table until a player has quit the game and cashes in.

String or Slow Betting

String or slow betting refers to a bet that is not completed or verbally declared immediately. In short, the player fails to announce the size of his bet and only puts a part of it in the pot, then hesitates before placing the remainder of his bet in the pot. It's this hesitation that's illegal. The reason is that during the hesitation period the player making the string or slow bet can study the reactions of his opponents, and depending on these reactions he either makes only a partial bet or continues increasing the size of his bet.

How Chips or Cash Bets Must Be Placed in Pot

Chips or cash representing antes, call bets, raises and reraises placed in the pot must be kept separate from the rest of the chips or cash long enough for other players to see that the correct amount is being placed in the pot. The same rule applies to taking change from the pot.

Criticism

A player is not permitted under any circumstances to criticize another player's methods. Poker is a game in which each man plays his own hand as he elects. No consideration should be expected by one player from another.

SCARNE'S RULES FOR PRIVATE OR SOCIAL POKER

Personally I feel that when playing Poker for money, friendships should be left behind and that a player may do anything to try and fool his opponents, as long as he does not cheat. I frown on a game where the betting is restricted by rules and a player must bet a specific amount at certain times. I consider it part of the skill of the game to vary the amounts of my bets in certain situations. I also consider it scientific Poker to check on a good hand in the hopes that someone else will bet and then I can raise or reraise as the situation dictates. I also consider it good Poker playing to make a big-limit bet in an attempt to steal the pot ante. However, I do know that the women who play Poker together once a week don't care much for my style of Poker, preferring the Poker-playing rules where sandbagging is prohibited and a more social form of Poker playing prevails. Twenty years ago a Poker club in my home town made up of both women and men asked me to formulate a set of Poker rules for them that would: (a) discourage the so-called Poker professionals and Poker hustlers from joining their group; (b) simplify the play of the game and minimize the betting-skill factor in Poker for the benefit of the poorer players; and (c) avoid sandbagging, which is the number one factor in breaking up a friendly Poker game.

I did formulate their club rules, and this same group still meets regularly and no one has really been hurt financially over the years. I have revised these rules slightly to agree with the changing times and offer them as my social or friendly Poker-playing rules.

All the basic preliminaries before actual play and the rules of actual play discussed in this chapter and those in Chapters 3, 5 and 11 hold good, except for the following betting regulations:

1. Three units must constitute the betting limits, such as 1, 2, and 4 cents, or 5, 10, and 15 cents, or $1, $2, and $4—or any other three-figure limit, regardless of the amount. Players are permitted to bet only the three specified figures as dictated by the rules previously established before the start of the game.
2. Draw Poker and its variants. The player who opens the pot is permitted to bet only one unit. After the draw, the opener must bet two units. He is not permitted to check, nor can he bet anything other than two units.
3. Stud Poker and its variants. The player who holds high card on the first betting round must bet one unit; he cannot check or drop out. During each succeeding round of betting, the high hand must bet one unit. But if the high hand shows a pair or better, the holder may bet two units. He may, however, check or drop out (fold).
4. After the first bettor of a particular round has made a legal bet as described here, other players may raise either one, two or three units.
5. If a player checks, he is not permitted to raise in the same betting round. In other words, sandbagging is illegal in a friendly or social Poker game.
6. The maximum number of raises during any given betting round cannot exceed three.

Dealer's Choice

This Poker variation is highly recommended for private or social Poker. Dealer's Choice is exactly what the name implies. When it is your turn to deal, you have the privilege of naming the Poker variant to be played, and it is often necessary to give a lesson in playing your version of the game. The dealer may select any game he knows how to play, and he is not limited to the common forms of Poker. He may select a game of his own invention or knowledge which can be easily explained to the other players without too much loss of time.

The Kitty

In a private or social game in which the same players meet once a week to indulge in their favorite recreation, Poker playing, it is suggested that a special fund be established by majority agreement into which are placed chips or cash drawn from pots possessing an agreed minimum amount of chips or cash. This fund, called "the kitty," may be used to defray expenses of the Poker session such as refreshments, cards, chips, etc., or it may be turned over to the establishment in which the Poker playing takes place; or any chips or cash left in the kitty at the end of a given period may be divided equally among the players.

SCARNE'S GENERAL RULES FOR COMMERCIALIZED POKER

In a commercialized Poker room, club, or house game, the management 1. Supplies all the essentials for Poker playing, namely, the room, club or house, a special kind of kidney-shaped Poker table that seats up to ten players, the cards, the chips, and a professional dealer. 2. In return for these goods and services takes a rake or cut, or an hourly charge. The amount of the rake or cut or the hourly charge is exactly what the traffic will bear.

My latest scouting survey of more than one hundred legal and illegal Poker rooms or clubs situated in Nevada, California, New York, Chicago, Miami, Atlanta and New Orleans failed to show two Poker clubs with the same general house rules. Furthermore, I failed to find one Poker room or club whose general house rules could not be vastly improved. Some of the rules were good, others fair, and some bad. So I selected the best of these hundreds of different Poker rules, perfected those that needed improvement, and added a number of rules that I personally developed. A combination of the best of these rules has been incorporated into Scarne's General Rules for Commercialized Poker. Add these to the rules governing the specific game to be played that are covered in detail in the following pages, and the end result is the best set of Poker rules for Poker rooms, clubs and house yet devised.

1. *The Color and Value of Chips.* Those I recommend are as follows: 1. White, one unit; red, five units; blue, ten units; and yellow, twenty-five units. The value in cash of the units is entirely up to management.

2. *The Size of the Initial Chip Buy-in.* The initial chip buy-in that permits a player to gamble at a commercial Poker club table should be ten times the size of the minimum-limit bet allowed.

Examples: In the $1–$3 limit, the buy-in is $10. In the $3–$6 limit, the buy-in is $30. In the $5–$10 limit, the buy-in is $50. In the $10–$20 limit, the buy-in is $100. In the $20–$40 limit, the buy-in is $200. In the $300–$600 limit, the buy-in is $3,000.

3. *The Pot Ante.* The size of each player's pot ante is about 15 to 25% of the size of the minimum-bet limit.

Examples: in a $1–$3 limit, the ante is 25 cents. In a $3–$6 limit, the ante is 50 cents. In the $5–$10 limit, the ante is $1. In the $10–$20 limit game, the ante is $2. In the $20–$40 limit game, the ante is $5. And in the $300–$600 limit game, the ante is $100.

4. *The House Charge, Cut or Rake.* In the $1–$3 limit, rake is 4% on pots totaling more than $5, maximum rake per pot, $3. In the $3–$6 limit, rake is 4% of all pots totaling more than $10, maximum rake per pot $2. In the $5–$10 limit, rake is 4% of all pots totaling more than $15, maximum rake $2 per pot. In the $10–$20 limit, rake is 4% of all pots totaling more than $20, maximum rake $3 per pot. In $20–$40 limit, rake is 4% of all pots totaling $25 or more, maximum rake $3 per pot. In the $300–$600 limit, the charge is fixed at $18 a seat per hour.

5. *House Dealer, Shuffle, Cut, Burnt Cards, and Buck or Button.* As in Nevada Poker rooms, Scarne's club rules do not permit a player to shuffle, cut or deal the cards. The house dealer does all. He collects the played hands, shuffles, cuts and deals the game. Under no circumstances is a player permitted to cut the deck. This ruling eliminates the possibility of a card-cheat player doing his crooked business on the cut. Furthermore, after each betting interval has been completed and before the next round of cards is dealt, the house dealer burns the top card of the deck by dealing it face down onto the table in front of himself.

At the beginning of the game and before the first round of play is dealt, the dealer places a buck or button (a chip marked "button") in front of the player to his left to identify the first imaginary dealer. Thereafter the buck or button is moved by the dealer around from player to player in clockwise sequence to keep track of the next imaginary dealer.

6. *Unlimited Raises and the Raise Freezer.* The raise freezer, my own creation, is probably the most important Poker ruling to come along in the past thirty years. This ruling permits active players to raise and reraise each other to their hearts' content, with no limit placed on the number of raises or reraises allowed. However, after three raises have taken place, any active player, at his turn of play, may put an end to all further raises merely by placing (calling) an amount equal to the last player's bet and calling "Freeze." This freeze announcement puts an end to all further raises for that particular betting interval.

7. *Check and Raise.* Check and raise, known as sandbagging, is permitted.

8. Each player is responsible for protecting his own hand. An incorrect number of cards constitutes a dead hand.

9. In the event that an extra card of like suit and value should appear in the deal, all chips in pot will be returned to players.

10. If a card other than the first active player's hidden card is exposed, there will be no action.

11. If a player "tapping out" has less than half the required bet in the pot, the next player to act can call the "tap-out bet" as completed —he cannot raise. If the tap-out player has half or more of the required bet in the pot, the next player can call the tapped-out bet and raise the bet.

12. A player folding or throwing his hand in on a deal where all players have checked is dealt out of the next deal.

13. When there are insufficient cards to complete a deal, all discards plus burnt cards will be shuffled and dealt to remaining players.

14. If a player does not call the full amount of a bet (unless tapping out) on his turn to act, he must make up the difference or throw in his hand and forfeit the amount he put in the pot.

15. In Draw, playing hands turned face down are considered dead unless call has been made and hand is still in possession of player.

16. The open or face-up cards in Stud must remain face up on the table in front of player at all times. Placing one or more of the open or face-down cards in a player's hand constitutes a dead hand, and the offender forfeits the amount he put into the pot.

17. No string or slow bets permitted at any time.

18. No splitting of pot permitted at any time except when hands are tied on the showdown.

19. In the event of a turned-up card, the dealer will deal and dis-

card a number of cards off the top of the deck equal to the number of active players in the pot.

20. When a hand has been called on the showdown, anyone playing in the game may ask to see all active players' hands.

21. Players are not permitted to look at burnt cards, discards or cards remaining on top of the deck at any time.

22. Husband and wife and immediate relatives are not allowed to play at the same table.

23. No game with less than four players is allowed.

24. Only one short buy-in is permitted after each full buy-in. One buy for less than "buy-in" is a short buy.

25. Under no circumstances are players permitted to touch the pot. If a player wishes change, the dealer will accommodate him. Furthermore, players' bets such as ante, call, raise and reraise must be placed outside the pot perimeter to be counted and pushed into the pot by the dealer.

26. All disputes between players or players and dealer not covered above must be settled by management.

Note: Many of the rules described above may be incorporated in the General Rules for Poker on pages 39 to 60.

4

General Strategy

TIPS, HINTS, SUBTERFUGES AND BITS OF STRATEGY THAT WILL IMPROVE YOUR POKER GAME.

At the very outset, I can make this promise: No matter how good a Poker player you are, this General Strategy chapter will improve your game. It is a collection of tips, hints, subterfuges, bits of strategy, Do's and Don't's that I have gathered over the years from the world's best Poker players in Las Vegas, Los Angeles, New York, New Orleans, Chicago, London, Paris, Rome, Cairo, South Africa, etc.

Let me say this right now—I'm not going to insist on the fiction that Poker is played for pastime only. It isn't. Poker is played for money, and big money at that. If Poker lacked the gambling element, the profit motive, it would never have attained its worldwide popularity.

Watching tens of thousands of Poker players and thousands of Poker games down these many years, I've made it my business to observe the small fleeting mannerisms of winning and losing competitors, to cross-examine hundreds and hundreds of experts (including several winners of the yearly Las Vegas World Series of Poker) and big-time Poker players, to measure the difference imposed on the play by the stakes of the game, to observe not only that sober citizens do indeed bet $100,000 or more on a single Poker hand, but also how they bet it.

And so, I can tell you this: Every Poker player who is a consistent winner has little tricks of his own. There are in the mass scores of such tricks developed over the lives of these players by trial and error and by costly experience into a very substantial body of Poker learning. No one player has mastered all of them. Perhaps no one player can. But I'm going to tell you about them.

First, let's consider what is meant when the professional gambler says of a fellow Poker player, "He has no card sense at all."

What is card sense? Of what is it made up? Well, its components are not so many. Card sense is knowing what to do and when. At Poker, should you drop out of the pot or play? Should you take your chance and try to raise on the first betting round or just play along and send it in at the last betting round? Should you break up a pair and try for a flush? Should you try a bluff against a winner or a loser? Is your opponent bluffing or not? To be a good Poker player, to have good card sense, you must have a reason for making any of these decisions and countless more. And reasoning is the application of intelligence.

Following are a collection of tips, hints, bits of strategy, subterfuges and warnings that, if practiced and put into action, are guaranteed to improve your Poker playing.

The most important thing to remember if you want to win at Poker is to *be alert.* Every little movement has a meaning all its own. Every draw and every card shown has a vital bearing on the strategy you employ. You must watch every player in the game to see that you are not being cheated or chiseled; you must watch every active player so that you can gauge the strength of his hand and judge his reactions to a raise or reraise, to a draw of two cards or three cards, etc. In Stud, especially, you must observe each card dealt carefully to see (1) how it affects your own chances of improving your hand; (2) whether it improves the chances of each other player, including the player who received the card. Finally, you have to watch yourself so as not to betray your hand or give clues to your opponents. Yes, you have to be alert.

You *can't* be alert if you are overtired or mentally disturbed by something either in or outside the game. And you can't be alert if your alcohol content is too high. Don't play Poker for sizable stakes if you've had a tough day at the office, if you're worried about business or about Junior's behavior or if you've had a few too many martinis. And don't drink liquor while playing—not if you want to win.

You must always be keen about sizing up situations. If you are, you have a good chance of winning even if you are just an average player. For there will always be one or more players who because of fatigue, irritation, recklessness or fuzziness will play badly and give you the edge.

Whether the game be Stud or Draw Poker, Seven Card or Five Card, Deuces Wild or Nothing Wild, there are three very important rules of play. If you remember these rules, it is almost impossible for you to lose in an evening of Poker unless you are playing with a group of experts who also know them. If you play Poker regularly with the same group of players and find that there are a few who win consistently while the rest of you lose—leaving the possibility of dishonesty aside—it is because these players are aware of these rules and play accordingly.

The first rule is: *When you have nothing, get out.* More money is lost by Stud Poker players who go in with two indifferent cards and drop out later, or by Draw Poker players who stay with a low pair and fold after the draw, than is ever lost by having three kings beaten by three aces. The player who has the patience to stay out of pot after pot, for hours if necessary, is the player who, in the long run, will win.

The second rule is: *When you're beaten, get out.* You may have a pair of queens back to back in a Stud game—a high hand good enough to win 99 pots out of 100. But if, on the next card, one of your opponents should show a pair of kings or aces, in most cases the smart play is to *drop out at once.* You may improve your hand, but the odds are against it. Even if you improve, your opponent may improve also—and his pair was better than yours to begin with. Except for going in on nothing, trying to beat a big pair with a small one loses more money than anything else in Poker.

The third rule is: *When you have the best hand, make your opponents pay.* If *you* have the pair of aces back to back, make it as expensive as possible for the man with the pair of queens to play. It is true that every once in a while he will outdraw you, but you will beat him much more often, and you can afford his occasional victory.

There are many fine points to the game of Poker; but if you get nothing out of this section of the book but these three rules, you will be a consistent money winner against most players.

The following tips, hints, bits of strategy and warnings added to the above, if studied seriously and applied faithfully, should make you a winner at Poker.

I have selected for discussion those traits possessed by gamblers who make their living or a part of it from Poker, i.e., Poker hustlers. Some of the warnings to the reader were inserted after watching numerous Poker games in which cheaters operated.

If the reader believes that a few of the tips given are too severe—such as "Never give a Poker player a break even if he is your best friend"—then he can simply declare his attitude at the start of the game by saying, "Boys, if you get them, bet them up, because that is what I am going to do." If you fail to bet a cinch hand for all it's worth when you hold one, you will rarely, if ever, be a good Poker player. The best gamblers have a slogan: "You must pay to look."

Poker is a money game, not just a pleasant way to spend an evening.

If you want to play cards simply for recreation, there are many games more interesting than Poker. Remove the gambling spirit from Poker and it is a bore.

Do's and Don't's

Insist that all players put the proper amount in the pot at all times. Many card hustlers obtain a decided edge by playing shy and forgetting to make good. Nickels and dimes stolen in this fashion amount to dollars at the end of a Poker session. Don't be a sucker for a card hustler: make him put up.

Learn the correct rules of the game so that in an argument you can protect your money. A bad decision against a player can break him for the evening. If you know the rules, no smart aleck will be able to cheat you of a pot by a bad decision.

If you are a neophyte Poker player, don't get into a game in which the boys are old hands. Experience is a big factor in Poker and very hard to overcome with mere talent. If you are lucky in a game with such players, you win little; if unlucky, you lose heavily. Find a game where the players are in your class.

Before joining a Poker game, ascertain the minimum and maximum limits, find out if the game is being played with any special house rules and whether the number of raises is limited or unrestricted. You need this information to determine whether you have enough money on your person to sit in the game. There is no law at Poker that says a player can't sit in a $5 limit game with a $10 bankroll, but you must realize that you will probably lose your $10 on the first pot and get plenty of criticism from the other players. Only very rarely will you be lucky from the start and win many times the $10 invested.

The smart Poker player has a couple of hundred dollars as a cushion in a $5 limit game, and the same ratio applies for smaller or larger limits. For example, a player should figure his cushion at $40 for a $1 limit; at least $20 for a 50¢ limit, etc. The smart Poker player reasons that his skill will win for him over several hours of play but if he lacks sufficient money to overcome a streak of bad luck, which may occur in the first few hands, he has, for that evening, lost any opportunity of putting his skill to work.

Before you sit down to a Poker game with strangers it is suggested that you observe the game for at least an hour, studying the players' characteristics. See who plays the cards loose and who plays tight. When you do join in, play a conservative game at first, just in case it might be a steer game (crooked game). If you are dealt an exceptionally good hand in a strange game, don't bet everything you have with you. Be satisfied with small winnings on the hand; if it is a steer game your losses will be small, and perhaps the cheaters will decide you are too hep to be taken in.

Don't lend money to another player in a Poker game. The money you lend will often help break you. Also, it is an even bet you won't get it back. Gambling debts aren't paid back as often as legitimate debts.

If you desire to improve your game, play as often as you can, because skill develops with experience. But don't play in a big-limit game during the learning period.

Poker skill consists of six elements:

1. Knowledge of the game's mathematics.
2. Money management.
3. Psychological deception.
4. Card memory and table analysis.
5. Playing position.
6. Betting courage.

The extent to which a player can use these elements will determine his Poker ability.

It is almost impossible to teach anyone to become a good Poker player by setting a standard pattern, because all players have different traits. Some are nervous and crave to be in every pot; others like to raise just for the thrill of the game; others are very conservative; others have no courage (afraid to bet up their cards at the proper time).

I do not believe that giving sample problems and their solutions can lead to better Poker playing. Even if you memorized their solutions, you would grow old waiting for one of these sample hands to occur in an actual game. And even if such a sample hand did turn up, it would be most unlikely that the other players would have the same Poker characteristics and the same amounts of money as the illustration specified. Therefore, sample problems in this book will be held to a minimum.

There are certain fundamental rules a player must follow if he hopes to play well.

Know the Mathematics of the Game. It's not difficult. You simply use some common arithmetic plus a little patience to guide your playing. You should remember, for instance, that in Poker the average hand becomes less valuable with the addition of more players.

For example: A pair of jacks is worth holding in a two-handed game, but in a seven-handed game it is very weak. A Poker player will better his game immediately if he remembers this.

Next, a player must have some knowledge of the chances of bettering certain hands. Study the Poker tables in this book. Don't try to memorize them; merely absorb the general implications. Some of the best Poker players just play a tight game, knowing little of specific probabilities but applying the general principles.

Keep a Poker Face. Don't complain when losing or show elation when winning. Emotional displays prohibit clear thinking and the proper evaluation of your hand. Don't indulge in unnecessary conversation. Keeping a poker face means keeping the same disposition at all times. Such restraints are very difficult to acquire overnight, but they are essential requirements of a good Poker player. When you achieve them, not only will you play your best game, but your opponents will not be able to figure your hand so easily.

Forget Friendship. Upon entering a Poker game leave friendship behind. If you hold a "cinch hand" at Stud and you allow a friend to see your hole card without putting in the last bet to call your hand, I can assure you that you won't be a winner. If you want to play a good game, you must bet your hand for what it is worth. Top money winners do. Poker is a game for blood.

Know Poker Psychology. A good Poker player must be a good psychologist. During a big money game, every type of human emotion comes into play. I used to play Stud with a player who, whenever he was dealer and had a pair back to back, would almost always fail to deal himself an upcard until his attention was called to it. He was concentrating so much on his pair that he forgot he could better the pair by drawing.

Another player at Draw Poker would always ask, "Whose play is it?" When he asked this question, I knew that he probably had openers or a four-card flush—at least he was going to play. When he had a poor hand he would keep quiet and put his cards down before him. These are little mannerisms, if noted by the smart Poker player, that will help him win because they help him to know what to do at the proper time.

Study Your Opponents' Style of Play

Most players follow a pattern of play without realizing it. Some are loose players, some play tight or close to the vest. I know a player who has never tried to steal or bluff a pot in twenty years of Poker playing, and I know another who tries to steal almost every other pot he is in. This knowledge has directed my play with both. In every group you will find players with similar idiosyncrasies. Study your opponents' play. It will pay off. Whenever you get an opportunity to watch the mannerisms of players in a game before you sit down, do so. You can learn much more about technique by watching than by playing.

Study particularly the playing mannerisms and techniques of winning players. They must have something on the ball (if they aren't cheaters) to win most of the time.

When you hold a good hand, don't be too anxious to put your money into the pot until it is your proper turn; don't even have your bet ready. Untoward eagerness will inform an opponent, before he need know, that you intend to play. Most beginners or poor Poker players are very anxious to bet on a good hand and conversely, when holding a weak hand, they turn down their cards before their turn of play.

THE BLUFF AND ITS STRATEGIC IMPORTANCE

Only in Poker, business and politics can a person publicly lie to his friends and indulge in various forms of chicanery and deception (excepting cheating or stealing) and still be considered respectable by his friends.

The bluff is an attempt to convince opponents that one possesses a higher-ranking Poker hand than all other participants when the truth of the matter is that the bluffer possesses an inferior hand. In short, the bluffer is trying to steal the pot by trying to frighten his opponents into believing that he holds the best hand—thereby causing them to fold and throw in their hands. This the bluffer tries to accomplish by a verbal show of assurance as to the strength of his hand followed by a series of raises and big bets.

The purpose of the bluff is threefold:

1. To confuse your opponents' playing styles.
2. To attempt to induce your opponents to throw in their hands because of your seemingly high-ranking hand.
3. To induce your opponents, aware of your bluffing tactics, to call many more of your better hands than they normally would have done.

The following true story demonstrates the strategic value that the bluff plays in Poker. Doyle "Texas Dolly" Brunson, winner of the 1976 and 1977 Las Vegas World Series of Poker, is in my opinion today's number one big-money bluffer in Poker, as was proven by the final two hands of the 1976 and 1977 Hold Em World Series of Poker Championship. The final hand in the 1976 tournament involved Brunson and a nonprofessional Poker player named Jess Alto. To reach the two-player finals, Brunson told me, he made five bluff plays, stole four pots, and was caught trying to steal the fifth. According to Brunson, in a high-limit table-stakes game, when you know your opponent has a good hand, that's the most successful time for a bluff because your opponent doesn't think you're bluffing at that time.

Getting back to the final hand of the 1976 World Series Hold Em Championship between Brunson and Alto—Brunson's table-stakes chips totaled $147,000, Alto's $73,000. Brunson's initially dealt two hole cards were the deuce of spades and the ten of spades, a pair of trash cards that Brunson would have folded at any other time but now—for the simple reason that at this stage of the tournament Brunson and Alto each had to make either a $1,000 opening blind bet or a blind raise bet of $2,000. As Brunson remarked to me, "If you sit around and wait for a good hand putting in that kind of money in every pot, you'll go broke faster than one can say John Scarne."

Brunson was on the button (turn to bet) and made an opening bet of $4,000. Alto on the blind exercised his option and raised $7,500. Brunson called. The flop (the first three community cards dealt face up on the center of the table) showed a jack of diamonds, deuce of hearts, and ace of spades. After the flop, Alto bet $8,500. Brunson called with his pair of deuces and the ten of spades. The fourth community card was the ten of diamonds. Brunson now had two pairs, tens and deuces. Alto moved all-in (tapped out) with $67,000.

Brunson studied Alto for a minute or so and then called the $67,000. After Brunson made the call he asked Alto what he had. When Alto said, "Two pair, aces and jacks," Doyle replied, "That's good." He barely finished that sentence when the dealer turned up a ten of clubs as the fifth community card, giving Brunson a full house, three tens and a pair of deuces, to win the 1976 World Series Tournament Championship and its top prize award of $220,000.

Soon after the 1976 tournament I ran into Brunson in Las Vegas and asked him about that particular hand. His reply follows: "Scarne, I thought Alto was bluffing and I was going to try to outbluff him and steal the pot. So I got lucky and made a hand. However, if I hadn't got lucky and caught that winning hand, I still had $74,000 in chips to battle Alto again."

In the last pot of the 1977 World Series of Poker, the two remaining finalists, Brunson, possessing $275,000 in chips, and a young pro named Gary "Bones" Berland, battled it out for the championship and the prize money of $340,000. Strange but true, Brunson again was dealt a ten and a deuce in the hole, and as before made a full house, three tens and a pair of deuces, winning the championship and taking home $340,000 in new crisp $100 bills as the prize award.

During the writing of this book I visited Doyle Brunson, publisher and author of *How I Made Over $1,000,000 Playing Poker* (1978), several times at his B and G office in Las Vegas. On one of these occasions I met with Doyle Brunson, Bobby Baldwin, the sensational young winner of the 1978 World Series Hold Em Tournament, and "Crazy Mike" Caro, who in my opinion is one of the five best Five Card Draw Poker players in the world. This meeting turned out to be a five-hour Poker talkathon with a good portion of time devoted to my entertaining Brunson, Baldwin and Caro with a number of card tricks with which I have at one time or another baffled the world's top magicians including Houdini, Thurston, Nate Leipsig, and Dunninger. Brunson reached into his desk drawer and produced a deck of playing cards. After thoroughly shuffling the deck he handed it to me and said, "Scarne, let's see you do one of those card miracles I've seen you perform on dozens of television shows."

"Okay, Brunson, I'll do just that," I replied as I fanned the deck face down across his office desk. I continued, "I'm now going to turn my back to you gentlemen and while my back is turned, I want each of you Poker champs to select one card from the deck, memorize its value, and return it to the deck face down. After the three cards have been replaced in the deck, I want Brunson to shuffle the deck."

While Brunson was shuffling the deck, I faced my audience, took the shuffled deck from Brunson, flipped the deck from hand to hand accordion-fashion several times, and followed this by several two-handed double fan shuffles. After completing the fan shuffles, I fanned the deck face up across the desk top in such a manner that the card value of each of the fifty-two cards was visible to all.

I then requested Baldwin to look through the face-up deck and remove his selected card. Baldwin spread the cards farther apart seeking his selected card and after a minute of fruitless searching said, "My four of hearts is no longer in the deck." Caro and Brunson also failed to find their selected cards in the deck.

"Gentlemen, watch this," I said as I reached into my inside jacket pocket and produced Baldwin's selected four of hearts. Caro's selected card, the three of hearts, I produced from my right-hand trouser pocket. Brunson's selected card, the two of spades, I extracted from my right-hand trouser pocket.

Brunson remarked, "Scarne, how in heaven did you get those cards into your pocket?"

In the meantime Baldwin had picked up the deck of cards and was closely examining them when Caro said, "Bobby, that's Doyle's deck of cards, not Scarne's."

"I know it's Doyle's deck. I'm looking for some sort of marks or crimps in the deck but there are none that I can find," replied Baldwin.

"Gentlemen, you haven't seen anything yet. The mental card effect that I'm now going to perform is one that once seen is never forgotten. Now, please watch closely."

Just then the office door opened and in walked Bruce McClenahan, Brunson's general manager. I immediately faced him and while gazing into his eyes said, "Bruce, would you please think of a card, anyone of the fifty-two cards? Not the joker."

As I backed away Bruce said, "I'm thinking of a card."

"Please don't change your mind. Just remember the same card you are now thinking of," I said.

Next I had Caro select a card from the face-up deck. He selected the king of hearts. I took the king of hearts and placed it face down on the desk. I then placed an empty water glass on top of the face-down king of hearts and requested Caro to place his hand on top of the glass and hold it firmly. Caro did as I requested.

I again faced Bruce, the general manager, and said, "Please name the card you are thinking of."

Without any hesitation Bruce replied, "I am thinking of the king of spades."

Next I pointed to Brunson, Baldwin and Caro and said, "Gentlemen, do you believe it's possible for me to make that king of hearts now resting under the glass Caro is holding down change into the king of spades that Bruce is thinking of?"

Brunson and Baldwin remained silent while watching the face-down card like hawks, but Caro shouted aloud, "Scarne, not while I'm holding this glass on top of that king of hearts."

Next with a dramatic bit of showmanship I shouted, "Change, king of hearts, into the king of spades!"

Turning to Caro I said, "Okay, Caro, it's changed. Now, please removed the glass from the top of the face-down king of hearts and slowly turn the card face up."

Everyone's eyes were glued to the card as Caro slowly turned it over and exposed its face value. It had changed into the king of spades! Caro threw his both hands in the air and said, "I saw that king of hearts as you placed it under the glass. How in good heaven did it change into the card Bruce was thinking of?"

Upon completion of this mental feat, I noticed that everyone in the room was shaking his head from side to side as if to say, "I saw it, but I don't believe it."

Getting back to the World Series Hold Em Championship Tournament, I asked Brunson to explain his feelings during the play of each of his two final winning hands of the 1976 and 1977 World Series Hold Em Poker Championship Tournament described earlier.

Brunson replied, "Scarne, you must remember that the tournament starts with each participant making a fifty- or a hundred-dollar blind bet. And as the players are eliminated, the blind opening bet and the raise blind bet get bigger and bigger as the tournament progresses. When it gets down to the final two contestants, the blind opening bet starts at one thousand dollars and the blind raise bet at two thousand dollars. If you put in that kind of money and sit waiting for two good hole cards, you'll go broke waiting. You've got to play many a trash hand when you're betting that much loot just to get a look at the flop. The only thing surprising to me when winning the final hands in the 1976 and 1977 tournaments was not that I won with trash hands, but that both hands were almost identical.

"Furthermore, Scarne," Brunson continued, "after hearing a lot of adverse comment about those two hands, I can promise you this—that should I ever be dealt a ten or a deuce as the hole cards in any no-limit game [actually he meant high limit] I'll just fold and toss them in even though I know they're my lucky cards. One more thing, Scarne, you must remember that I'm an aggressive player and my opponents never know if I'm bluffing or not—take this bluff factor out of no-limit Poker and you take all the skill out. Many a time in tournament play I started out with a bluff trying to steal the ante and got lucky and caught a good hand on the flop."

And now for some bluffing advice for the limit Poker player. Don't try to win a small pot with a big bet. Example: A player makes a 25-cent opening bet at Stud Poker, holding the high card; another player raises the bet $2 for a total of $2.25 in the pot. The first player drops out; the player who raised wins the 25 cents with a lower hand than the hand of the player who dropped out. That is not considered a bluff. This sort of play may win a few quarters, but it will eventually lose much more on one hand whenever the opponent has that high pair backed up. Winning small amounts with big bets doesn't pay off in the long run.

Don't attempt to bluff a pot when four or five players are still in the game. Don't keep raising before you have your full hand because you intend to bluff. The legends of money won by bluffing at Poker are greatly exaggerated. Good Poker players seldom attempt a bluff, simply because when they have a weak hand they are not usually still in the pot at the showdown. The best time to bluff is when one or two players are in the pot—and if they are heavy losers. If they are heavy winners, forget it; it's 99 to 1 you'll be called. Don't try a bluff on a beginner; he almost always calls. Really good Poker players can be bluffed more easily than the beginners because a beginner or bad player will play when he has some kind of a hand and will fold when he doesn't have a hand.

But when a pot contains $50 and the limit is $2, and you were not the opener or high hand, you will be called at least 24 times to 1.

Never attempt a bluff at Stud unless you have a little something in your hand. In Draw Poker you must start the bluff by raising before the draw in order to sell the other players on the idea that you have a strong hand.

If you get caught bluffing twice, it's about time to stop for that evening. It is too costly to continue bluffing after being burned once or twice. But don't stop trying to bluff entirely. This would mean a considerable loss of call money on the showdown as soon as you become known as a player who never bluffs. The other players would hesitate to call you when you do bet.

It is good practice not to show a hand after a successful bluff unless you do not intend to bluff for the remainder of the session. And if a player does not call on the showdown, bluff or no bluff, don't show your hand. This merely gives the other players more information about your playing methods. Conversely, a player should sometimes call a hand even if he knows he is going to lose, just to gather information concerning his opponents' methods.

If you ever have had the opportunity to watch a $25,000 buy-in table-stakes game in Las Vegas or elsewhere, you'd notice that in these games the bluff is used four or five times as often as in a $3 and $6 or a $5 and $10 limit game and twenty times as often as in a 25-cent and 50-cent game.

Card Memory and Table Analysis

These are valuable assets in Poker. If you play Draw or any of its variations, practice remembering the number of cards each player draws; that information is vital. Memory also serves in Stud. Several players may, for instance, turn down their hands after the third-card draw, and those cards may include three kings. If you draw a king for your fourth card in a no-pair hand, and the king is your high card and another player has queens, you might—if you don't remember that three kings are dead—gamble on drawing a king because the pot is big. You gamble on an impossibility. Observation plus memory will save you money.

Beware of Kibitzers at Poker

A kibitzer is usually defined as a nonplayer who stands behind the players to watch a Poker game for his own pleasure. There are three different kinds of kibitzers: the honest, the bad, and the cheat.

An honest kibitzer is one who after having folded his own hand peeks into his once-opponent's hand or takes a peek at his hole card. Even though the opposition may be stupid enough to give him permission to look at his cards, the practice should be prohibited because it leads to a possible tip-off of a player's hand accidentally or purposely. Example: Suppose you have a weak hand at the time the kibitzer looks at it. The kibitzer is inclined to lose interest, which can give an observant opponent vital information. Or, if you hold a cinch hand, the kibitzer's reaction can also easily be read by an observant opponent.

An example of the harm an honest kibitzer can do to a $250,000 Poker pot follows. The time, 1947. The place, the Flamingo Hotel Casino on the Las Vegas Strip. The game, Five Card Stud Poker table stakes with a $150,000 chip buy-in. The ante, three hundred dollars, and the low hand had to bet five hundred. The two opponents, "Nick the Greek" Dandolos, the most famous gambler of this century, and Joe Bernstein, the legendary Las Vegas big-time gambler. It must be noted that Bernstein would never sit in a high-stakes Poker game unless he could sit with his back against the wall, leaving no room for anyone to stand behind him. Nick the Greek had his date for the night, a beautiful showgirl named Marie, sitting alongside of him observing his play.

After an hour's play, Bernstein, who sat against the wall, was a $25,000 winner, making his table stakes total $175,000. The Greek possessed $125,000. Then the hand which was to beat Nick the Greek popped up. The pot held a total of $90,000 when Bernstein and Nick the Greek received their last upcard. The Greek drew an ace, and Bernstein's hand showed an open pair of deuces. Nick the Greek decided to tap himself out for $80,000. Then he made the mistake of taking a last peek at his hole card and Marie, his girlfriend, also took a peek. After the peek the Greek pushed his $80,000 worth of chips to the center of the table, making the total pot $170,000. Seconds after the Greek had pushed his $80,000 in the pot, Marie rose from the table, excused herself and said she was going to the ladies room.

Nick, in his staccato Greek accent, needled Joe Bernstein to call the $80,000 bet. Bernstein eyed the Greek's four upcards—ace, jack, six, and five (Bernstein himself possessed a pair of shown deuces). Then Bernstein recalled Marie's getting up from the table after seeing the Greek's hole card, and he reasoned that if the Greek's fourth upcard or any one of the three previously dealt cards had paired the Greek's hole card, he was beaten. Then he figured Marie's leaving the table as a losing hand for the Greek because Marie realized the Greek could not beat his (Bernstein's) pair of deuces and didn't want to be around when her boyfriend lost the pot. Bernstein called the $80,000 bet. The Greek immediately threw in his hand and remarked, "You win, Joe. Marie blew the pot for me—you read her actions."

"You're right, Nick. If Marie hadn't left the table I would never have called your $80,000 bluff."

So-called "innocent" kibitzers often work in collusion with a confederate to whom they signal the value of a player's hand.

Kibitzers of any kind are a Poker liability and should not be allowed in high-stakes Poker, but at penny ante they perhaps can be tolerated. However, for the best protection, even in a friendly game, do not permit a kibitzer player or nonplayer to scout your hand; a nonplaying kibitzer will learn your style of playing simply by watching, and once he becomes an opponent, he'll be harder for you to beat.

Playing Positions

Generally speaking, the Poker player who must speak first is in a bad position. The player who speaks last has a superior position. This applies in all kinds of Poker.

But you can't get enough action if you confine your play to hands in which you have a favorable position. You must act on what you know about the habits of the players in the game. Suppose the player on your right is the first to speak and opens or bets. If you believe the pot will be a big one and will offer you favorable odds, you should play in anticipation of a big pot. In a game where players play the cards close to the vest, you would not play any doubtful hand without waiting to see how some of the cards fall; but then, in a game with close-to-the-vest players, you should not play a doubtful hand anyway.

In the final round of betting, position is most important. The best possible position is when you are last to speak and there is only one player you are afraid of. Your turn will come after his and you will already know his decision.

The worst possible position is between two players that you fear. If the player before you bets, you are fearful to call even if you think you hold a better hand—the other dangerous player bets after you and may raise.

You should always try to anticipate what your position will be on the final betting round. At times you can create a good position from a situation in which your position happens to be a bad one.

Opportunities such as these arise constantly in both Draw and Stud. Keep on the lookout for them, and by so doing you will make more money with a winning hand and lose less with a losing hand. And one must always bear in mind that the object of playing Poker is to win money, not the most pots.

Giveaways of Player Hands

Most top winning professionals that I have scouted here and abroad try hard to vary their Poker-playing mannerisms and style of play. This is done to prevent their opponents from spotting any giveaway habits. To the pros, these giveaway habits are called "tells." Most Poker players possess a tell of one sort or another—those giveaway verbal or physical gestures are almost as revealing to a sage opponent who has spotted them as seeing an exposed hand.

Doyle Brunson, twice winner of the Las Vegas World Series of Poker, hinted to me that one of the first things he does when seated at a Poker table is to look at the neck of each opponent to see if the pulse is visible. If it is, he pays special attention to this player during the game—and should this opponent bet $10,000 or more, and Brunson spots his neck throbbing wildly, he knows the opponent is excited and is bluffing.

The effervescent Amarillo Slim Preston, Poker's goodwill ambassador, and winner of the 1972 Las Vegas World Series of Poker, had a tell on Doyle Brunson during that championship series. Brunson's giveaway habit was that he would count all his chips when he held a good hand and when he was bluffing he would just push in his bet without counting his remaining chips.

Eric Steiner, one of London's top five Poker wizards, and my companion on my London scouting Poker club mission, offered this sage advice: "Make sure to spot your opponent's tell before he spots yours." When looking for an opponent's giveaway, Steiner takes into account the way his opponents are sitting, their previous playing habits, how they bet, and even their conversation. It's a combination of all these things that reveal an opponent's tell.

To be a winning Poker player, one must adopt a style of one's own.

Some do best to sit pokerfaced at the table, others find it more effective to keep up a constant line of chatter. Neither type should overdo it. Every winning Poker player must be a good actor to prevent his opponents from spotting his tell. However, overacting can become a heavy liability if it becomes a habit other players can spot.

The best strategy is to adopt the style of play and demeanor that best suits you, but then to vary this from time to time. You must occasionally vary your manners and mannerisms and, most of all, your style of play. If you are a tight player, you must occasionally play a trash hand. If, in Draw, you ordinarily draw three cards to a pair, vary your style of play and hold a kicker. If in Five Card Stud you generally call or raise with an ace, king, or queen in the hole, then occasionally you must play with a low five or six in the hole. If you seldom play a weak hand, occasionally you must do so. If it is not your style to bluff, occasionally you should bluff. Even in a tight game, where one must necessarily play tight to win, you must make an occasionally unsound loose play.

I have known dozens of superb professional Poker players here and abroad who had only one weakness. And that one weakness cost them a fortune. They were masters in the art of dissecting the playing habits of their opponents for the smallest giveaway, but it never occurred to them to analyze their own playing habits in the same way. If they had done so, they could have gotten rid of some dead-giveaway habits of their own, which in time made them sure losers instead of possible winners.

Sandbagging and Slowplaying

When you hold a good hand and you either check or bet weakly with the intention of raising or to let your opponents take the lead in the betting, you are either "sandbagging" or "slowplaying." Sandbagging is checking with the probable best hand with the idea of raising later. Slowplaying is betting a strong hand weakly to try to mislead your opponents into believing you had a mediocre hand. Both of these psychological playing semibluffs can be put to good use in various betting situations.

In standard Draw Poker, playing position is most important when attempting to sandbag. The obvious reason is that when playing this draw game the dealer acts last and the leader (player to the left of dealer) acts first, thereby giving the dealer the positional advantage, since he acts after all other players have spoken. However, after the draw, the opener acts first, rather than the leader, thereby diminishing the dealer's positional advantage. This is where slowplaying comes into its own.

Why are playing positions so important in standard Draw? Here is my analysis. First, let's take the draw. If you open as the leader (first position) or in other early positions, you are subjecting yourself to one or more possible raises by players seated in the middle or late positions. The earlier your position, the more risk you are taking, especially should you be holding just a pair of openers. You probably would have checked your pair of openers if you suspected that one or more strong opening hands were lurking in the middle or late positions. After one or more raises, you'll probably fold your pair of openers, giving up your ante and opening bet without drawing cards.

To help minimize these early positional disadvantages in Draw, I submit the following recommendations. If there are five or fewer players in the game, there is no point to sandbagging, since you run the risk that the pot will be passed out. However, in an eight- or nine-handed game sandbagging may prove to be profitable for the first, second, or even the third person to act. True, the hand may be passed out, but the chances of this happening are considerably less than in a five-or-fewer-handed game.

When deciding whether or not to sandbag, it is most important to carefully analyze your five-card hand. For example, suppose your hand is made up of three sixes, a four, and a three. Your opponents' hands must be made up from the remaining forty-seven cards, and the chances that one of your opponents will hold a pair of jacks or better as openers is considerably greater than it would be if you, for instance, held three kings, a queen and a jack. This is due to the fact that each jack, queen, king or ace in your hand has a diminishing effect on each opponent's chances of holding openers.

With the above in mind, we may establish a general principle that the best time to sandbag is when you hold three of a kind or better, when there are five players or more to act after you, and when your hand is composed of low-valued cards.

In Draw Poker, recent attempts have been made by several mathematicians to make use of a point count card system to aid the player in determining whether or not he should open on the draw. I've analyzed this system thoroughly and have found it to be ridiculous and unworkable—but these mathematicians seldom give up, and I believe that in the very near future they'll add a point count card system to Poker and swear on a stack of Bibles that it will beat the top pros in the world.

Speaking of point count card systems brings to mind today's countless so-called winning Black Jack systems being sold to the gullible and unsuspecting public. The reason for the continuous sale of these worthless Black Jack systems is that casino bosses work in cahoots with the so-called card counters by "supposedly" barring them from their casinos. It's good for casino business because it brings millions of Black Jack suckers to the casinos believing that the game of Black Jack can be easily beaten and it makes money for the so-called card counters by the sale of their worthless systems. For a complete exposé of this racket, pick up a copy of *Scarne's Guide to Casino Gambling* (1978).

A player's position is considerably more important in Hold Em (Seven Card Stud Poker variant) than in Draw Poker or in any other major Poker games. As in Draw, Jacks or Better, the dealer acts last and the leader acts first. Furthermore, Hold Em, due to its community cards, has four betting intervals where possible sandbagging can take place, as opposed to Draw Poker's one. One must also bear in mind that if you are in first position in games such as Hold Em, you will remain there for the entire hand. Sometimes, however, it is to your advantage to be in first position, particularly so when you make a big bet to try and drive all players out so as to steal the ante, or just to gain the advantage of playing against fewer opponents.

In Stud games in which the value of the players' face-up cards determines the player's first betting position, slowplaying takes the place of sandbagging as a sort of semi-bluff in reverse.

Money Management Versus Probabilities

Most Las Vegas big-time Poker players, including several top winners of the Las Vegas Hold Em World Series of Poker, make their crucial big-money bets in limit games after considering three factors. (1) The total sum of money in the pot. (2) The amount of money required to play. (3) The chances of winning the pot. In other words, before they put additional big money in the pot, they compute these three factors and base their decisions to call, raise, reraise or drop out on their end result. In big-time table-stakes games, Poker experts consider a fourth factor—the sum total of the money in front of each opponent.

I recommend this method of strategy for the $2, $4 or higher limit game. This betting system is best described as follows: Suppose you are playing in a $2-limit game and there is one more betting turn. Before putting any money in the pot on the last betting turn, you must compare the amount of your next bet with the money already in the pot that represents the favorable or unfavorable odds you'll be taking. Suppose the pot holds $20 and it will cost you $2 to play—the pot is offering you 10-to-1 odds.

Now you must calculate your chances of bettering your hand and winning the pot. Studying the mathematical tables in this book can help you do so. At times you will employ a combination of mathematics and personal judgment. The point I am trying to make here is that if the pot offers you 10-to-1 odds and you know that the odds are only 7 to 1 against your making a winning hand, you have an excellent bet.

At this point, however, if the pot odds are 10 to 1 in your favor and the odds of filling in a winning hand are 11 to 1 against your winning (which are the correct odds against filling an inside straight), then it is a very bad bet to put your $2 in the pot.

It is important to remember to treat the pot as a separate odds bet. Any money you previously contributed to the pot belongs to the pot and not to you. Forget that you ever had it.

Here we find a good reason for that old Poker expression, "Don't throw good money after bad." The fact that you previously contributed $10 or more to the pot doesn't justify your betting a dollar more if the odds of winning the pot don't justify it.

The betting limits will have a great deal to do with your decision, partly because they affect the size of the pot and partly because they can help your future betting decision, if any.

Most Poker games have a fixed limit that is fairly low. However, it can be quite a stiff game. For example, a game in which you can bet $2 on openers and $4 after the draw (or in a Stud game, $2 on high card, $4 on an open pair, and $6 on the last betting interval) is a stiff game, but it is still a relatively low-limit game. In such a game, you can often stay in for $2 when there is already $40 or more in the pot. You are being offered fine odds and your risk is minimal.

Compare it with a table stakes game in which the average bet is the same $2 or $4, but in which every player has $100 or $200 in front of him and can later bet the $100 or $200 at any betting interval. Suppose in such a game you toss your $2 or $4 into the pot hoping to better your pair. With $40 already in the pot, you are getting excellent odds, but you are risking a situation in which you may better the pair and then be confronted with a $200 bet. Yet, if you better your pair, nobody is likely to call a $200 bet unless he believes he can beat your hand. Therefore your potential risk is much greater than in the $2 or $4 limit game.

In any form of Poker it usually pays to play only when your hand, even without improvement, has a chance to win the pot, and when you believe your chance of improvement is as good as all other players'. For example, you have a pair of aces and another player has kings showing. If neither of you improves, you win. You have as good a chance to improve as your opponent has, and if you both improve equally, you'll still win.

Whatever the style Poker game you play, don't play against a single opponent unless you feel you have a better hand. Don't play against two, three or four opponents unless you believe there is a chance that you have the best hand. And with five or six opponents you should be pretty sure that you have at least a third-best hand going in and that, should you get lucky and improve your hand, you will win the pot.

Betting Courage Is a Must for Winning Poker

A winning Poker player, in addition to possessing the knowledge described earlier, must also possess betting courage. The knowledge part is what you can acquire by studying this book for whichever form of Poker you are playing. The factor of courage cannot be taught; but you can't become a winning Poker player without it. When you sit down at a money Poker game, you aren't there to have fun only. You're there to win. And to do just that, you must bet up your good hands to the limit and risk your money when you believe you're right.

Lack of heart (courage) is the reason so many otherwise good Poker players are at a disadvantage once they start losing. Every time an opponent makes a big bet, their first reaction is one of fear. They check when they should raise, and drop out when they should bet, thus collecting small money on their winning hands and losing money on hands they should have won.

I know a number of Las Vegas gamblers who were formerly rated among the thirty top Poker players in Las Vegas until they lost their courage, either through a reduced financial position, family responsibilities or a long losing streak. These men changed from top players to fair ones.

If the amount of Poker money at stake is frightening to you, I can only recommend that you put aside the amount of money you can afford to lose and play that money as if it were an unlimited supply. If you lose it all, quit the game. In this way, while you're playing Poker, you'll have a better chance to win because you'll be betting with courage.

However, let's not confuse Poker courage with betting stupidity. In Stud, it is not courage to chase a pair of open kings with a pair of queens by making a big bet and hoping to catch the third lady. That is reckless stupidity, not betting courage. Millions of unknowledgeable Poker players mix up the two, believing that tight players are shy and courageous players are those who are in most of the pots, raising and reraising to their hearts' content while chasing superior hands with their weaker hands, hoping for some miracle to take place.

Courage at the Poker table is the ability to take control of each favorable situation. *Example:* In Stud, when you have the table beaten with one more card to be dealt, then you must have the courage to bet the limit and try to force some of your opponents to fold and thereby increase your winning chances. And those who do play will have to call your big bet at a disadvantage to themselves.

When the game runs into high betting limits, big-money table-stakes games, or the yearly Las Vegas World Series of Poker, that's the time psychological pressures take over.

To acquire "betting courage" in big-time Poker games, one must first learn to cope with the tensions that are sure to arise in big-money games—the excitement, fear, frustration, nervousness, trepidity, etc. Few of the millions of nonprofessionals know how to cope with these tensions, since it takes years of Poker hustling to become hardened to them. However, I've seen many a Poker professional entrant in the yearly Las Vegas World Series Hold Em Tournament lose a $100,000 pot or more, get up from the table, and chalk it up to a bad day, adopting a "tomorrow's another day" attitude. On the other hand, I know of some twenty-odd nonprofessionals who have dropped dead at the Poker tables in the past decade. Cause of death? They could not cope with the tensions that arose in the Poker game they were involved in.

Joey Hawthorne, the sensational young Las Vegas pro and one of the five best Lowball players in the world, had two nonprofessional Poker players drop dead on him in a high stakes Lowball game. Let Hawthorne tell us about these two unfortunate incidents.

> I tell you, Deuce-to-Seven can be brutal. It's a game where you need that killer instinct.
>
> And you can just about take that literally, because I've had two players drop dead on me right at the table. One had just suffered a twenty thousand dollar beat with a 7-6-4-3-2. And the other one, a few years later, had the nuts (7-5-4-3-2), but he never got to rake in the chips. He actually dropped dead from the excitement of holding "the name of the game."

Now, perhaps, you understand what I've been saying about the excitement, the frustration, and brutality of big-money Poker. For the above-stated reasons, I recommend that nonprofessionals with limited bankrolls do not enter the yearly Las Vegas World Series Hold Em

Tournament or play against seasoned professional gamblers in high-stakes Poker games. Big-money Poker games play havoc with most nonprofessionals. And the pros usually eat up the nonpros.

SCARNE'S POKER-PLAYING SYSTEM

At the very outset, be you an expert or an average Poker player, I can make you this promise—if Scarne's Poker-Playing System is put to proper use, it will decrease the amounts of money lost during your losing sessions and increase the number of your winning sessions.

The basic principle that makes Scarne's Poker-Playing System work is the manner in which you handle your pocket bankroll. This money management can be broken down into three parts.

1. How much money a player should take to a game in the form of a pocket bankroll.
2. The maximum sum of money a player can afford to lose of this poker bankroll in one game session.
3. The maximum sum of money a winning player can add to this pocket bankroll in any one game session.

A player should not enter a game with a short pocket bankroll (insufficient money to play an aggressive game). Should he do so, he will be gambling with what is known among professional gamblers as "scared" money, and playing under such conditions he can't possibly play his best. Scared money also means the lack of betting courage, which has been covered earlier. Scared money doesn't afford a player too many opportunities to play in big-money pots to the showdown. In addition, a player with a short bankroll is a target for bluffers and ante stealers.

So, in order to play your best Poker game, you must enter any game with a proper pocket bankroll calculated on the maximum betting limit of each specific game. I recommend that the proper pocket bankroll must be sixty times the top-limit bet permitted in the game. In that way, your playing ability will not be handicapped with scared money. The amount of pocket bankroll required for each limit game follows:

Game	Pocket Bankroll Required
50¢ and $1 limit	$ 60
$1–$2 limit	$120
$3–$6 limit	$360
$5–$10 limit	$600, etc.

These figures may appear high to some players but the fact remains that twenty of the nation's top Poker professionals that I recently consulted with agreed that my bankroll Poker game figures listed above are correct for most Poker players.

Next, we must know where this pocket bankroll money is coming from, and more importantly, we should play only with money we won't miss if we happen to lose it. Playing with rent or food money that should be paying household bills is considerably worse than scared money and is known among professional gamblers as "losing" or "desperado" money that should not be gambled with—because your winning chances are greatly reduced when gambling with this kind of money.

This brings us to "What is the biggest amount of money you should lose in any one Poker session?" We should always know in advance before we sit down to play Poker how much we are prepared to lose. By so doing, we will protect ourselves from being tapped out. The losing limit I recommend should never exceed the pocket bankroll required to sit in the game as shown above. In a 50¢ and $1 limit game, you should lose no more than $60; in a $1 to $2 limit game, no more than $120; in a $3 and $6 limit game, no more than $360; in a $5 and $10 limit game, no more than $600—and so forth.

What happens when we lose the recommended amount? We simply get up from the table and go on our merry way. We've had a losing session, we've held bad cards, we didn't play well, we competed against better players, and there's also a possibility we may have been cheated.

And now, to help prevent you from continuing play in an attempt to recoup your losses, bring with you only the recommended pocket bankroll that you are prepared to lose at the Poker session, and stick with it—don't borrow money to continue to play under any circumstances.

Last, and most important, we now discuss the maximum amount of money you are permitted to win by sticking with Scarne's Poker-Playing System. You'll recall your recommended pocket bankroll was sixty times the top betting limit of the game being played. Scarne's Poker Betting System demands that your winning goal should be to win a sum equal to your pocket bankroll. In short, when you have doubled the amount of your pocket bankroll, you quit the game. Examples: If you are playing in a $1 and $2 limit game and your beginning pocket bankroll was $120, and the last pot you collected doubled it to $240 or more, you must quit playing. This forces you to quit the game when cards seem to be coming your way and you are a winner. Quitting a game when you are on a winning streak is a very difficult thing to do.

But quit the game you must. It is only by quitting the game once you have doubled your pocket bankroll that you will increase the number of your winning Poker sessions. If you fail to abide by any or all of the three main rules that make up Scarne's Poker-Playing System, it will not work.

TWENTY STRATEGY RULES EVERY EXPERT POKER PLAYER MUST KNOW

So that the reader may review at a glance most of the tips, hints, subterfuges and bits of strategy discussed in the preceding pages, they have been condensed into the summary that follows:

1. The prime rule of Poker is: Don't try to beat the other players; let them try to beat you. This isn't just an introductory sentence; it is probably more important than all the tips and hints that follow. Do yourself a favor by memorizing it.
2. Be sure you know the rules of the game. The player who knows the rules has a decided advantage in any game against players who are vague about them.
3. Study the mathematics of Poker in Chapter 10. A player who knows the Poker probabilities of drawing and improving hands has a decided edge over the player who thinks he knows. But don't become a slave to Poker probabilities. They are probabilities, not laws; and they do not supply a surefire recipe for winning.
4. Observe your opponents; learn their Poker mannerisms. Are they loose or tight players? And avoid giveaway mannerisms of your own.
5. Play as often as possible; experience is the best teacher.
6. Always remember that in a Poker game the average hand becomes less valuable the more players there are.
7. Treat every round of betting as if it were the first. Forget the previous betting rounds and the money you have contributed to the pot.
8. When you hold a cinch hand, wait till the last two betting intervals to raise.
9. Fold a doubtful hand at the start rather than in the middle or at the end.
10. Call your opponent or opponents when you believe your hand is good enough to win, not merely because you suspect a bluff.
11. As a general rule, don't try to steal a pot by trying to bluff a poor player, a heavy winner or a heavy loser.
12. When you're in a losing streak, don't let yourself get panicky.

The more reckless you feel, the wiser it is to get away from the table at once. An excited player or a player plunging to recoup losses is a player at his worst.

13. You must expect to lose the pot unless you believe you have the best hand going in.

14. Most Draw Poker players would win instead of lose if they never tried to outdraw the opener.

15. Bet your big hands to the hilt and make every active player pay to see your hand.

16. Vary your playing strategy. The player whose game is always the same becomes an easy mark for smart Poker players.

17. Try to keep a poker face. Don't complain when losing or show elation when winning. The emotional aftermath will prohibit clear thinking and proper evaluation of succeeding hands.

18. Try to sit with your back to the wall and try to avoid kibitzers who watch your hand. Many good hands are tipped off by onlookers who don't keep poker faces.

19. Trust no one at Poker; it is a game for blood. If you want to play a good game you must forget friendship and bet your hand for what it's worth. Top-money winners do.

20. When you play Poker, give the game all you've got, or get out. That is not only the best way to win at Poker; it's the only way you and the rest of the players can get any fun out of what ought to be fun.

Draw Poker: The Granddaddy of Modern Poker

It is an established fact that straight twenty-card Poker (minus the draw) is the granddaddy of all forms of Poker. It also is established that Draw Poker, also known as Jackpots, Jacks or Better, Closed Poker, and Five Card Draw, is the granddaddy of modern Poker and therefore will be the first to be discussed in these pages. Draw Poker (and its countless variations) is one of the more popular games at men's and women's friendly weekly sessions. Today, big-money gamblers prefer Stud or Hold Em to Draw Poker. Every adult and every teenager have probably played penny ante Draw Poker at one time or another. Children learn to play it before any other adult card game. It is the world's most popular family card game.

RULES FOR DRAW POKER, JACKPOTS, JACKS OR BETTER

Requirements

1. Two to six players make the best game, although up to eight players may play—with the following rule added: Should the pack become exhausted and there are players who still must draw cards to complete their hands, the discards are assembled, shuffled and cut, and the draw is continued. But when playing for high stakes, the maximum number of players is six.
2. A standard pack of 52 cards is used. It is best to have two packs available of different backs and colors, so a player may call for a change of decks upon completion of any deal.

The Object of the Game

For a player at the showdown to hold a higher-ranking five-card hand than any of the other players. The player (or players) having the best hand is declared the winner (or winners), and collects the pot. A player may also win by forcing the other players to drop out of the pot.

Preliminaries Before the Deal

All the preparations before the start of the actual play are as described under the basic General Rules for Poker: selecting the banker, his duties, rank of hands, royalties, time limit, betting limits, preparations before play, selecting the dealer and seating positions at the table, irregularities in cutting the cards, the shuffle and cut, etc.

The Ante

Two types of ante used in Draw Poker are as follows:

1. Each player, before the cards are dealt, antes an equal amount into the pot. All players must ante in turn, starting with the player to the dealer's left and rotating clockwise.
2. Dealer's edge. The player whose turn it is to deal antes an amount into the pot. In dealer's edge a new player entering the game must wait until it is his turn to deal before he is permitted to play.

The Deal

Dealing clockwise, starting with the player on the dealer's left, the dealer deals a card face down to each player until each has five cards. The dealer gets the last card. The remaining cards are put to one side in front of the dealer for future use in drawing.

Openers

The player who opens the pot must hold in his hand a pair of jacks or a higher-ranking hand. It is essential for the stability of the game that a player have jacks or better when opening. If this rule is not enforced and a player opens the pot any time he feels like it, one of the greatest factors of skill in the game is automatically eliminated—that which depends on knowing that the opener holds at least a pair of jacks.

Splitting Openers

The player who opened the pot has the right to discard his openers or part of his openers, but he must announce "splitting" and place his openers or the discarded part of his openers face down beneath a chip or coin to one side to verify at the showdown the fact that he had them. If the player splits but fails to declare he was splitting, that player's hand is declared foul or dead.

Player's Turn of Play

The leader (player to the dealer's left) has the first privilege of play. After examining his cards and determining that he holds a pair of jacks or a hand of higher rank, he must do one of two things:

1. He may open by putting a bet into the pot.
2. He may pass, which indicates that he does not desire to start the betting. Should he fail to hold a pair of jacks or a hand of a higher rank, he is compelled to pass.

If all the players pass, they must ante again, and the new dealer deals another hand to each player; and, if playing dealer's edge, the new dealer must ante.

When a player opens by putting an amount within the limit into the pot, each succeeding player in turn can do one of these three things:

1. He may pass; and, should he pass when the pot has opened, he merely folds his cards and puts them aside on the table. This is "folding up."
2. Should he decide to play, he must put up an amount equal to the bet of the player who opened the pot.
3. If he wants to raise, he merely says "Raise" and puts into the pot an amount equal to that put into the pot by the opening player, plus an amount for the raise.

All the other players may now either play by putting into the pot an amount equal to the total amount of the raise or, should they already have put the opening bet into the pot, merely put into the pot an amount equal to the raise. Or a player may reraise by putting into the pot an amount equal to the raiser plus an amount for the reraiser. Or he may drop out by folding his cards and throwing them into the discard pile on the table. This procedure of dropping out, playing, raising and reraising is continued until the players stop raising. If all the players drop out but one, he wins the pot. Should he be the player who opened the pot, he must show his openers to the rest of the players. If he is not, he does not have to expose his hand.

Burning Top Card of the Deck Before the Draw

Upon completion of the first betting interval and before the draw takes place, the dealer must "burn" the top card of the deck by dealing it face down onto the table in front of himself.

The Draw

When all the players have either dropped out or put into the pot an equal amount, and there are no uncovered bets in the pot, and when the active players number two or more and the dealer has burnt the top card of the deck, these remaining players may, if they desire, draw either one, two or three cards from the undealt portion of the deck in an attempt to improve their hands or stand pat. This procedure is called the draw, and it is played as follows:

The dealer must ask each player (starting with the nearest active player to his left and rotating to the left, clockwise) at his proper turn of play how many cards he wants to draw, if any; to each player he says, "How many?" The player either says he's standing pat or tells the dealer how many cards he wants to draw. The dealer must wait until the player discards a like number before dealing the new cards; or he passes the player by should the latter say "I stand pat or no cards."

In Draw, every player must take the cards he asked for if the dealer has dealt them off the deck. If too many, player must discard to make a legitimate hand. If too few, he has fouled his hand, as he has fewer than required for a playing hand. Dealer must take the exact number of cards he dealt off the deck for himself. Cards once discarded cannot be taken back. If a player does not get the correct number of cards he asked for, the dealer must rectify the mistake—provided no one at the player's left has drawn cards.

The Betting After the Draw

The player who opened the pot has the first turn of play after the draw, and the play goes on to each active player, starting with the player to the opener's left and moving clockwise. A turn of play now consists of either checking, betting, calling, dropping out, raising or reraising. But a player cannot check at his turn of play after a bet has been made. The play continues around the table until one of the following situations develops:

1. A player has made a bet and is not called by any player, in which case he wins the pot and does not have to expose his hand, unless he was the opener. Then he is compelled to show his openers only.

2. All players have passed; and now the opener must be the first player to expose his hand for the showdown. This is done by announcing the rank of his hand and turning his five cards face up on the table. The same holds for all the remaining players, continuing with the first remaining player to the opener's left and rotating clockwise.

3. Or, an equal amount has been put into the pot by betting on the part of two or more active players. In this case the first bettor or raiser is being called, and he must be the first to announce the rank of his hand and turn it face up on the table for the showdown. The first active player to his left does the same, the showdown rotating clockwise. The player holding the highest-ranking hand wins the pot. For rules pertaining to two or more tied hands see "Object of the Game," under General Rules for Poker, page 39.

Showdown

In Draw Poker the cards in the showdown speak for themselves. If a player calls a lower- or higher-ranking hand than he holds and this error is noticed before the pot has been collected, the error can be rectified. But if it is noticed after the pot has been collected, the error cannot be rectified. The same rule regarding the showdown holds true should all the players pass after the draw.

Misdeals

Whenever a misdeal occurs, there must be a new shuffle and cut. The same dealer deals again, but should the dealer make two misdeals in a row, the deal passes to the player at his left. The following will determine if a misdeal has occurred or not:

1. If one or more cards are exposed in cutting or in reuniting the cut packets, there is a misdeal.

2. If the pack has not been offered to the proper player to cut, and the pot has not been opened yet, there is a misdeal. If the pot has already been opened, and the irregularity has not been discovered, the deal stands—there is no misdeal.

3. If the pack has not been cut and the betting has not started, there is a misdeal.

4. If one or more cards are observed face up in the pack before each player has received his five cards or the betting has not yet started, there is a misdeal.

5. If a player's card is exposed by the dealer before the draw, there is a misdeal.

6. If the dealer exposes one or more of his own cards at any time, the deal stands—there is no misdeal.

7. Should a player expose one or more of his own cards at any time, the deal stands—there is no misdeal.

8. If an imperfect pack is being used with fewer cards than the standard pack or with duplicate cards and it is discovered before the pot has been collected, there is a misdeal. Play immediately stops when the imperfect pack is discovered, and all the players get back the amounts they put into the pot.

9. If the cards have been improperly dealt—for example, more than one card at a time—or any player has received improper cards and this is noticed before the pot is opened, there is a misdeal.

10. If too few or too many hands have been dealt, there is a misdeal.

11. If too few or too many cards have been dealt to one or more players and this is discovered before the pot is opened, there is a misdeal unless it can be properly corrected before any one player has looked at his hand.

12. If the wrong player is dealing and this is discovered before the pot has been opened, there is a misdeal.

Exposed Cards on the Draw

The following will cover situations involving an exposed card on the draw:

1. Should a dealer expose one or more of a player's cards on the draw, the player is not permitted to take the exposed cards. They must be put into the center of the table face up, and are out of play. The dealer deals the player whose card has been exposed another card in its place.

2. Should a player expose one or more of his drawn cards, he must take them.

3. Should a dealer expose one or more cards on his own draw or if they are found face up on the draw, the dealer must take them.

Betting

A bet once placed in the pot, regardless of whether it's a player's proper turn or not, must stand. It cannot be taken out of the pot. If a player should put into the pot an amount less than the amount of the previous bettor, he must add the required sum so that his bet is equal to the previous bet. Should he fail to do so, his hand is dead, and the amount he bet must remain in the pot.

Betting out of Turn

The following rules apply to playing, calling or raising out of turn. A player making a bet out of turn must leave the bet in the pot. He cannot take it back, and the play reverts to the proper player. When it is the proper turn of the player who bet out of turn he must do one of the following:

1. If no bet has been made by any preceding player, the bet stands as is.
2. If a bet has been made by a previous player smaller than the bet made out of turn, it stands as a raise.
3. If a bet has been made by a previous player equal to the bet out of turn, it stands as a play or call.
4. If a previous bet was raised by another player and the bet is in excess of the amount bet by the out-of-turn player, the out-of-turn player may either drop out of the pot, play or call by equaling the bet made by the previous bettors, or reraise the pot after equaling the raised bet.

Verbal Betting

If a player in his turn of play announces his bet he must abide by the announcement. He cannot increase or decrease the oral bet. Should a player make an announcement at an improper turn of play and has not placed any money into the pot, it should be disregarded and considered a joke or an attempted bluff.

Passing or Checking out of Turn

If a player passes out of turn before the draw and still holds his cards in his hand, there is no penalty. He just waits for his proper turn of play, but he is not permitted to raise should a preceding player make a bet. The same holds true for passing or checking after the draw, provided no previous bet has been made.

False Openers

1. A player opening a pot with false openers forfeits his right to the pot, and his hand is dead. Remaining players in the pot, if any, will

play the pot out as though it had been opened legitimately. If no one stays, the opening bet remains in the pot, and a new deal is declared.

2. If an opener bets with false openers and his bet is not called, the amount of the bet shall be withdrawn, but any ante remains in the pot.

3. If the bet is called, the false opener loses the entire pot to the best legitimate hand.

Foul or Dead Hand

1. If a player holds more or fewer than five cards on the showdown, that player's hand is declared foul or dead, and he has no interest in the pot. But if the irregularity is discovered after the pot is collected, the hand must stand as legitimate.

2. If a player forgets to draw cards or permits another player to draw cards at his turn of play, he must play his hand as is. If he has discarded and failed to draw, his hand is dead.

Improper Fold-up

If a player decides to drop out of the pot or fold up, he cannot give an indication of this, verbal or otherwise, until it is his proper turn of play. Should he fold up out of turn, his hand is dead. Strict observance of this rule makes for a better game.

Optional Betting Limits at Draw Poker

The most popular betting limits are as follows:

1. Penny to 5 cents, 5 to 10 cents, 25 to 50 cents, $1 to $2, $2 to $4, $5 to $10, etc. Only two amounts are specified, the minimum and the maximum permitted; which means that at a player's turn of play he must conform with one of the following rules:
   - (a) A player cannot bet an amount less than the minimum limit.
   - (b) A player cannot bet an amount larger than the maximum limit.
   - (c) A player may bet any amount between both limits.
   - (d) The ante is usually 20% to 25% of the minimum bet, except in penny ante, and 5 to 10 cents limit where the ante usually equals the minimum bet.

2. *Variation in betting limit.* Often three figures are mentioned such as 5 cents, 10 cents, and 15 cents, or 50 cents, $2, and $4—which indicates that the ante and opening bets are the low amount, and after

the draw a bet must be either the middle or highest amount. The same holds true for any other three-figure limit, regardless of the amount.

3. *Jackpot.* Should all the players pass on the first deal, the amount of the opening bet on the second deal can be any amount not higher than the ante already in the pot, provided the limit bet is less than the amount in the pot before the opening. Thereafter, each bet after the draw can also be the amount of the possible opening bet. The dealer must announce the jackpot limit to the opening player, and that amount cannot be exceeded in betting, except if it be lower than the maximum limit.

4. *Pot Limit.* Undoubtedly the fastest betting limit of all the limits played today at Poker. A player at his betting turn is permitted to bet any amount up to the total amount in the pot.

5. *Table Stakes.* Each player puts up a specified amount of money on the table, but not less than a minimum agreed on beforehand. A player may increase or decrease the amount he has on the table, but only after a showdown and before the next deal. He may not take any money off the table before he leaves the game. On any bet a player is permitted to bet any or all of the amount he has in front of him. (See "Tapping Out" under General Rules for Poker.) But, after the tapping-out hand, the player may continue playing by putting more money on the table.

6. *Freezeout.* After the style of Poker to be played has been determined, each player puts an equal amount of money on the table. The game ends when one lone player has won all the table money.

7. *Open Blind Betting.* Players ante a specified amount into the pot. Then the leader (player to the left of the dealer) opens blind or "force in" as it is sometimes called. In other words, the leader must open and bet before looking at his five dealt cards. The amount of the blind bet is usually the minimum bet permitted. The open blind game is designed for one purpose—to force everyone to play liberally. Sometimes the game is played so that not only does the leader open blind, but the second position (player to the left of the leader) raises blind. And occasionally this blind-betting procedure is carried through to the third position and becomes open blind, raise blind, and reraise blind. This type of betting is favored in Nevada casino Poker rooms with high stakes and in most of California's four hundred licensed Draw Poker clubs, where only Draw Poker is allowed by law.

For additional betting methods see the basic betting rules under Scarne's Rules for Private or Social Poker, and Scarne's General Rules for Commercialized Poker, Chapter 3.

DRAW POKER STRATEGY

With all the general tips, hints, subterfuges, bits of strategy and warnings described in Chapter 4 pretty well absorbed, the Draw Poker player might need some expert advice on specific money-making decisions at Draw Poker.

The correct money-making decisions at Draw Poker are generally made the moment the player receives his five dealt cards. It is then that the player must decide whether to stay or fold, to take advantage of every opportunity of winning or to avoid every likelihood of losing. In order to achieve these goals it is absolutely necessary for the player to make an accurate estimate of the playing characteristics of his opponents. Whether opponents are tight or loose players is an important factor to check out because often a winning hand with tight opponents may be a losing hand with loose opponents.

There is an old Poker saying in Las Vegas which goes like this: "A tight player will always beat a tableful of loose players." I go along with that. However, the same tight player has little or no advantage in a game that involves several other tight players. Therefore a good Draw Poker player must adjust his game to the playing traits of his opponents as spotted by him during play, or as a spectator before joining the game.

Aside from his estimate of his opponents, when the player first looks at his five dealt cards he knows nothing except:

1. The value of his own hand.
2. The mathematical composition of the 52-card deck.
3. The number of players he is out to beat.

Before he can make any judgment of his winning chances of the kind of hand he holds, he must consider the following factors:

1. The strength of the probable best hand among his opponents.
2. The chances of his bettering his own hand.
3. The likelihood of being outdrawn and losing the pot.
4. The probable size of the pot and what it will cost him to play.
5. Whether the strength of his hand calls for him to play or not to play.

Nearly every average Draw Poker player has in the back of his mind, consciously or unconsciously, an answer for each of these factors. Generally speaking, few of these answers are correct. Most top-notch Draw Poker players follow a set of rough opening guides that don't vary much from the following.

1. In a seven- or eight-handed game, if you are next to the dealer and first to speak, don't open on less than a pair of aces. In a seven- or eight-handed game, second and third man should open on kings or better, fourth and fifth man on queens or better, seventh or eighth on jacks or better.
2. Should the pot be opened ahead of you, play with kings or better and fold with any lesser pair.
3. If you hold any two pairs, raise immediately, especially if you follow the opener. With queens or better don't raise if two or more players are still to speak after you.

As I mentioned earlier, these are very tough rules to follow, but if followed diligently, they will reward the player with many more winning pots.

When to Open at Draw Poker

You will recall my general advice in Chapter 4: Don't bet unless you think you have the best hand going in except when the pot odds are extra tempting. So that the reader can see at a glance the usual one-pair hands that have an even chance to be the best prior to the draw, they have been placed together in the following table.

VALUE OF HANDS TO OPEN WITH

Number of Players to Speak	Hands to Open With
6 or 7	A pair of aces or better
5	A pair of aces or better
4	A pair of kings or better
3	A pair of queens or better
2	A pair of queens or better
1	A pair of jacks or better

Our mathematics tells us that if you hold a pair of kings in an eight-handed game, the odds are slightly better than even that an opponent has a pair of aces or better. In a six- or seven-handed game, the odds are even that your pair of kings are high. In a five-handed game, the odds are 1.1 to 1 that your pair of kings will be high, since the odds of one of your opponents' holding a pair of queens is even. Remember that these hands are not expected to win the pot, they are high hands only before the draw.

At this point I must add that the three odd cards that accompany your pair affect your chance of being high. A pair of queens with an ace-king-ten will be the high hand in a six-handed game as often as a pair of kings. These three odd cards better the value of your hand very little but they do reduce the possibility of other players' holding a pair of aces and kings. Even when discarding these three odd cards, their values should be remembered because they limit the chances that a player holding aces or kings will make three of a kind on the draw. If you hold Q-Q-A-K-X at the start and catch a queen on the draw, you should bet them up as if you had three aces.

As stated earlier under General Strategy, the player who opens early is in a bad position because he must bet first after the draw. Therefore I suggest that the player under the gun in an eight-handed game should not open with any pair less than aces. The only exception to this ruling is when the pot is extra big and offers better than favorable odds.

A pair of aces or any two pairs are always worth opening with, regardless of position. At times, with a big pot and six or more players, and if you speak first or second, it's a good bet to pass with aces or two pairs for strategic purposes, then to come in and raise if anyone opens. But, I must warn you, it's not smart to do this with tight players.

Value of Hands to Stay in With

With a pair of kings you have a reasonable chance of holding the high hand in any game, and in an eight-handed game you can expect to be second or third best, which may be profitable if there were several pass hands, antes, and if the pot is big. A lower pair should usually be folded.

The following table depicts the hand you must possess to have a reasonable chance of holding the best hand before the draw when the pot has been opened before your turn to speak.

Players Who Speak Before You	If Players Are Tight	If Players Are Loose
1	A pair of kings	Pair of queens
2	Two small pairs	Pair of aces
3	Queens up	Two small pairs
4	Kings up	Jacks up
5	Aces up	Queens up
6	Three of a kind	Kings up

The above table is intended only as a guide. When the pot is extra large, a lower-rank hand than stipulated above may be quite in order.

Raises

There are a couple of reasons for raising. One is to increase the size of the pot. The other is to drive other players out. It may appear wrong to want to drive other players out of the pot when you have the best hand before the draw, since, as I have mentioned, the best hand going in usually wins the pot. However, chance and probabilities don't always act as expected, so at times it's best to try and drive other players out, and at times to let them stay.

The following table shows the percentage win after the draw for a hundred pots comprising two to seven players, each of whom puts one chip into the pot.

PERCENTAGE AND CHIP WIN BY HOLDING TWO LOW PAIRS IN A HUNDRED POTS

Number of Players in Pot	Percentage of Pots You Are Expected to Win	Total Chips Expected to Win
2	73½	47
3	53	59
4	39	56
5	29½	47½
6	23	38
7	17	33

You will note that the maximum chip win is scored on two low pairs when you have only two opponents in the pot besides yourself. The chip win is least when everyone stays. So, in short, you are better off to drive most of the players out.

The reason for these happenings is that two low pairs afford you the best opportunity when no one improves his hand, but rarely win when one or more players improve their hands. The odds are 3 to 1 in your favor that your two low pairs are high before the draw, but the odds after the draw are roughly 11 to 1 against improvement, and the only chance for improvement is to make a full house.

It's a different story when you hold two high pairs such as aces up. In this case you do not want to drive out competition, but instead to fatten the pot. In this situation you figure to win against players who improve, but who get no better than kings up.

If the pot is opened and you follow the opener, you simply stay with the aces up. In a loose game you should refrain from raising as long as there are players behind you still to speak. Such hands profit most from position—you raise after nearly all players have spoken and have already decided to play or fold. Thus you increase the size of the pot if other players meet your raise, you give yourself a better chance of winning against fewer players, and the pot is about the same size as if all players stayed and you didn't raise.

Reraising depends on the betting limit, the size of the pot, and your appraisal of your chances to better your hand with the draw. Suppose you have opened with three kings, the player to your right has raised, and another player after him has reraised. This time you simply call (play). You don't want the original raiser to fold, since you expect to win the pot.

At this point I would like to remind my readers of my previous remarks in the General Strategy chapter about courage. It is true that three kings are not a sure bet to win the hand. One of the other players may have a straight going in, either of the other players may improve and wind up with a full house with the draw. Nonetheless you must play your three kings, on the assumption that you hold a winning hand, and you must find a way to make the pot as big as possible regardless of whether you win it or lose it. Let yourself become fearful of losing the pot with three kings and you won't be a winner at Poker.

Draw Poker Probabilities

The number of possible five-card combinations to be made from a standard 52-card deck with no wild cards are 2,598,960 and are made up of four royal flushes, 36 straight flushes, 13 four of a kind, 3,744 full houses, 5,108 flushes, 10,200 straights, 52 three of a kind, 2,808 two pairs, and 78 pairs. It may appear strange that there are more than 5,000 flushes and only 78 pairs. The explanation is that each of those 78 pairs is teamed up with three differently valued cards to make a five-card hand. The true number of five-card hands containing a pair is 1,098,240 and the probability of a player's being dealt a pat pair hand is .422, or roughly, 1½ to 1 against. However, when playing Five Card Draw, the probability that a player will be dealt a pair of jacks or better in the five dealt cards is .206, or roughly, 4 to 1 against.

The following table depicts the approximate probability and odds against being dealt a pair or better in the first five dealt cards.

The probability and odds against holding a specified pair is .033, or 29 to 1.

If all your opponents were poor Poker players, you would get best results by consistently drawing three cards to a pair. Since most likely they are not, you should occasionally hold a kicker (an odd card).

Rank of Hand	**Probability**	**Approximate Odds Against**
Any pair or better	.499	1 to 1
Pair of jacks or better	.206	4 to 1
Pair of queens or better	.174	5 to 1
Pair of kings or better	.141	6 to 1
Pair of aces or better	.109	8 to 1

True, by holding a kicker your chances of improving the hand are lessened. The exact chances of improving a pair with a kicker are 1 in 3.86, whereas the chances of improving a pair without a kicker are 1 in 3.48. But the player holding a kicker has added a certain deceptive value to his hand. Your judgment must decide if it is worth holding. Your decision must be made after analyzing both the players' characteristic methods and the number of cards each player has drawn before your turn to draw.

Here is a hint on whether to stay in with a four-card flush, which I have found sound both in theory and in actual play. Calculate the amount of money in the pot and recall the chances of drawing the fifth card to make the flush. The chances of drawing one card to make a flush are 1 in 5.2. Therefore, the pot should contain at least five times the amount it will cost you to draw a card. In other words, if the opening bet was $1, there must be at least $5 in the pot before it is worth your risk in paying $1 to draw a card in an attempt to make a flush.

"But," you say, "should I make the flush, it may not win; therefore, shouldn't the pot make me better odds?" The answer is no, for as a rule there isn't too much money in the pot before the draw; and, second, a flush will win many more times for a player than it will lose.

The Draw Poker tables shown in Chapter 10, The Mathematics of Poker, are intended as an aid to better Draw Poker playing. A player who has a fair idea of the chances of improving his hand in Draw will have a great advantage over the player who does not have the vaguest idea. It is suggested that a player try especially to memorize the exact chances of bettering certain hands, such as a pair, a four-card straight and a four-card flush.

Betting After the Draw

Another general-strategy Poker rule like the ones cited in Chapter 4 is: Don't bet into a one-card draw. It is true that a hand that drew one card may turn out to be a straight, flush or full house made on a one-card draw to two pairs. The theory is that it is not smart Poker playing to bet against a one-card draw when you have something like three of a kind or two pairs, because if the hand did not make a straight or flush, it would fold, and if it did not improve its two pairs it might just call. If the hand improvement made a straight or flush and your hand failed to improve, it has you beaten. It's as simple as that.

However, if you never bet into a one-card draw, you will lose considerably more than you should have collected with your winning hand than that lost to a successful one-card draw that beats your hand. What you must do is to decide to your own satisfaction what the one or more one-card draws mean. Suppose there are six active players in the pot. You opened under the gun with three aces. The next five players played, the first two players drew three, and the following drew one each. It would be foolish for you as the opening bettor to check. Of the two players who drew three cards each probably had a pair of kings or less and could not beat you if each made three of a kind. The other two players probably had two pairs and the odds are about 5 to 1 that neither made a full house. The last player may have had a four-card straight or flush and the odds are roughly 5 to 1 that he failed to fill the straight or flush. If you check and no one improved his hand, the players holding two pairs will also check and you will have lost the amount of the call bets. The odds favor your chance that some player will call a bet, rather than that some player will have bettered his hand with the one-card draw. Furthermore, if your bet is raised, the chances are that your three aces are beaten, but it will cost you only one bet more to call the raise than it would have cost to check in the first place and call a bet later, which you would have had to do unless you are a mind reader or know your Poker-playing opponents awfully well.

Whether to raise and bluff in Draw Poker is determined by the situation involved. A player must take into consideration the temperament of the players with whom he is competing, the amount of money in the pot, the number of cards drawn, and the relative value of the player's own hand. All these factors are learned over years of Poker playing, and so is the faculty of evaluating them correctly. It isn't necessary to do these things perfectly to win money at Poker. All you must do is to play a better Draw Poker game than your opponents. If you can't do that with the information contained in this book, I suggest you look for a Poker game with younger and greener players.

6

Draw Poker Variations

POKER HERE AND ABROAD

In my capacity as casino gambling consultant for the Hilton International Hotel chain, the United States Senate, the British Home Office, the Puerto Rican Government, and various other governments, I scouted dozens of casinos and Poker games the world over. These Poker games included Draw and Stud Poker variations found in England, France, Italy, Egypt, South Africa, Macao, Panama and other Caribbean countries. These, added to the dozens and dozens of Poker variations I picked up during my travels all over the United States, make a very impressive list. From this endless group, I have selected the most popular variations. Here, then, are the greatest number and the most popular variations of Poker games collected by me from years of scouting and analyzing all kinds of Poker being played here and abroad.

I have divided the Draw or Closed Poker-style games and the Stud or Open Poker-style games into seven separate categories:

1. Basic variants of standard Draw Poker
2. Low and High-Low Draw Poker variants
3. Draw Poker variations of Spit in the Ocean
4. Miscellaneous Draw Poker variants
5. Five Card Stud Poker
6. America's seven most popular Seven Card Stud games
7. Five Card Stud Poker variations and miscellaneous Stud Poker variants

Specific Poker games can be found in the index. However, you may know certain games under other names. In this case, determine the type of game you are interested in and look through the relevant category. You should find either the game itself or a close cousin.

BASIC VARIANTS OF STANDARD DRAW POKER

The player will find the rules governing the Draw or Closed Poker variants that follow in Chapter 3, under General Rules for Poker, in Chapter 5, under Rules for Draw Poker, Jackpots, Jacks or Better, and under each game heading that follows. For pointers in strategy, the player may refer to Chapter 4, General Strategy, and Chapter 5, under Draw Poker Strategy. For easy reference the Draw Poker and other Poker variants that follow have been numbered.

1. California Draw Poker with the Bug

This game is played more often in California than in all other places combined. Its popularity is due to the fact that Draw Poker is legal in California and Stud Poker is not. And so, California Draw with the Bug and all other Draw Poker-style games have a monopoly in its four hundred-odd licensed Poker clubs. Therefore it was natural for Draw Poker with the Bug to spread to private homes in California. However, this fantastic Draw Poker variant is rapidly gaining in popularity among Poker players throughout this country and abroad.

All the rules of standard Draw Poker apply to this variation with the following two exceptions:

1. Some California Poker clubs permit players to stand pat or draw one to five cards at the draw, other clubs one to four cards. I recommend a one- to three-card draw.

2. The game is played with a standard 52-card deck with a joker added, making it a 53-card deck. The joker is referred to as a "bug." However, this bug, or joker, has limited wild powers. It can be used only as an ace or to complete a straight flush, a flush or a straight. A player can have five aces but not five of any other kind. Rank of hands in descending order are as follows:

1. Five aces (A-A-A-A-Bug)
2. Royal flush
3. Straight flush
4. Four of a kind
5. Full house
6. Flush
7. Straight
8. Three of a kind
9. Two pairs
10. One pair
11. No pair

A standard 52-card deck possesses 2,598,960 possible five-card hands. A 53-card deck with the added bug (joker) possesses 2,869,685. The difference is 270,725 additional hands in a 53-card deck. The majority of these hands use the bug as a high card. The bug livens up the betting quite a bit and furnishes the players with more playable one- and two-card draws and more good hands, in general, than one gets in standard Draw.

A player making use of the strategy exactly as described under standard Draw in this California variation is sure to be rewarded with a losing game.

A California Draw player must take many factors into consideration when deciding whether or not to open, fold, call, raise or reraise.

How many players are yet to act? What is the size of your bet relative to the size of the anticipated pot? Following are the ranks of hands needed as an opening requirement for the average game.

Playing Position	Rank of Hands
8th (dealer)	A pair of jacks or better
7th	A pair of queens or better
6th	A pair of kings or better
5th	A pair of aces or better
4th	A pair of aces or two pairs, tens up or better
3rd	A pair of aces or two pairs, jacks up or better
2nd	A pair of aces or two pairs, queens up or better
1st (leader under gun)	A pair of aces or two pairs, kings up or better

Following are a number of important one-card draws you will confront with the bug in a 53-card deck. With an open-ended three-card sequence 4,5,6, all of the same suit, and the bug, the player has a perfect combination that will give him nearly an equal chance to fill in, 22 in 48 or a 45.83% chance of making a straight flush, a flush, or a straight. This is known as a 22-way hand. This hand deserves a raise before the draw. Another 22-way hand is the 10, jack, queen, all of the same suit, plus the bug. Twelve cards will make a straight for this 22-way hand, six cards a flush, and four cards a straight flush. Same odds and percentage figure as shown in the above 22-way hand prevail. This hand is also worth a raise before the draw.

A one-card draw to 6,7, and 9, all of the same suit, and the bug, is a 19-way hand, and 19 times out of 48, or about 40% of the time, will fill in.

And there are hands such as A-K-Q of the same suit, and the bug, that permit a player to hold a pair of aces and still draw one card to a possible straight, flush, or straight flush. Should the player miss filling in the hand, he still has the chance of making three aces or aces up. At the worst, he'll still hold a pair of aces, a good hand to raise before the draw.

Basically, California Draw is a game of aces and the bug. Any player who doesn't take aces and the bug into consideration is bound to lose. The following list proves the importance of aces with the bug.

1. There is only one five-of-a-kind hand, and it is comprised of four aces and the bug.
2. There are five times as many four-ace hands as any other specific four of a kind.
3. There are 2.3 times as many full houses involving three or two aces as any other specific full house.
4. There are 2.5 times as many three-ace hands as any other specific three of a kind.
5. There are 1.66⅔ times as many one pair of aces as any other specific one pair.

Furthermore, there are 1⅓ as many flushes and straight flushes and two times as many straights as are found in Draw Poker minus the bug.

It now should be obvious to the reader that, should he hold an ace and the bug before the draw, he is the boss man and should raise the limit. On the other hand, when you don't possess the bug, the odds favor an opponent's holding the bug, and you must play cautiously. And since check and raise is permitted, be on the alert for players "backing in." There is no advantage in making two-card draws to possible flushes or straights. Should you possess the bug and three adjacent cards of the same suit, you should raise regardless of the number of active players left when you possess a 19-way or 22-way hand. The best time to bluff is before the draw.

Now that you have a general idea which hands to play and which not to play, don't ever forget that California Draw Poker is a game of aces.

To further improve your game to the expert level, I suggest you study the tips, hints, subterfuges, bits of strategy and warnings described under General Strategy, Chapter 4.

2. *English Draw Poker, or Blind and Straddle*

This is the basic English Draw Poker game, also known as Australian Poker, South African Poker, Tiger, and Blind Tiger, each of which possesses several minor variations—but none is materially different from any other. Blind and Straddle began to lose popularity throughout the globe with the introduction of Jackpots or Jacks or Better, but it still remains a very popular Draw Poker game in England, Australia, South Africa and neighboring countries.

The standard Draw Poker rules prevail except in the following respects, which concern principally the first betting interval and the showdown.

Whether or not there was any ante before the deal, at the conclusion of the deal the player on the left of the dealer (leader), who is called the "blind," must put up an ante of one unit before looking at his cards. Next, the player on the left of the blind, known as the "straddle," must ante two units into the pot before looking at his cards. In effect, he raises the blind one unit. The third player to the dealer's left is the first to act. After looking at his hand, he has two options available—he may open for four units (he cannot bet more or less than four units) or he may fold (passing out) and throw in his hand. Should he fold, the player on his left has the same options available, opening for four units or folding. If everyone folds before the blind, the blind is required only to bet three units above his one-unit ante. If the blind folds, the straddler collects the three units in the pot.

Once the pot is opened, the game proceeds in the usual Draw Poker way, each succeeding player having the choice of folding, calling or raising. When the turn of play reaches the blind and straddle, who have already anted one and two units respectively, these units are credited to any bet they choose to make. Example: Suppose a previous player has opened the pot for four units, the blind may call for only three additional units and the straddler for only two additional units.

Recently on a casino investigation for the government in Lesotho, Southern Africa, I witnessed a big limit Blind and Straddle game played with optional straddles. If the second player to the dealer's left decides not to straddle, he becomes the first to act after looking at his cards. In this instance, he can open for two units or fold. If the second player decides to straddle, he must bet two units without looking at his hand.

Once this voluntary straddle is made, then each succeeding blind player may straddle by betting double the previous bet. Usually the number of voluntary straddles is limited to four.

After the last straddle, each player may look at his hand. At his proper turn of play, each player, beginning with the player to the left of the last straddler, must either fold or bet. The first player to act must either fold or raise the last straddler's bet by an amount equal to the last straddler's bet.

Once a player has made the last voluntary blind bet, each player after him may either fold, call or raise. When the turn of play reaches the blind and the straddle, who have previously contributed one and two units respectively, the units are counted as part of any call or raise bet they may choose to make.

When the turn of play reaches the blind, he counts his opening bet toward his call, and each straddler counts his previous bet toward his call. If all non-straddlers have dropped out when the blind's turn to play comes around again, he may drop, call or raise, and so may each successive straddler. If no one calls the last straddler, he wins the pot and everything in it. If one or more players call, and as soon as all player bets are equalized, players may either stand pat or draw one to four cards. Then a second betting interval takes place. The raise betting limit after the draw is four units regardless of the number of straddles.

The advantage of voluntary straddling is to try to gain a favorable table position, since the last player to straddle becomes the last player to bet after the draw. The disadvantage is that the last straddler is obliged to raise on a hand which may be worthless.

The following table depicts the number of active players who have acted before you and the rank hand you should hold to call or raise before the draw.

Active Players Who Have Acted Before You Excluding Blind and Straddle	Rank of Hand You Should Hold
1	Kings or better
2	Tens up or better
3	Queens up or better
4	Aces up or better
5	Three of a kind or better

In practice, I've noticed that most players rarely weigh the pros and cons carefully but simply straddle to increase the size of the pot. A player who straddles or restraddles when others are only calling at their turn of play is surely not theoretically justified. If he continues to play under these conditions, it's a sure bet he'll not be a winner over the long run.

Note: To improve your Blind and Straddle game to expert level I suggest you study the tips, hints, subterfuges, bits of strategy and warnings described under General Strategy, Chapter 4, and Draw Poker Strategy in Chapter 5.

3. *Old-time English Blind and Straddle*

This variant of Blind and Straddle has lost its popularity in England, Australia and South Africa. In this game high- and low-rank hands compete against each other. The purpose in including these low-rank hands was to speed up Blind and Straddle play by increasing the number of hands, thereby increasing the betting action and livening up the game. The names and the ranks of these low Poker hands follow.

1. Big Cat or Big Tiger: King to eight low, mixed suits, no pair. Loses to a flush, beats any lower-ranking hand.
2. Little Cat or Little Tiger: Eight to three low, mixed suits, no pair. Ranks below a Big Cat or Big Tiger.
3. Big Dog: Ace to nine low, mixed suits, no pair. Beats a straight or any lower-ranked hand.
4. Little Dog: Seven to deuce low, mixed suits, no pair. Ranks next below a Big Dog, beats a straight or any lower-rank hand.

In the case of two cats or dogs of the same rank, highest-rank hand wins. Examples: K-Q-10-9-8 beats K-J-10-9-8, as would 7-6-4-3-2 beat 7-5-4-3-2.

A Blind and Straddle Game I'll Never Forget

I will always harbor mixed memories of a Blind and Straddle game that took place many years ago at the swank Pair of Shoes casino in London. I was in London on official business for the British Home Office with regard to a revision of England's casino laws when I visited the Pair of Shoes casino to say hello to my friend, dapper Eric Steiner, the crack English Poker expert, mentioned earlier, who at the time was the operator of the Pair of Shoes casino. It was an "in" place for celebrities. On this night Lee Marvin, Sydney Chaplin, Henry and Clare Luce, Nicky Hilton and Sophia Loren were present.

It all began while Steiner and I were having a drink at the casino bar when Steiner whispered, "Scarne, see those two men at the end of the bar? They just dropped twenty-five thousand dollars at the roulette table."

Later I learned they were two French multimillionaires from Paris (whom I shall refer to as Mr. X and Mr. Y). They were both big-time gamblers. Mr. Y had once lost $300,000 at a single dice session in George Raft's London Colony Club without ever batting an eyelash.

"Eric, what's their business?" I asked.

"They head a law firm in Paris," replied Steiner with a nonchalant shake of his head. "Scarne," he continued, "the tall one loves to play Poker. He pictures himself as a champ Poker player and whenever he's here in London he spends a couple of hours at the downstairs cardroom playing Blind and Straddle."

"What limit do they play?" I inquired.

"Oh, it's a small twenty- and forty-dollar-limit game—and do you know what? Mr. X never fails to invite me to play. He's a Poker degenerate and likes to play with our top English Poker experts regardless of his losses. Furthermore, Scarne, he thinks of himself as one who knows everything there is to know about Poker and is always bragging that he can't be cheated at Poker."

"One of those guys," I thought to myself.

Several minutes later, as Mr. X and Mr. Y were leaving the bar, Mr. X shouted, "Mr. Steiner, how about you and your friend joining us in the cardroom for a little Poker playing?"

I nudged Steiner and said, "Eric, that's the first Poker game invitation I've received in years."

Steiner, turning on a big smile, said, "Scarne, how about you and me playing a joke on those two Frenchmen? We'll both sit in the game, you put your sleight of hand to work, and we'll take them to the cleaner's. We'll give them a good going over and at the end of the game we'll return their money and we'll all have a good laugh."

"Eric," I replied, "I don't believe Mr. X will like the idea of being made a fool of at the Poker table even though he gets his money back. And there is always the chance that I'll be recognized by someone in the cardroom before we return the money to those two Frenchmen. If that happens we might have a lot of explaining to do to make them believe we were only playing a joke and not really cheating. But, if you really want to do it, I'll take the gamble of not being recognized and go along with your joke."

I asked Eric to get me two decks of cards—a red and a blue—with the same back designs as used in the Poker game and gave him the lame excuse that I wanted to go to my room and practice dealing out some cheating Poker hands. When Eric Steiner handed me the two decks of cards he said, "Scarne, be back as soon as possible."

"Okay, Eric, shall do," I replied.

A half hour later, Steiner, Mr. Joe Brown (my alias at the time), Mr. X and Mr. Y were battling each other at a $20 and $40 limit game of Blind and Straddle, each of us having bought in $1,000 in chips. For the first fifteen minutes or so the betting moved at a slow pace. I noticed that Mr. Y was giving me the once-over, too close to suit me.

It was then that I decided before I was recognized to put my cheating skill to work and get the joke over with.

The moment had arrived. It was Mr. X's turn to deal. Mr. X gave the deck several thorough flat table riffle shuffles, then placed the deck in front of me to be cut. After I had completed the cutting of the cards, Mr. X placed the deck in his left palm and proceeded to deal out four Poker hands. Steiner, who was seated at Mr. X's left, was the blind and without looking at his cards made a blind ante of $20. Mr. Y, seated at Steiner's left, being the straddle, was forced to make a $40 bet. It now came my turn to bet and I made a voluntary blind straddle bet of $80. Mr. X called, as did Steiner and Mr. Y. The pot now contained $320.

I studied Mr. X as he looked at his hand and noticed that his previous poker-face composure had completely disappeared and his face had turned a pinkish red. I quickly glanced at Mr. Y as he studied his hand and noticed him shaking his head from side to side. Mr. X picked up the remaining undealt cards, faced Steiner and asked in a weak, choking voice, "How many cards?" Steiner discarded and called for two cards.

Mr. X's hands were visibly shaking as he dealt Steiner his two requested cards. Mr. X next turned to his law partner, Mr. Y, and looked him straight in the eye as if he were trying to convey a message. He softly asked, "How many, please?"

There was some thirty seconds of silence as Mr. X and Mr. Y kept looking into each other's eyes before Mr. Y responded meekly, "I'll play these."

As Mr. X faced me, I discarded three cards and called for three. Mr. X nervously dealt me two cards instead of the called for three. He dealt me the third card after I reminded him that I called for three, not two.

It was now Mr. X's turn to draw cards. He placed the deck face down on the table, picked up his five-card hand from the table and after nervously looking at his cards for a while said, "No cards for me."

Since I was the last voluntary straddler, Mr. X was the first to act. Mr. X pushed $40 in chips into the pot and, wearing a big smile, half-shouted, "I bet forty dollars."

Steiner raised and bet $80. Mr. Y without a second wasted cried aloud, "I call the eighty and raise forty."

I pushed $120 into the pot and said, "I call."

Mr. X reraised $40. And so it went around the table several times, reraise, reraise, reraise, call, reraise, reraise until all of Mr. X's and

Mr. Y's chips were in the pot. Steiner and I collectively had some $100 or less in odd chips still left. I pushed my odd chips into the pot and muttered, "These few chips won't help me any. Let the winner take all."

Steiner followed suit and pushed his remaining chips into the pot. The pot now contained the total $4,000 chip buy-in.

Mr. X was first to act on the showdown. As he placed his hand face up on the table for all to see, he jubilantly announced, "Gentlemen, believe it or not, I dealt myself the invincible Iron Duke, a royal flush. Did you ever see anything more beautiful? The ace, king, queen, jack, and ten of spades, the first royal flush I have ever held in all my forty years of Poker playing—and gentlemen, I dealt it myself."

While Mr. X was talking, I felt a pain in my stomach thinking how he was going to react when he learned his hand was just a joke. To lessen the shock to come I hurriedly placed my diamond royal flush face up on the table and meekly said, "I also have a royal flush."

Steiner followed immediately and spread out his club royal flush.

Mr. Y, like Mr. X, remained stunned and speechless at this chain of events, as he silently placed his heart royal flush on the table.

After a minute or so of silence, Mr. X, who had by this time regained his composure, said, "If I hadn't dealt the cards myself, I would say there was something crooked about these four royal flushes. But, since I shuffled and dealt the cards, I don't know what to make of it."

I didn't want this joke to continue any further so I told Steiner to explain what had happened. Steiner rose from the table, faced Mr. X and said, "Gentlemen, these four royal flushes are of equal rank so the hand is a draw. No one wins, no one loses. I'll return the thousand dollar chip buy-ins to each of you. I don't know what else to say and I don't know what in heaven really did happen, but what I do know is, the man responsible for these four royal flushes is that man sitting alongside of you, the one and only John Scarne, the world's greatest card magician and gambling authority."

Mr. X and Mr. Y stood up and appeared stunned by Steiner's announcement. Mr. X shook my hand vigorously and said, "Imagine me sitting in a Poker game with *the* John Scarne. I'll never forget this game if I live to be a million."

Mr. Y joined in and said, "Mr. Scarne, during the game I kept thinking I knew you from someplace. Now I remember, I saw your film, *Cheating in Gambling*, in a Paris theater a couple of months ago. In that film I saw a close-up of you dealing four of a kind to four different men and giving yourself a royal flush."

Mr. X turned to me and asked, "Mr. Scarne, how did you make me deal those four royal flushes?"

"Magicians never reveal their secrets," I replied. "However, if we all amble upstairs, I will demonstrate some card-cheating manipulations at the casino bar." That night I demonstrated my gambler's card-cheating techniques for two full hours while Mr. X and Mr. Y watched in amazement, as did a couple of dozen casino patrons who had left the gaming tables to watch my performance.

As the sun began to rise in the east, Steiner, while accompanying me to my room at the nearby London Hilton Hotel said, "Scarne, since you told me you were going to switch in a stacked deck on Mr. X's deal when he offered you the deck to cut, I watched you like a hawk each time you cut the deck and never did I see you make a move. I was as surprised as Mr. X and Mr. Y when I was dealt a royal flush. Your deck switch tonight was a masterpiece."

Some years later I had the pleasure of being the technical adviser to the 1973 Academy Award-winning film, *The Sting*, which starred Paul Newman, Robert Redford, and Robert Shaw. In addition to my duties as technical adviser to *The Sting*, I performed all the card manipulations seen in the film. Of particular delight to movie patrons was the Poker game scene which took place aboard a train. In one scene, the villain, Robert Shaw, was shown switching a stacked deck into the Poker game to fleece Paul Newman. The stacked deck switch was not faked. They were my hands that actually switched decks. I've seen *The Sting* a dozen or more times, and believe you me, the switch was executed so smoothly that even I can't spot the switch. This is the same deck switch I executed at the Poker game described above. If you happen to see a rerun of *The Sting*, try to spot the deck switch. I'm sure you won't.

4. Draw Poker—Blind Openers

This variation of Draw Poker, commonly referred to as Open Blind, is being played in many commercial Poker clubs across the country from New York to California. The reason for its recent popularity in Poker clubs is that it speeds up the game of Draw Poker be it standard Draw Poker, or California Draw Poker with the Bug, or any other form of Draw Poker. And it earns more money for the house.

All the rules for the specific Draw Poker game being played prevail, except here the leader to the left of the dealer opens the pot for a stipulated amount before looking at his cards.

Most of the Draw Poker strategy found under standard Draw Poker or in California Draw Poker with the Bug will be of value. Stay out of high-stakes Open Blind games until you've mastered Draw Poker Jacks or Better.

Sometimes the game is structured after Blind and Straddle so that not only does the leader open blind, but the next player to his left raises blind, and occasionally this is carried through to the next player and becomes open blind, raise blind, reraise blind.

For rules and strategy of this type of game, see game number 2, English Draw Poker, or Blind and Straddle.

5. *Straight Draw Poker, or Anything Opens*

Straight Draw Poker, or Anything Opens, the granddaddy of standard Draw Poker, is played very little today throughout the globe and that's because of the availability of the countless new and more interesting Draw Poker variants.

The game is played exactly as is standard Draw Poker with the following two exceptions: 1. A player may open the pot on any hand he desires. 2. A player may stand pat or draw up to five cards on the draw.

Straight Draw Poker for five or fewer players is a superior game to standard Draw Poker because in these five- or fewer-players games standard Draw Poker pots are won all too frequently by the opener, and often require a number of redeals because no player possesses a pair of jacks or better as openers.

The game requires a very similar strategy to standard Draw Poker except that there is considerably more sandbagging (check and raise), refusing to open with a good hand in order to raise the eventual opener. So the first three players under the gun should exercise restraint in opening.

Generally speaking, in a six- or seven-handed game, if you should happen to be one of the first three players under the gun, you should not open the pot regardless of how good a hand you hold. If you possess a good hand, there is no sense in committing yourself that early. If you possess an excellent hand, there's no reason in playing it from the opener's unfavorable position. In Straight Draw Poker, unlike basic Draw Poker, there is little hope that all players will fold or drop out—some player nearly always opens.

In the end game positions, to open you need a pair of aces or better in an eight-handed game, a pair of kings or better in a seven-handed game, a pair of queens or better in a six-handed game, and a pair of jacks in a five-handed game. If you are the last player to act, regardless of the number of players, open on a pair of tens or better.

Following is the rank of hands it takes before the draw to have a better-than-even chance to beat a given number of players regardless of where you sit and the number of players that have not yet committed themselves.

Rank of Hand Required	To Beat Opponents 50% or More of the Time
A pair of aces or better	8 opponents
A pair of kings or better	7 opponents
A pair of queens or better	6 opponents
A pair of jacks or better	5 opponents
A pair of tens or better	4 or fewer opponents

At times I recommend that a late player open on a four-card straight opened on both ends and a four-card flush just to see if he fills in. Anyway, it's a good spot for a bluff, and even if he loses to the hand because his bluff didn't work, he will keep his opponents guessing as to the type of player he happens to be.

Note: To improve your Straight Draw Poker game to an expert's level, I recommend you study the tips, hints, subterfuges, bits of strategy and warnings described under General Strategy, Chapter 4, and Draw Poker Strategy, Chapter 5.

6. *Straight Draw Poker—Pass or Drop*

Also known as Bet or Drop, the play is the same as in Straight Draw Poker (above) except that a player may not check. He must either bet or drop out of the game.

7. *Showdown Straight Poker*

This variant of standard Draw Poker, also called Cold Hands, is strictly a game of chance where luck wins out. This game is usually played by big-time gamblers toward the end of a Poker session.

The only betting in Showdown is done before the cards are dealt, as if anteing into the pot. Then five cards are dealt each player, one at a time, face up, starting with the leader and rotating to the left clockwise. The player holding the highest hand wins the pot. There is no draw. All other rules are identical to those for Draw Poker.

8. *Draw Poker High Spades*

This is a side bet at Draw Poker between two or more players that one will hold a higher-ranking spade card than any of the other players in his first five cards dealt. Players announce the approximate value of their hands—for example, a player says, "I have a low spade." The other player says, "I have a high spade," then shows it to all players betting on spades. The reason for this is not to expose too many cards. Although spades is a popular bet at Draw Poker, it often exposes a player's hand and gives other players, not betting on spades, a slight advantage in the game. This type of spade side betting affords no opportunity for skillful play and is generally played by professional or big-time Poker gamblers.

9. *Progressive Draw Poker*

If you think standard Draw Poker Jacks or Better or Jackpots is too slow a betting game and you'd like bigger pots without increasing the betting limits, then this is your game.

Progressive Draw Poker is very popular in England, where it is known as Jackpots. It is also a favorite at men and women's social and private weekly games in this country.

Progressive Draw Poker is played like standard Draw Poker with the following exceptions.

1. On the draw, a player may stand pat or draw one to five cards.
2. The player to open is required to hold a specific rank hand, which increases in rank with each successive deal.
3. The first deal requires that a player's hand must possess a pair of jacks or better to open.
4. Should all the players pass (not open the pot) on the first deal, the requirement for openers on the second deal becomes a pair of queens or better. If the pot is not opened on the second deal, a pair of kings or better is required as openers for the third deal, and a pair of aces or better for the fourth deal.
5. The requirement for the fifth deal is kings or better; for the sixth, queens; and for the seventh, jacks; and then back up to aces and back to kings, etc.
6. Once the pot has been opened by a player, the game reverts back to Draw Poker, jacks or better as openers, etc.

If you like to increase the size of the Poker pots, add this progressive ante variation to your game. When the original ante is two units, the second ante must be four, the third, eight, up to a previously agreed maximum ante of sixteen units. With such an ante, the betting limits should be two and four units. This variation is not recommended for small-time players or pikers.

In a game of this type where the compulsory antes in the pot at any one time vary according to the number of passed hands, most players feel justified in playing with a trash hand. However, the better player, who usually wins more often than he loses, is more cautious about opening the pot unless he believes he has a good chance of winning it.

With progressive antes, these general strategy rules apply:

1. In a five-handed game, the player should play with a pair of jacks or better regardless of the opening requirement.
2. In a six-handed game, the player should play with a pair of queens or better regardless of the opening requirement.
3. In a seven-handed game, the player should play with a pair of kings or better regardless of the opening requirement.

The above general strategy rules are applicable only when the size of the pot has been fattened by successive antes due to passed hands.

To improve your Progressive Draw Poker game to the expert level, I suggest you study the tips, hints, subterfuges, bits of strategy and warnings described under General Strategy, Chapter 4, and Draw Poker Strategy, Chapter 5.

10. Leg Poker

This fascinating addition to standard Draw Poker or any of its variants is sometimes called Leg in a Pot. In Leg Poker the pot stays on the table until one player has won two legs (won it twice); then it is his to keep. The legs need not be won consecutively. *Warning:* If you are in a five-, six- or seven-handed game, don't play this near quitting time, because it might be several hours before one player does win two legs.

11. Draw Poker—Joker Wild

This variation of standard Draw Poker, commonly referred to as Joker Wild, is played exactly like standard Draw Poker, Jacks or Better, except that a joker is added to the standard 52-card deck, making it a 53-card deck. In this game the joker has unlimited powers and can be made to represent any card the holder desires. The addition of the joker to the standard deck adds 270,725 more hands—an increase of about 10½%.

In an eight-handed game the favorable odds are about 3 to 1 that one of the eight players will be dealt the joker. However, unlike the Bug in California Draw Poker, the workings of the joker are found throughout most rank hands.

For a player to play an expert game of Joker Wild, the player must be adept at the strategies described under standard Draw Poker and those involving California Draw Poker with the Bug. Study the distribution table that follows, which depicts the rank of hands in Joker Wild in descending order, and you'll develop a feel for how often the various rank hands are expected to appear pat when dealt from a 53-card deck.

CHANCES OF HOLDING VARIOUS POKER HANDS IN THE FIRST FIVE CARDS DEALT WHEN THE JOKER IS ADDED MAKING A 53-CARD DECK

Rank of hand	Number of each	Chance
Five of a kind	13	1 in 220,745
Royal flush	24	1 in 119,570
Straight flush	216	1 in 13,286
Four of a kind	3,120	1 in 920
Full house	6,552	1 in 438
Flush	7,768	1 in 369
Straight	20,532	1 in 140
Three of a kind	137,280	1 in 21
Two pairs	123,552	1 in 23
One pair	1,268,088	1 in 2¼
No-pair hand	1,302,540	1 in 2⅕
Total hands	2,869,685	

I bring to the attention of the reader a very unusual mathematical situation that arises in Joker Wild regarding the relative value of three of a kind and two pairs. Studying the above chart closely, the reader will observe that the chances of drawing three of a kind are one in 137,280 and the chances of drawing two pair are one in 123,552. Since there are more chances of drawing three of a kind than two pairs, two pairs should be of a higher rank and beat three of a kind. But they don't. This peculiar situation is caused by the fact that there are 82,368 possible five-card Poker hands that contain a pair plus the joker. When a player holds one of these 82,368 hands, he values his hand at three of a kind, making the joker count the same denomination as the pair he is holding.

12. Spanish Draw Poker

This variant of standard Draw Poker is played the same as ours, and all the rules that apply to standard Draw Poker apply to European, or Spanish, Draw Poker, with the following exceptions:

1. In Spanish there are from two to five players; four make the best game.
2. A 32-card deck is used, made by stripping out twos, threes, fours, fives and sixes.
3. If there are not sufficient cards to satisfy each player's draw, the discards are picked up, shuffled and cut, and the draw continues.

13. Canadian Draw Poker

Canadian Draw Poker is played like the standard game of Draw Poker with the following exceptions: A player may open on a four-card straight or a four-card flush, and on the showdown a four-card straight or flush beats a pair, not two pairs or better, and a four-card flush beats a four-card straight.

14. Draw Poker—Deuces Wild

This is standard Draw Poker, Jackpots, or Jacks or Better, with the four deuces wild. Deuces have unlimited wild powers and each deuce can be counted as any card a player desires to call it. The deuce may even be counted as a duplicate of a card already held by a player. Therefore the highest-ranking hand a player can hold is five aces. A player should take extreme care in calling the rank of his hand because the rank called must stand, contrary to the practice in standard Draw Poker, where the cards speak for themselves. Take, for example, a hand like this: two of clubs, two of diamonds, two of spades, six of hearts, ten of hearts. The average player very often calls four tens instead of a ten-high straight flush. Deuces and natural cards have the same value.

Four deuces wild and other wild cards that number four or more cannot be analyzed with the same accuracy as non-wild cards. The four wild deuces have too many different mathematical probabilities because the probabilities depend upon the denominations of the four deuces claimed by the players.

In standard Draw Poker, minus wild cards, the content of a player's own hand does not drastically affect the contents of opponents' hands, but when four wild deuces are involved, the possession of one or two of them does affect opponents' hands considerably. The opponents' hands are weakened in proportion as a player's own hand is strengthened with wild deuces.

The game is played most often by women at their weekly Poker sessions, or by others who play for small stakes and don't take the game seriously. However, in Australia, where it is called Freak Pot, it is a regular feature in many big-money Poker sessions.

The purpose of introducing the four wild deuces is to increase the action—and that it does. The whole level of the hands found in a 52-card deck (no wild cards) except for no pairs and two pairs is considerably increased in Deuces Wild. Examples: There are seven times as many three of a kinds, six times as many straights and almost fifty times as many four of a kinds.

As mentioned earlier, the total number of possible five-card hands dealt from a 52-card deck are 2,598,960. Although this same total figure holds true when the four deuces are wild, the division of the number of hands in each rank has changed considerably. The following table shows the many mathematical changes that take place in a 52-card deck when the four deuces are wild.

CHANCES OF HOLDING VARIOUS POKER HANDS IN THE FIRST FIVE CARDS DEALT WHEN THE FOUR DEUCES ARE WILD

Rank	Number	Chances
Five of a kind	672	1 in 3,868
Royal flush	484	1 in 5,370
Straight flush	4,072	1 in 638
Four of a kind	30,816	1 in 84
Full house	12,672	1 in 205
Flush	13,204	1 in 197
Straight	66,236	1 in 39
Three of a kind	355,056	1 in 7
Two pairs	95,040	1 in 27
One pair	1,222,048	1 in 2⅒
No pair	798,660	1 in 3¼
Total	2,598,960	

The first thing to note in the above table is that there are 672 possible five of a kinds and only 484 royal flushes. Nonetheless, in this Draw Poker variation, five of a kind outranks a royal flush. The next thing to notice is that a two-pair hand is rare compared with three of a kind. But most important, note that four of a kind will appear about 2½ times more often than full houses and flushes. And last but not least, the above table reveals that two out of three players seated at the card table can be expected to have been dealt a pair or better.

The average winning hand in this game is three aces, but not three natural aces. The fewer wild deuces you hold, the higher ranking hands you can expect your opponents to hold. Two pairs seldom win a pot, and should you hold them before the draw, the lower pair should be discarded. Two wild deuces always justify a play and it is better to draw two cards to two deuces and an ace or king than to draw three cards to the two deuces. A natural three of a kind, except aces, is a weak opening hand. A four-card straight or a four-card flush including a deuce should be played.

15. Fives and Tens

This game, also called St. Louis Draw or Woolworth Draw, is played like standard Draw Poker except that all fives and tens are wild cards. But, to open the first round of betting, a player must hold at least one five and one ten in his hand as openers. (The game cannot be opened if a player holds all four five spots, but does not have a ten.) If no player has the minimum openers—a five and a ten—the deal passes, the players ante again, and new hands of five cards are dealt. This procedure is repeated until someone has the necessary openers. While the obtaining of a wild five and ten as openers may appear difficult to achieve, in reality there are slightly more passes in this game than in standard Draw Poker Jacks or Better. To be exact, the chances of being dealt a wild five and ten in the first five dealt cards are 1 in 8.28, or 7.28 to 1 against. Once the pot is opened, standard Draw rules are followed. Since there are possibly eight wild cards in the game, three of a kind, straights, flushes and full houses seldom win. Four of a kind is the average winning hand, but straight flushes and five of a kind occur frequently.

Low and High-Low Draw Poker Variants

THE BIRTH OF LOW AND HIGH-LOW POKER GAMES

The first time that I ever witnessed a Five Card Draw Low Poker game was in the cardroom of the Dempsey Vanderbilt Hotel in Miami Beach, Florida, during the month of August 1935. I was on vacation with my childhood buddy, James J. Braddock, then the World's Heavyweight Champion. We were on a month's holiday celebrating Jimmy's title win over Max Baer on June 13, 1935, at the Madison Square Garden Bowl on the flats of Astoria, New York.

Jimmy approached me in the lobby of the hotel one night and said, "Professor [that's how Braddock usually addressed me], I just played in the screwiest Poker game ever. It's Five Card Draw, but listen, the lousiest hand wins over straight flushes, four of a kind, full houses, straights, and all other regular Poker winning hands."

"You're sure, Jimmy, that the lousiest hand always wins?"

"Yes, I'm sure. Go into the cardroom and see for yourself. The game's in progress at the third table on the left as you enter."

After watching this Five Card Draw Poker game for about a half hour, I realized Jimmy had told me the truth. I was watching for the first time a Poker game where the worst hand on the showdown was winning all the pots.

After leaving the cardroom, I rushed to my room, grabbed paper and pencil and jotted down the rules of play for this unusual Draw Poker variation.

The Low Poker game that I witnessed played that night back in

1935 is still popular in Southern states and is now called Lowball Deuce to Seven. By 1945 this Lowball Draw Poker variation introduced a new family of countless Low Poker, Lowball, and High-Low variations of both Draw and Stud Poker. Today, we have four different kinds of Low Draw Poker games being played throughout the world, and they are: 1. Lowball Deuce to Seven; 2. Lowball Ace to Six; 3. California Lowball Ace to Five; and 4. Five Card High-Low Draw Poker.

16. Lowball Deuce to Seven

Now let's take a good look at the granddaddy of the family of Low Poker, High-Low, and Lowball, where the worst high Poker hand really does win on the showdown.

The rules of play for this game are the same as those governing standard Draw Poker, except that the rank of hands is just the opposite of those in the standard Draw game, and anything opens. In addition, the ace may be used as high card only, and must not be used to rank as low with a value of 1. Straights, flushes and straight flushes count high and against you. The low hand is evaluated by the rank of its highest card. If there is a tie between highest cards, it is evaluated by the rank of its second highest card, etc. The value of the lowest card is irrelevant to the hand's value except when on the showdown the four higher cards are exactly matched by one or more players. Example: A nine high mixed suit hand such as 9-7-6-5-3 would beat a nine high mixed suit hand 9-7-6-5-4. In this Deuce to Seven Lowball variation, the lowest-ranking cinch hand and certain winner is the 7-5-4-3-2 in mixed suits.

Here, beginning with the cinch hand, I have listed the ten best hands. There are mixed suits, of course. Any hand in a superior rank beats any hand listed below it.

1. 7-5-4-3-2 (cinch hand)
2. 7-6-4-3-2
3. 7-6-5-3-2
4. 7-6-5-4-2
5. 8-5-4-3-2
6. 8-6-4-3-2
7. 8-6-5-3-2
8. 8-6-5-4-2
9. 8-6-5-4-3
10. 8-7-4-3-2, etc.

For the purpose of this discussion, a low-ranking hand will be considered to be any one of 123,420 comprised of seven high, eight high, nine high, and ten high hands. These four categories consist of all hands containing five different denominations that do not together make a straight, flush or straight flush, and in addition do not possess an ace, king, queen or jack.

Study the probability table that follows and you'll develop a feel for how often a passable hand is expected to appear in the first five dealt cards.

Rank of Hands	Number of Hands	Chance
A pat cinch hand (7-5-4-3-2)	1,020	1 in 2,548
Any pat seven	4,080	1 in 637
Any pat eight or lower	14,280	1 in 142
Any pat nine or lower	34,680	1 in 49
Any pat ten or lower	70,380	1 in 21

The above table of probabilities is based on 2,598,960 possible five-card hands that can be dealt from a 52-card deck. The probability for each specific hand in this Deuce to Seven Lowball game is 1,020. In other words, there are 1,020 ways to be dealt a hand of specific rank not including high hands such as straights, flushes, straight flushes, four of a kind, etc. As an example, a pat cinch hand 7-5-4-3-2 and an eight high (8-7-6-4-3) have an equal chance of being dealt in the first five dealt cards. The odds against each of these hands being dealt pat are 2,547 to 1.

More important than any of the above probabilities is to know that the odds are 20 to 1 of being dealt a pat ten high or lower. And the odds are 2 to 1 against anyone holding such a pat hand in a seven-handed game.

Most Poker writers that I've read maintain that there is only one fixed strategy for the draw and that is never to draw more than one card because drawing two cards to a low three-card hand is simply nonsense and a waste of money.

Surely on any specific dealt round of hands, the player whose hand merits a one-card draw has a decided advantage over a player who's compelled to draw two cards.

But, let's consider the money outlay of a supposed smart player whose policy is to play pat hands only, nine high or lower. The game is $1 and $2. There is a 50-cent ante. Four dollars or possibly more to play gives us a minimum of $4.50 per played hand. Since the chances of being dealt a pat hand nine high or lower are only once in 49 deals, than in 48 deals the player simply forfeits the antes and on the remaining one deal he bets $4.50. In 49 games, at this rate, he would have paid out $28.50 and he would have played only once. It would have cost him $28.50 per played hand—and this smart player faces the possibility of losing the played hand. For this reason, I recommend a two-card draw.

However, I do not recommend a two-card draw from an early speaking position because there is not enough money in the pot to justify the odds of 20 to 1 to make a seven high and 6 to 1 odds of making a nine high. I further insist that any three-card draw hand must possess a deuce. The best possible four-card draw hand is 7-4-3-2 in mixed suits. Another good draw hand is 6-4-3-2 in mixed suits. And always remember that any two-card draw must possess a deuce. Not only does the deuce reduce or eliminate your chances of going bust with a straight, but it prevents your opponents from getting your valuable deuce.

The best possible two-card draw is a hand consisting of 7-3-2-2-2. Such a hand makes it difficult for your opponents to possess a top-notch hand because there's only one possible remaining deuce available to them. However, most top Las Vegas professional Lowball players such as Doyle Brunson, Bobby Baldwin, David Reese, Joey Hawthorne and Mike Caro know better than to draw two cards to a possible straight. But any time they make a good two-card draw to three really small cards without a deuce, they often have a possible straight looking down on them, should the first drawn card make a four-card straight. Example: I draw two cards to a 6-4-3 and the first card I look at is a five. I now possess a hand even a sucker wouldn't draw one card to. A seven or a deuce would make that 6-5-4-3 hand a disastrous straight, and the best hand I could make with my fifth-card draw would be an eight high (8-6-5-4-3). If you look at the ten best-ranking hands in the table on page 125, you'll see that it's the ninth-best hand in Lowball Deuce to Seven.

However, I still insist that there are times that a two-card draw is not only a good draw but a mandatory money draw.

The best hands you should try to make are low nines (9-5-4-3-2) and eights, or any sevens. You should draw to these hands at a minimum money risk. Let your opponents play the tens and the high nines. Of course, at times when the pot warrants it, you'll have to play such hands too.

17. Kansas City Lowball Deuce to Seven

A big favorite among big-time Midwestern Poker players, this game is usually played Blind and Straddle table stakes with a $1,000 buy-in. The game rules are identical to those of Lowball Deuce to Seven described above except that a small straight A-2-3-4-5 is considered a low hand and beats any pair.

18. Lowball Ace to Six

During my five-year term as gambling consultant to the United States Armed Forces and *Yank: The Army Weekly* during World War II, I learned that Lowball Ace to Six was the most popular Lowball game being played by our 12 million servicemen stationed throughout the globe. Since that time, this Lowball version has become a regular feature in tens of thousands of Army and civilian Poker sessions being played all over the world. In England, Australia and South Africa Lowball Ace to Six is called Misère.

Lowball Ace to Six is played like standard Draw Poker with the following exceptions. In this game, as in all Low Poker and other Lowball games, the value of the hands is reversed, i.e., one wishes to make as low a hand as possible. Consequently a pat nine (9-5-4-3-2) is a sure loser in standard Draw but becomes a good hand in this game. In addition, aces count low and straights and flushes are considered high and count against the holder. Playing this version of Lowball, when you draw one card to 6-4-3-2, you would hope for an ace. This, provided the hand is not a flush, would give you a cinch and an unbeatable sixty-four (6-4-3-2-A). If you were to draw a nine, that would still be a good low hand. However, if you drew a five, that would make you a straight, and in effect, a disaster.

In short, at the showdown the lowest-ranking five-card hand wins the pot. If all players pair or stay until the showdown, one pair of aces wins the pot, since they are lower than a pair of deuces or any other pair. If some players fail to hold one pair or better, the hand having the lowest-ranked high card wins the pot. If two or more players have the same-ranked high card, the second-lowest-ranked card wins the pot. If the second-highest cards in each hand are equal in rank, the third-highest card determines the loser. And so it goes with the fourth and fifth cards. If all five cards are the same denomination, the pot is split equally. Furthermore, anything can open the pot and a player may draw up to five cards.

As noted earlier, there are 2,598,960 possible five-card combinations to be made from a 52-card deck with no wild cards. Among these 2,598,960 combinations, 1,296,420 consist of one pair or better and 1,302,540 hands are made up of five cards of different denominations that do not together make a straight, flush, straight flush or royal flush.

For the purpose of this discussion, the 1,302,540 hands that do not make one pair or better will be considered as low hands in this Lowball variation. It is true that a Lowball game may be won on occasion by a pair or better, but such hands will not here be classified as low hands.

The following table will give you an idea of the frequency with which you may expect to be dealt a pat low hand in order of priority, starting with a cinch and unbeatable (6-4-3-2-A) hand. The pat five high hands are not listed because they are straights and count against the player.

CHANCES OF BEING DEALT A PAT FIVE CARD LOW RANK HAND

Rank of Specific Hand	Number of Specific Hands	Chances of Being Dealt Specific Hand	Chances of Being Dealt Specific Hand or Better
A pat cinch hand (6-4-3-2-A)	1,020	1 in 2,548	1 in 2,548
Any six high	4,080	1 in 637	1 in 637
Any seven high	14,280	1 in 182	1 in 142
Any eight high	34,680	1 in 75	1 in 49
Any nine high	70,380	1 in 37	1 in 21
Any ten high	127,500	1 in 20	1 in 10
Any jack high	213,180	1 in 12	1 in 6
Any queen high	335,580	1 in 8	1 in 3
Any king high	502,860	1 in 5	1 in 2

More important than any of the above probabilities is to know that the odds are 20 to 1 against being dealt a pat nine high or lower. And the odds are 2 to 1 against anyone holding such a pat hand in a seven-handed game. A pat king, queen, jack, or ten high or lower shown in the above table is usually drawn to. Competition in this Lowball variant is usually restricted to pat hands and one- and two-card draws. The two-card draw is a luxury that you should indulge in from time to time. About half the hands dealt are three low cards to a nine. Such hands have roughly the same probability of success in this Lowball game as a pair of deuces, threes, fours, fives or sixes have in standard Draw. A pat seven high or eight high is a good hand to open, raise or reraise, since the chances of your opponent's catching a pat six high to beat you are 1 in 637 and his chances of catching a seven high are 1 in 182. A good pat ten high (10-6-4-3-2) is worth opening with in certain situations. A pat jack, queen or king high may be a possible one-card draw hand.

If you draw, watch out for the possibility of making a straight or flush and in effect winding up with a disaster.

The following table gives the odds against improving (assuming that you possess a hand that will not readily fall into a disastrous straight or flush) when drawing one or two cards.

ODDS AGAINST IMPROVEMENT WITH A ONE- OR TWO-CARD DRAW

Drawing One Card	Odds Against Improvement
Finishing ten high or lower	1 to 1 (even)
Finishing nine high or lower	5 to 4
Finishing eight high or lower	2 to 1
Finishing seven high or lower	3 to 1
Finishing six high	5 to 1
Drawing Two Cards	
Finishing jack high or lower	1½ to 1
Finishing ten high or lower	2¼ to 1
Finishing nine high or lower	3½ to 1
Finishing eight high or lower	6 to 1
Finishing seven high or lower	10 to 1

After the draw an eight high in the early and middle positions and a seven high are worth a raise in any position. Any six high is normally worth a third raise. A seven high should not be rated higher than, say, a full house or a low four of a kind in standard Draw Poker. If your seven high is beaten, you can be disappointed, but you shouldn't be amazed, since there are 4,080 hands that will beat the best seven high. And don't be shocked if an opponent beats your seven high with a cinch 6-4-3-2-A hand, because cinches are by no means unknown in Lowball Ace to Six.

Generally there is considerable more bluffing after the draw in this game than in standard Draw Poker. Example: An active player who has made a disastrous straight or flush will often try a bluff by making a maximum-limit bet. At any rate, with two or three active players remaining, since he knows that if he checks he cannot possibly win, he will bluff and bet. It is difficult to call such a limit bet when each of the remaining players has paired his hand. However, it's worth noting that against an opponent who has bet the limit and drawn either one or two cards, a small pair of aces or deuces will win nearly as often as a ten high.

When only you and one opponent remain and both of you have drawn cards, if your opponent drew one card it's an even bet that he will finish better than ten high. If you finish with a high nine and are first to speak, you should bet the limit. Don't give your opponent a possible free ride. Similarly, if you speak last and your opponent has passed (checked), your nine high will win unless he is aiming to sandbag (check and raise) you. By all means take that risk, since the only way one can win real money at Poker is by being aggressive.

19. California Lowball Ace to Five

California Lowball, also known as Loball, is the most popular Draw game in the 400 licensed California Poker clubs and in the 100-odd legalized casino Poker rooms in the state of Nevada. In California, where only Five Card Draw Poker and Five Card Lowball are legal, Lowball accounts for most of the action.

The way California Lowball is played in the clubs varies. Some clubs play the game with a 52-card deck and no joker. Others play the game so that straights and flushes are considered high. However, the Lowball variation we will focus on is California Lowball Ace to Five. It is the most popular Draw action game west of the Rocky Mountains. It's a favorite of most Western professional Poker hustlers, mainly because the average Draw player is a perfect sucker because he suffers under the illusion that it's only a game of chance. That is, until he's taken to the cleaner's a number of times. It is then that he realizes that Lowball possesses a great amount of skill, countless angles, subterfuges and bluffs not found in regular Draw Poker.

All the standard Draw Poker rules of play apply to this variation of Lowball, with the exceptions that follow. Lowball Ace to Five is a five-card draw game with no minimum opening requirements, allowing a player to draw up to five cards. On the showdown, the lowest-ranking hand wins the pot. Flushes and straights count as low hands. Thus a hand reading 9-8-7-6-5 in Lowball is considered a nine high. The straight doesn't count. The same thing would apply if this hand were all of the same suit—it wouldn't be a straight flush, just a nine high. The ace ranks low, counting as 1. If all players pair and stay until the showdown, one pair of aces wins the pot, since this is lower than one pair of deuces or any other pair. The lowest hand is 5-4-3-2-ace, and is called a wheel, or bicycle.

This Lowball variation is played with a 53-card deck that includes the bug (joker). The power of the bug is similar to that of California Draw Poker with the Bug (page 106) except that it is more advantageous to hold the bug in Lowball Ace to Five, as it can be used as a wild card to represent any card the holder desires, whereas in California Draw it can only be used as an ace or part of a straight flush, straight or flush.

Some Lowball clubs have instituted what is known as the Sevens Rule. This means that after the draw, if a player checks with a seven high or better, he forfeits any further profits from the pot. He may still win the pot of course, but if another player bets and the player with the seven high calls and wins the pot, the player who made the bet is entitled to remove it from the pot.

Here are the twenty best-ranking hands, starting with the bicycle.

1. 5-4-3-2-A (bicycle)
2. 6-4-3-2-A
3. 6-5-3-2-A
4. 6-5-4-2-A
5. 6-5-4-3-A
6. 6-5-4-3-2
7. 7-4-3-2-A
8. 7-5-3-2-A
9. 7-5-4-2-A
10. 7-5-4-3-A
11. 7-5-4-3-2
12. 7-6-3-2-A
13. 7-6-4-2-A
14. 7-6-4-3-A
15. 7-6-4-3-2
16. 7-6-5-2-A
17. 7-6-5-3-A
18. 7-6-5-3-2
19. 7-6-5-4-A
20. 7-6-4-3-2, etc.

Usually, when played in California Poker clubs, this game is played eight-handed with three different betting styles: Blind, Blind and Straddle, and Pass-out.

1. Blind. After the ante and before the players receive their five cards, the leader (player left of the dealer) puts in a blind one-unit bet. Player to the leader's left raises two units blind.

2. Blind and Straddle. There is no ante in this transported English game variation. There are usually three blind bettors, starting with the dealer. The dealer places one unit into the pot. The leader places two units into the pot, and the player to his left places three units into the pot. Thereafter the betting and raising limits usually amount to three units.

3. Pass-out. In this variation there is no blind. Players ante. If you pass or check before the draw, you must fold (throw your hand away).

Sometimes the game is played with a 52-card deck minus the joker.

However, I consider this Lowball variation a weak sister to Lowball with the Joker (bug).

The following table will give you an idea of the frequency with which you may expect to be dealt a best pat hand with a 53-card deck which includes a joker. California Lowball with the Joker, a 53-card deck, possesses 2,869,685 possible five-card hands. Of this figure, slightly less than half, or to be specific, 1,302,540, are low hands. However, since straights and flushes count low in this California Lowball variation, we must add 7,768 flushes, 216 straight flushes, 24 royal flushes, and 20,532 straights to this low-hand figure of 1,302,540 for a total of 1,331,084 low hands. The table that follows will give you an idea of the possibilities of your catching a valuable pat hand.

CHANCES OF BEING DEALT A PAT HAND IN CALIFORNIA LOWBALL

Rank of Specific Hand	Number of Specific Hands	Chances of Being Dealt Specific Hand	Chances of Being Dealt Specific Hand or Better
Cinch bicycle (5-4-3-2-A)	2,304	1 in 1,246	1 in 1,246
Any six high	7,680	1 in 373	1 in 287
Any seven high	20,480	1 in 140	1 in 94
Any eight high	44,800	1 in 64	1 in 38
Any nine high	86,016	1 in 33	1 in 18

The player should realize that when playing Lowball, a pair, particularly a high pair (from jack up), is almost worthless. Only when the pot is extra big or when the player holds the joker should he play a hand after an opening bet on the strength of having three low cards with the hope of getting two low cards on the draw. The best possible odds against drawing two cards to fill in a nine high or lower hand are 5 to 1. Drawing two cards to a medium three-card hand without the joker is a foolish bet in Ace to Five. If you draw two low cards, you have the possibility of pairing your other three low cards; and you then hold a pair or probably two pairs. So, as an overall tip, the best hand at Lowball is a good pat hand. But you don't always get good pat hands—therefore I suggest you draw one or two cards as the situation dictates.

Hands such as six high are equal to a straight flush in Draw Poker, and a good seven high is equal to a full house. These hands usually will win the pot.

CHANCES OF IMPROVING A CALIFORNIA LOWBALL HAND WITH A ONE-CARD DRAW OR A TWO-CARD DRAW

Cards Held After Discarding	Chance
4-card bicycle with joker	1 in 6
4-card bicycle without joker	1 in 9⅗
4-card six high with joker	1 in 4
4-card six high without joker	1 in 5⅓
4-card seven high with joker	1 in 3
4-card seven high without joker	1 in 2⁷⁄₁₀
4-card eight high with joker	1 in 2⅖
4-card eight high without joker	1 in 2⅘
3-card bicycle with joker	1 in 23½
3-card bicycle without joker	1 in 47
3-card six high with joker	1 in 11⅘
3-card six high without joker	1 in 18⅘
3-card seven high with joker	1 in 7
3-card seven high without joker	1 in 10
3-card eight high with joker	1 in 4¾
3-card eight high without joker	1 in 6¼

The above probability chart is based on the premise that all 4-card hands have discarded either a king or queen and all three-card hands have discarded a king and queen, or a king and jack.

After the draw has taken place, one of the best things you should learn to do when playing Lowball is not to call when you believe you are beaten. Most of the time it's mandatory to call when your opponent bets into you, just because the size of the pot warrants it. More often than not this policy dictates your Lowball strategy. If you hold a seven high (7-4-3-2-A) and one or more opponents have raised before you, it's a must that you should stay to the finish, especially if your opponents had drawn one or two cards. Furthermore, you should occasionally call with a small pair or king or queen high against loose opponents who usually bet with a pair. Also, the best bluff attempt is made with a big pair, a near-full table of players and big money in the pot. Of course, you must respect opponents who just will never call without a hand of sorts. It is such players you should try the bluff on more often than on a loose opponent.

And a very important rule to remember is: Don't try a bluff in last position when checked into. When players check, they are usually laying back for either a call or a raise. In big-money Lowball Ace to Five games, the best position in which to try your bluff is from first position—or not at all.

20. High Back to Low Draw Poker

My Poker research convinces me that Jacks and Back, a game I played in the late 1930s, was the forerunner of High Back to Low Draw Poker. To my knowledge, Jacks and Back was the first game in which players alternated playing both high and low Poker.

Each dealt round of hands in High Back to Low Draw Poker is either played as standard Draw Poker or California Lowball Ace to Five. Each dealt round begins play as standard Draw Poker (Jacks or Better). If no one opens with jacks or better, instead of anteing and reshuffling and redealing a new hand, the same hands are played as in California Lowball Ace to Five. The leader (player to the left of the dealer) must now open blind for low. The remaining players must either call, raise or drop out. If no one calls or raises, the leader collects the pot, then a new deal is dealt as in standard Draw Poker, and the round of play continues as described above.

If you've read and studied this book this far you should be pretty well equipped to play this game.

When the hand shifts to Lowball, which happens about once in four times, the low hands are usually better than those encountered in California Lowball; this is caused by the absence of high cards, which makes the presence of low cards mathematically more available. Probably the reason for the shift is that since no one opened for high, it naturally follows that most players are holding low cards.

The problem that confronts the average High Back to Low player occurs when he is dealt a weak mixed high and low hand and can't make up his mind whether to play for high or to fold and hope the round becomes Lowball and he can play for low with a three- or four-card low hand. The best advice I can give is to study the standard Draw Poker strategy on pages 98 to 104 and play the high hand accordingly. If it doesn't warrant a play, drop out, regardless of your low-hand possibilities. And when it's Lowball time, make use of the strategy pertaining to California Lowball Ace to Five described above.

21. High-Low Draw Poker

We now turn our attention to High-Low Draw Poker, the game that my research reveals to be the first Poker game that gave both holders of high- and low-ranking hands equal opportunity to share the pot. In this five-card game each player can make either a low hand or a high hand, but not both.

The rules of play for this Poker variation are the same as those for standard Draw Poker with the following exceptions.

1. Two to eight players may participate. However, six to eight make for the best game.
2. The high- and low-rank hands split the pot. The rank of high cards is the same as regular Draw Poker, and the perfect low hand is a sixty-four (6-4-3-2-A) of mixed suits. For a detailed description of the ranks of low Poker hands, see General Rules for Poker, pages 43–45.
3. Players may draw from one to five cards.
4. A player can open on any hand (jacks or better are not required), and no high or low announcement is made. Cards decide at the showdown.

In playing for high, I recommend that you play any hand that you would play in regular Draw Poker, and in addition, remember that any possible low four-card flush or straight may turn out to be a low hand. The majority of players usually draw for low rather than for high. The high hands may run slightly higher than those in Draw Poker, and the low hands not much worse than the low hands in Lowball. As a rule it is better to draw to a good high possibility than to a good low one.

22. *Draw Poker, High-Low Declare*

Played the same as Draw Poker High-Low with the following exceptions. The big difference is that if a player declares for a high hand, straights and flushes count. If he declares for a low hand, straights and flushes don't count. The ace is considered the lowest-ranking card, and bicycle (5-4-3-2-A) is the cinch low hand. The game is played with a simultaneous declaration described under General Rules for Poker, page 46.

In this variation draw, it is rare for a player to win both high and low hands, but it is possible; that is, if a player holds a low straight such as A-2-3-4-5, which will win the high, and because straights don't count in determining the low-hand winner, he calls a bicycle and takes the other half of the pot as well. This is an exceptional case. Therefore, generally I do not recommend that a player declare high-low.

23. *High-Low Draw Poker Roll Em Over*

This game is played the same as High-Low Draw Poker except that after the second betting interval (after the draw) there are four more betting intervals, which are as follows. After the draw and the betting interval have ended, each player selects one of his five cards, and when he is ready the dealer calls "Turn" and each active player turns a card face up on the table in front of him. Once the rolling begins, the high man bets first. The game proceeds in this manner until four cards have been rolled over by each player and a betting interval takes place for each rollover. The game comes up with some real lulu hands in the sense that the active players on the showdown are all low or all high more often than in any other game. Otherwise it varies very little from High-Low Draw described earlier.

24. Laino High-Low Roll Em Over

The game is played like High-Low Draw Poker Roll Em Over except that the leader (player to the dealer's left) must open the pot regardless of the value of his hand. Players can stand pat or discard only one or two cards and draw a like number. After the draw, players arrange their cards face down on the table as they see fit. Each player then selects one of his five face down cards and when all players are ready, dealer calls "Roll Em," and each player faces up a card and a betting interval takes place starting with the openers. The game continues in this manner until four cards have been rolled by each player. The last round of betting is followed by a simultaneous declaration of high or low or both high and low as described under General Rules for Poker. Straights and flushes count both high and low and the best low hand is 5-4-3-2-A.

I have been asked often how a certain hand should be rolled. In most situations it depends upon the impression you want to create. Should you want to conceal the true strength of your hand, you should hold back a key card as your final hole card. The four cards may be turned in a number of ways. Sometimes you may want to present another posture and so you roll your cards accordingly.

Should you be on a bluff, then you must turn over your cards in a manner that will make your cards appear as a bluff. Should you hold a medium sort of low and you would like to cut down the raising, in this instance you turn your cards to show a potential cinch low early, in the hope of stopping other low players from raising.

Naturally, the most difficult rolling problems to solve are the two-way hands. Suppose you possess a sixty-five low and as rolling continues you figure an opponent for a cinch low and a good high hand. I recommend that you raise and try to convince him that he'll be tied for low even if he holds a perfect low hand.

25. *Seven Card High-Low Draw Poker*

Played the same as Laino High-Low Roll Em Over, with the following exceptions. After the ante has been made each player is dealt seven cards face down one at a time in rotation to the left. This is followed by a betting interval in which any amount up to the maximum limit can be wagered. After the first betting interval, each remaining player passes three cards to the player at his left, and in turn receives three cards from the player at his right. Each active player next discards two cards, making his best five-card high hand or his best five-card low hand. Then, starting with the leader, each player, in rotation to the left, rolls a card (turns it face up and places it on the table in front of him), and a betting interval takes place. Each player may turn up any four of his five cards, but he must, of course, always have one card face down. Three additional cards are rolled, each followed by a betting interval. After the last betting interval, the declaration for high, low, or high and low follows.

You're a sure loser if you don't remember the cards you passed and the cards you received. If the player to your left plays and you passed him nine, ten or king of mixed suits, he must be holding at least one of your passed cards among the five he plays, and under such conditions cannot be playing for low regardless of what cards he rolled over at the start. On the other hand, if you received three low cards from the player on your right, the chances are very good that he is playing for high. This game is tricky, and many unusual situations develop during the rollover. So play with caution.

Draw Poker Variations of Spit in the Ocean

THE BIRTH OF THE SPIT IN THE OCEAN FAMILY

No one knows surely when and where the first Spit in the Ocean game originated. The author has consulted several hundred books in various languages—English, French, German, and Italian—on Poker and card games in general and he has failed to find any mention of Spit in the Ocean prior to the late 1920s.

Contrary to the views held by many Poker writers, the basic principle involved in this game is not new in card games—it is quite ancient. As a matter of recorded history, the now obsolete French games of Ambigu and Brelan embraced the identical basic principle centuries ago.

The original Spit in the Ocean game that follows undoubtedly sprang from Five Card Draw. Today there are countless Draw and Stud variations of the Spit in the Ocean family. However, this chapter will concern itself only with the best of those based on Draw Poker. Others based on Stud Poker will be discussed later under a separate heading.

Most Spit in the Ocean games embrace a common essential feature combining each player's dealt hand with one or more cards dealt in the center of the table, and are known as community cards, thus automatically made part of the hand of every player.

Spit in the Ocean games that involve three or more wild cards cannot be calculated with the same accuracy as natural cards. Four or more wild cards offer too many contingencies, and if they are all covered, the final analysis turns out to be too burdensome to be of any use. A major difficulty is that the probabilities depend upon the various denominations of the wild cards. Since the denominations of wild cards in Spit in the Ocean variations change with each new deal, so do the probabilities. Therefore, I have considered all unspecified wild cards that appear in the Spit in the Ocean games that follow to be wild deuces.

26. The Original Spit in the Ocean Game

The rules of play are those of standard Draw Poker with the following exceptions. Anything opens. Four cards are dealt to each player. After all players have received their four face-down cards, the next card off the deck is dealt face up in the center of the table. This card, which is common to all hands, is wild and so are the other three cards of the same denomination. To repeat—this exposed wild card forms the fifth card of each active player's hand and is referred to as a community card.

1
One Community Card

The game proceeds as in standard Poker or Straight Draw (Anything Opens), that is, there is an interval of betting, then each player may stand pat or discard from one to four cards from his hand and draw the same number of cards to replace them. This is followed by a second interval of betting and a showdown.

Although there are actually only four wild cards in the deck, one must assume that there are as many wild cards in play as the number of players plus three. Example: in a seven-handed game we must assume that there are ten wild cards in all.

In playing this game you must consider that every player is dealt one wild card and that there are three more wild cards available. In the seven- and eight-handed game, if you haven't got them, other players almost surely have. As a result, four of a kind is an average winning hand. Forget about drawing for straight flushes and full houses because anything less than four of a kind is taboo. You should drop out unless you hold three of a kind and you can draw for a possible four or five of a kind.

I would suggest the following minimum requirements for drawing cards: (a) an ace with the community wild card; (b) three of a kind including the community wild card; (c) a three-card possible straight flush plus the community wild card.

During the last betting interval, if you hold three of a kind, straight, flush, or full house and there was a raise before the draw and two or more active players have called a raise, fold and throw your hand in, because generally any of these hands is not good enough to win.

27. *Wild Widow*

This game, also known as Pig in the Poke, is a variation of Spit in the Ocean. However, in this game, only three cards are considered wild. Four cards are dealt in the usual way face down to each player, and after each player has received his four cards, the next card (community card) is dealt face up onto the center of the table. The three remaining cards of the same numerical value as this exposed card are wild and can be used by the players to represent any cards they desire. However, the face-up community card on the table is not wild; it is used simply as an indicator card.

1
One Community Card

There is a betting interval; then a fifth card is dealt face down to each active player. This is followed by another betting interval and a showdown. (To repeat, the community card in the center of the table is not counted as part of any player's hand. It simply denotes the rank of the three remaining wild cards.)

In playing this game you must consider that there are only three wild cards in play, plus the fact that there is no draw as in Spit in the Ocean. Therefore, three wild cards notwithstanding, a pair of kings or aces is a good hand to bet on in a five-handed game, and a pair of aces or two pairs is a good betting hand in an eight-handed game especially when you are holding a wild card. Three of a kind, straights and flushes are excellent ranking hands in this variation of Spit in the Ocean.

28. *Stormy Weather*

This version of Spit in the Ocean is a variation of standard Draw Poker, with extra draws. Each player is dealt four cards singly, face down, as in standard Draw Poker; but after the dealer has received his second card, he deals a community card face down in the center of the table, another community card face down in the center of the table after receiving his third card, and a third community card face down in the center of the table after dealing himself his fourth and last card of the deal.

1 2 3
Three Community Cards

The betting round and the drawing of cards is as in standard Draw Poker, except that a player may open the pot on any hand he desires (jacks or better are not required), and a player may draw up to four cards if he desires. If all the players pass, a new hand is dealt and all the players ante again, as in standard Draw Poker.

If the pot is opened and the active players have completed their draw, there is no betting at this time. Instead:

The dealer now turns up the first community card of the three cards in the center of the table, and a betting round begins, the opener making the first bet. When all bets have been met, the dealer turns up the second community card in the center of the table, and another betting round ensues, with the opener having the first turn. The same holds with the facing up of the third community card in the center of the table.

On the showdown, a player is permitted to make use, for his fifth card, of any one of the three community cards turned up in the center of the table. Player must indicate verbally, at his proper turn of play, which of the three upturned cards in the center of the table he is using for his fifth card. No mistakes may be rectified after his proper turn of play has passed.

Since there are no wild cards in this game and the three common center cards are exposed after the draw, the chances of pretty good hands are as follows. A pair before the draw is a fair hand to draw to. A pair of aces or better is an excellent opening hand, and should the pot be opened before you, such a hand is worth a raise. Three of a kind, straights and flushes are generally winning hands.

29. *Cincinnati, or Lame Brain*

A fascinating variation of Spit in the Ocean. In this game, five cards are dealt each player and five community cards are dealt face down in the center of the table. The dealer, after dealing himself a card on each round, deals one face-down community card in the center of the table. There is no draw in this game as in standard Draw Poker, and there are no wild cards.

1 2 3 4 5
Five Community Cards

After each player has looked at his five cards, the dealer turns the first community card face up in the center of the table. The betting now starts. The player to the dealer's left has the first turn of play. Betting and the rotation of play are as in standard Draw Poker.

On completion of the betting round, the dealer turns the second community card face up in the center of the table, and another betting round takes place. This procedure is followed until the five community cards in the center of the table are face up and five betting rounds have taken place. On the showdown, each active player must select his hand from his own five cards and the five community cards shown face up in the center of the table. In other words, he selects the best hand of five cards out of a total of ten—five in his hand and five face up in the center of the table.

Since the player selects the best hand of five cards out of a total of ten, a straight may win a pot, and a high flush has about an equal chance of winning a pot.

If as many as three cards of the same suit turn up among the five community cards, it's almost a sure bet that some player in a six- or seven-handed game will possess a flush. Should a pair turn up in the center, someone is pretty sure to possess a full house. As a matter of fact, without three cards of the same suit turning up, flushes occur with considerable frequency. A high full house or four of a kind will win 90% of all pots.

30. Cincinnati Ohio

In this variation of Cincinnati, the lowest-rank card of the five community cards in the center and all those of the same numerical value are wild. The only really good hand is five of a kind. Flushes and straights rarely stand up. A low four of a kind has a 50% chance of winning.

31. High-Low Split Draw Poker

Played the same as Cincinnati with five cards in the hand and five community cards resting in the center of the table. Hence there is plenty of opportunity for a player to win both high and low. The best low hand is 6-4-3-2-A, as shown under General Rules for Poker, pages

43–45. This game is played without a declaration. On the showdown, "cards speak."

1 2 3 4 5
Five Community Cards

Pay no attention to a possible straight, since even if made, this is seldom a winning hand. In the event that three low cards are among the community cards, it is not at all uncommon to find that two or more players tie for low. If you hold a pair of aces in your hand and the first and second face-up community cards don't possess a third ace or pair one of your three odd cards, fold (throw your cards in), the reason being that you still need two favorable cards to make a full house and must catch those two out of the three remaining face-down community cards. But, most important, pay attention to the betting in the early rounds. If two or more players show strength and if three or more active players remain for the showdown, usually the winning hand is a high full house.

32. *Twin Beds*

This is a variation of standard Draw Poker with the following exceptions. At the start of the game each player is dealt four cards. After the dealer has received his fourth card, two horizontal rows of five community cards each are dealt face down on the table. The betting round takes place, and the dealer turns up one community card from each row (1 and 6 as shown in illustration below). Another betting round, and another community card is turned up from each row. Continue betting and turning up a community card from each row until the last community card in each row has been turned face up and the betting round has been completed.

1 2 3 4 5
6 7 8 9 10
Ten Community Cards

The last community card to be turned up from each row is wild, and so are the three cards of the same denomination as the wild card. The player may use from one to five cards from either row to improve his dealt hand, but he cannot use cards from both rows to help his hand.

The strategy of this game must combine the best features of play of both Stormy Weather and Cincinnati. The average winning hands are flushes, full houses and four of a kind. However, because of the large number of community cards and betting intervals, it is important that, before you make your first bet, your five-card hand has sound values. Generally a Twin Beds player should not be betting in the game unless his present hand has such strength that he is prepared to play through to the showdown.

33. *Twin Beds Roll Em Over*

Twin Beds Roll Em Over is probably the most exciting Draw Poker Spit in the Ocean variation. The rolling adds lots of spice to the game, as well as four more rounds of betting. The game is best for eight players and is played like standard Draw Poker with the following exceptions.

After each player has received his five-card hand, ten community cards are dealt face down onto the center of the table arranged in two five-card horizontal rows as shown below.

1 2 3 4 5
6 7 8 9 10
Ten Community Cards

The first community card of each row (the 1 and 6 in illustration above) is turned up on completion of the deal and the leader is first to speak. He may check or bet. After the first betting interval, the second community cards of each row are turned up and the player to the left of the leader speaks first. This procedure is continued until all ten community cards are turned face up. After all the community cards are face up and after the fifth betting interval is completed, the rolling begins. Each player selects one card of his five-card hand, and when all players are ready, the card is faced up. In the earlier betting intervals the first to speak is determined by table position. However, after each player's card has been rolled, high card bets first. This procedure continues until four cards have been turned over by each player, leaving each player with one closed card. After the final betting interval (and before the showdown) a simultaneous declaration of high or low or both is made by each active player. The last raiser declares first. If no raise has taken place on the last round, the player who started the last betting round declares first. To make the best high or low hand the player may use from one to five cards from one row with his five dealt cards. However, if you call both ways, you are permitted to make the high hand from one row with your own hand and your low hand from the other row with your own hand. I repeat—in no instance are you allowed to use cards from both rows to create a high or low hand. (For the rules governing simultaneous declarations and rank of low hands, see General Rules for Poker, pages 43–47.)

There are nine rounds of betting in this game and second-best hands can take you to the cleaner's. The first major decision is whether to play or drop out. If you have nothing of value in your hand at the start, throw your hand in and save your bankroll. If you stay for the first roll and you fail to have a high full house or even a bad six low, throw your hand in. If you can't bear to concede a small loss on a small full house or bad six low before the rollover, you are a certain loser in this complex game. Generally you need a high full house or a good six low to win the money at this game.

34. Criss Cross

Also known as X Marks the Spot, Cross Widow, and Cross Over. With the exception of Texas Hold Em, this is more widely known than any other Spit in the Ocean variation. The game is played like Twin Beds Roll Em Over except that only five community cards are dealt face down onto the center of the table and are laid out in the shape of a cross.

```
    1
2   3   4
    5
```

Five Community Cards

The top card is turned up first, followed by a betting interval. Each adjacent card (except the center card) is turned up in clockwise fashion and a betting interval follows each. The card in the center of the cross is turned up last. This last card is wild and so is any other card of the same rank, including cards in the active players' hands and the other community cards on the table. After the fifth betting interval, the rolling as described under Twin Beds Roll Em Over takes place. A low or a high hand is made by using either the 1,3,5, or the 2,3,4 set of community cards with your own five-card hand.

The strategy in Criss Cross, like other games that make use of wild cards, is based on your judgment of the value of hands. Since each player will have at least one wild card, and three possible wild cards are lurking around, the player's hand values of high- and low-rank hands should be slightly increased over Twin Beds Roll Em Over.

35. *Rockleigh High-Low*

This fascinating High-Low variation of Spit in the Ocean was developed at an all-women's Poker session in my neck of the woods. In this fascinating High-Low variation, four cards are dealt to each player as in standard Draw Poker. After the dealer receives his fourth card, he then deals four groups of two cards each in a row face down in the center of the table as illustrated below.

1 2
3 4
5 6
7 8

Four 2-Card Groups of Community Cards

After the players look at their four cards and a betting round takes place, the dealer turns any two-card group he wishes face up. Another betting round, and another two-card group is turned face up. Continue betting and turning up a two-card group until the last two-card group from the center of the table has been turned face up, followed by the fifth and final betting round. On the showdown a player, announcing high, is permitted to select the best five cards for his hand, using either one or two cards from only one of the four groups. The same holds true when announcing low. Players on the showdown must stipulate and point to the two-card group they wish to incorporate in their high or low hand. When announcing both high and low, a player may make use of one two-card group for high and another two-card group for low—or, if desirable, make use of one two-card group for both high and low.

The crucial feature of this game is the eight community cards divided into four groups of two community cards each and the rule that a player may only make use of either one or two community cards from any one of the four groups.

One familiar with Spit in the Ocean variations would usually think that with eight community cards resting on the table, full houses and four of a kind would be the average hands. Quite the contrary. The average-rank winning high hand is two pairs or three of a kind. The best low hand is about a nine high. If a player is dealt a high four-card straight or flush, his chances of filling in are 8 to 1 in his favor. Should a player be dealt four low cards, the chances of catching a fifth low-card hand are about 7 to 1 of filling in. A medium or high pair dealt hand is worth one or two bets. The game is tricky: Be careful that when making use of a community two-card row you select the one that helps you most.

36. *Italian High-Low Draw Poker*

The first time I played this game was at the home of a member of the American Embassy in Rome. The game is played like standard Draw Poker except for the following. After each player has been dealt five face-down cards, the first betting round starts with the leader making the opening bet regardless of the value of his hand. However, after the draw and the second betting round, with the leader speaking first, the leader now has three options. He may drop out, check, or bet as he wishes.

Only three raises are permitted on this betting round and other betting rounds. Players may choose to stand pat or discard one or two cards. After the discard turn of play has been completed, the dealer places the two top cards of the deck in the center of the table face up, placing a coin on the first dealt community card for identification.

1 2
Two Community Cards

If a player has discarded one card he makes use of the community card with the coin on top for his fifth card. If a player has discarded two cards, he makes use of both upturned community cards. If he failed to discard, he cannot make use of the community cards. Straights and flushes may be considered both high and low hands. Example: A hand comprised of ace, two, three, four and five may be declared high or low, or both high and low. A deuce, three, four, seven, eight flush also may be declared as high or low, or as both high and low.

The strategy for Italian High-Low Draw Poker must combine the best feature of play of Rockleigh High-Low, standard Draw Poker and California Lowball. The average high winning hand is considerably lower than in standard Draw, and the average low winning hand much higher than in California Lowball Ace to Five.

37. *Teeko High-Low*

This is a Spit in the Ocean creation of my son, John (Teeko). The game is played the same as standard Draw Poker except for the following.

1. Five cards are dealt to each player as in standard Draw Poker. After the dealer receives his fifth card, he deals four groups of three face-down community cards onto the center of the table in horizontal rows.

1	2	3
4	5	6
7	8	9
10	11	12

Twelve Community Cards

2. After the players pick up their cards and look at them, the first betting round takes place.
3. Next, the dealer turns the first three-card group face up to the dealer's left, and a second betting round takes place. He continues turning a group of three community cards face up followed with a betting round, as each row is faced up until the last row of three community cards has been turned face up and the fifth and final betting round has been completed.
4. A player must make use of three cards from his hand and two cards from one of the four three-card community groups resting on the table. However, if a player calls "high-low" he may use two cards from one group to help form his high hand and two cards from another group to help form his low hand. Straights and flushes are not considered as low.

38. *Bing-O-Draw*

This game is played the same as Criss Cross (page 146) except that nine cards are placed in the center of the table in the shape of a square. These act as community cards.

1	2	3
4	5	6
7	8	9

Nine Community Cards

The four corner cards of the square are dealt face up and the remaining five cards face down. This is followed by a three-raise maximum betting interval. Thereafter the remaining five cards are faced up one at a time, with the center card reserved for the last turn. This last card is wild, and so is any other card of the same rank, which includes the cards in the player's hand or the cards laid out on the table. The player then proceeds by rolling and betting as in Criss Cross. A low or high hand is made by using a set of three cards from the square on the table (running horizontally, vertically or diagonally) with the five dealt cards.

39. *Klondike*

This game, which is known also as Tennessee, is played like Cincinnati or Lame Brain, except for a slight dealing variation. Five cards are dealt to each player, face down; then the dealer turns up five community cards from off the top of the pack, one at a time, with a betting interval after each.

1 2 3 4 5
Five Community Cards

In the showdown, each player selects the best hand from his five plus the exposed five cards.

Klondike is played with progressive betting. That is, each betting unit is increased one unit on each round and a raise must be double. For example, if the betting unit is one chip, the first interval would require a bet of one chip; the second round a bet of two chips; the third, three, and so on. If you wish to raise, say in the fourth round, you would have to double the bet, or put eight chips in the pot; a reraise in the fifth round would cost twelve chips. In this system of betting, there is no checking—you must bet, call or drop. The betting position progresses, too. In other words, the first position—at the left of the dealer—must bet first on the first round; the second position—the second player to the left of dealer—bets first on the second interval; the third position first on the third round; and so on.

40. *Scarney High-Low Draw Poker*

This game creation of the author's is one of the most bizarre, exciting and charmingly exasperating of all Poker variations. Scarney Poker combines the principles of High-Low Draw Poker with community cards, plus an entirely new Poker compulsory-discard principle. A player may possess a straight flush and moments later be forced to break up his hand by discarding part of his hand. The Poker purist can, and will, find holes through which he can drive a truck in the architecture of this game. Its compulsory method of getting rid of cards in hand, for instance, makes a farce out of Poker skill, but the stark fact remains that when Poker players like a game, as many seem to like this variation, the game fills the bill.

The rules for standard Draw Poker hold true, with the following exceptions and with additional rules. There are three to eight players. Six, seven or eight players make for the best game. The object of the game is for a player at the showdown to hold a higher-ranking Poker hand, or to hold fewer total points, or both at the same time, than any other active player.

The dealer deals five cards to each player, one at a time clockwise, starting with the player at his left. After the dealer has received his fifth card, two horizontal rows of five cards each are dealt face down on the table. The row farthest from the dealer is known as the "Poker row," and the row closest to the dealer is known as the "discard row." Poker row cards may be used to help form Poker hands; the discard row is used only to discard matching cards.

Poker Row	1	2	3	4	5
Compulsory					
Discard Row	6	7	8	9	10

Ten Community Cards

When playing Scarney High-Low Poker, the player holding the highest-ranking five-card hand, provided he has declared for high, and the player holding the lowest total-point count with zero, one, two, three, four or five cards, provided he has declared for low, share the pot equally. If a player calls "high-low," he must win both high and low to be declared the winner. When declaring high, the player may select the best five cards out of his hand and Poker row. Discard row cards cannot be used as part of a hand. The point value of cards when calling low are as follows: The ace is the lowest-ranking card, having a value of 1; the king, queen, and jack are valued at 10 points each. All other cards have their numerical face value. To repeat, standard Poker hands do not count when announcing low. When cards are used from the Poker row to fill in a hand, the player must state the value of his hand. If a player calls his hand incorrectly and the pot has not yet been collected, he may correct the error; but if the pot has been collected the error must stand.

If the low hand is comprised of zero, one, two, three, four or five cards, the rank of low is determined by the total number of points of the cards held by the player. Example: a player holds five cards—four aces, and a two-spot—the low point count is 6. A player holds four cards—four aces—the low point count is 4. A player holds three cards, three aces, the low point count is 3; a player holds two cards, two aces, the low point count is 2; a player holds one card, one ace, the low point count is 1; a player holds no cards, the low point count is zero, which is the best possible low-count hand.

For the rules for announcing high or low or both on the showdown, see General Rules for Poker, pages 45–47.

All the preparations before the start of the actual play are as described under General Rules for Poker, including rank of hands, betting limits, preparations before play, selecting the dealer and seating positions at the table, irregularities in cutting the cards, the shuffle, the cut and the ante.

After each player has picked up and studied his hand, the first betting round takes place. Next the dealer turns up (faces) the first card to his left of each row and a second betting round takes place. The second card is turned face up from each row and a third betting round takes place. The dealer continues turning up a card from each row, followed by a betting round, until the last card from each row has been turned face up and the sixth and final betting round takes place.

The play of the Poker and discard rows:

1. The Poker row: The player may, if he chooses, use from one to five cards of the Poker row to complete his hand.

2. The discard row: As each card is turned face up in the discard row, a player holding one or more cards of the same rank *must* immediately place these cards face up on top of the matching card or cards of the discard row. Example: A player holds the ace of clubs and the ace of spades; the dealer turns the ace of hearts face up in the discard row; the player must discard his two aces on top of the ace of hearts of the discard row, leaving him with a three-card hand. As other cards are turned face up in the discard row, all matching cards held by players must be placed on the discard row. If a player discards his five cards, he has zero points. If a player fails to discard a playable card onto the card of the discard row, and this irregularity is discovered on the showdown, the player's hand is dead and he must throw in his cards.

The strategy and skill in the play of Scarney High-Low Draw Poker involve six different betting intervals. However, it is foolish for a player at the start of the game to gauge his bets as to whether he should be anticipating a high or low hand or both. The conditions that determine a skillful player's opening bet, check, raise, or reraise, or whether to drop out, change for better or worse as the dealer turns up a pair of community cards resting in the center of the table. In this game, generally speaking, it is not unusual for a player to start out with a high cinch pat hand and wind up discarding his entire hand and possess a low cinch hand of zero points. In short, each time a pair of community cards are turned face up in the center of the table, a player must reevaluate his betting hand.

9

Miscellaneous Draw Poker Variations

There are countless miscellaneous Draw Poker variations that I picked up during my travels all over the United States and abroad. From this group I have selected those that I consider the most interesting. The rules governing standard Draw Poker hold true for the following miscellaneous games, with the exceptions and additional rules as shown under each specific game that follow.

41. Gin Poker

This game is known in Georgia as Get You One. It's a combination of Gin Rummy and Poker played by two players. The object of the game is to form a complete five-card Poker hand such as a royal flush, straight flush, four of a kind, full house, flush or straight.

After each player has been dealt five cards, the remainder of the deck is placed in the center of the table face down. This is the stock. The non-dealer makes the first play. He picks a card from the stock, making six cards in his hand. He next discards a card face up on the table, adjacent to the stock, forming a discard pile as in Gin Rummy. Thereafter each player in turn has the option of taking a card from the top of the stock or from the top of the discard pile, followed by a one-card discard. When a player announces, "Gin Poker," meaning he has a pat hand, he discards, and his opponent has an opportunity for one more pick from the stock or the discard pile. On the showdown, the best Poker hand wins the agreed-upon wager.

42. Three-Card Poker

Played the same as standard Draw Poker, except that any hand may open the pot, and each player is dealt only three cards on the first round and must draw two cards on the draw. Betting is exactly as described under Draw Poker. There may be three-card straights or flushes, and the cards rank as in standard Poker. But some players consider three of a kind as the highest hand.

43. Three-Card Monte, or Three-toed Pete

In this game, one card is dealt to each player face down and two cards face up, with a round of betting following the dealing of each card. The rank of Poker value is the same as Three-Card Poker.

44. Two-Card Poker, or Frustration

A variation of standard Draw Poker on a reduced scale. Each player is dealt two cards, singly, as in Draw Poker. On the draw a player must do one of the following:

1. Stand pat.
2. Draw one or two cards. The highest-ranking hand in this game is a pair of aces.

45. Hurricane

Each player receives two cards as in Two-Card Poker, but in this game, one is face down and one is face up. There is usually a previous ante as in all Two-Card Poker games. Wild cards may be used. The play may also be for high-low. This game is also known as Dynamite, Gruesome Twosome, and Double Trouble.

46. One-Card Poker

In this game, which is sometimes called Lazy Edna or Lazy Mary, each player is given one face-down card. This is the complete hand. The betting is for high-low. Tied hands divide the pot high or low. If a joker is used, it holds rank equal to an ace for high or to a deuce for low. The ace is played only as high.

47. *Show Five Cards*

Seven cards are dealt face down to each player, and each player looks at his cards. At a signal from the dealer, each player turns up one of his cards on the table. Before giving the signal, the dealer should inquire whether everyone is ready. After the cards are exposed, there is a round of betting. After the betting is completed, the dealer gives the signal for the exposure of the second card. All these second cards must be exposed at the same time. The process continues until all players in the game have five cards exposed before them for the showdown. The game is usually played high-low. It is not unusual for a player to change his mind during the game and try for a low hand rather than a high one, according to the cards exposed by the other players.

48. *Big Sol*

In this game, which is also called TNT and Snookie, each player receives three cards face down dealt in rotation one at a time. Then follows a round of betting. Then each player is dealt another closed card, followed by another round of betting. This continues until every active player has seven downcards, with betting after each round of cards has been dealt.

Each player now discards any two cards from his hand, leaving himself with five cards. Every player, beginning with the man at the dealer's left, then turns one card face up. This is followed by a round of betting. In like manner, three more cards are turned up, one by one, with a round of betting each time. The fifth card is kept face down. The players then declare for high-low, and there is a showdown.

49. *Draw Your Own*

Each player is given five cards face down, dealt in rotation, one at a time. Then, also in rotation and one at a time, each player is dealt three additional cards face down to form an individual stock from which to draw later.

There is a round of betting. Then each player discards a card from the first five in his hand and draws a card from his individual stock of three cards. He may not look at any of the cards from his individual stock except the card he draws. There is another round of betting, and then another card is discarded and a second one drawn from the individual stock. This continues until all the players have exhausted the cards in their stock. The game is high-low.

50. *Whiskey Poker*

This game is the ancestor of all Poker games, but is seldom played today. The dealer gives five cards face down to each player and deals an extra hand ("widow") of five cards face down in the middle of the table. He must deal to each player in turn around to the left, one card at a time, then to the widow, then to himself last. Each player, beginning at the dealer's left, has the option of exchanging his hand for the widow, or keeping it as it is. If he takes up the widow, he places his five cards face up on the table and they become the new widow. Each player in turn has the option of taking up one card or all of the new widow and replacing it with cards from his hand. If a player wishes to play his original hand, he signals by knocking on the table, but he cannot draw and knock at the same time.

The process of exchanging cards continues around the table until some player knocks. A knock means that this player will show his present hand when it is his next turn around the table, and that thus each player has only one more chance to exchange cards. No player may draw after he has once knocked. A player may knock before the widow is exposed, if he wishes to.

If no one takes the widow until it comes around to the dealer, the dealer must either take up the widow for himself or turn it face up on the table. Even if the dealer knocks and does not take up the widow, he must spread it on the table for each player to see and draw once more. A player may pass in any turn—he may decline either to exchange or to knock—but he may not pass in two consecutive turns. If he has passed on the previous round, he must either exchange or knock.

After the knock, and the final round of draws, all hands are shown to the table. The highest takes the pot. The lowest pays the forfeit agreed upon beforehand. Some players have a round of betting before the showdown.

51. *Knock Poker*

Knock Poker, or Rap Poker, is the direct survivor of Whiskey Poker. This fascinating game for three to five players is designed not only for Draw Poker fans but for Rummy players as well. At the start of the game, each player antes one chip into the pot, and is dealt a hand of five cards (as in Draw Poker) from a regular 52-card deck. The remaining undealt cards are then placed face down in the center of the table to form a stock from which players draw, as in Rummy. The top card of the stock is turned face up on the center of the table to begin a discard pile, as in most Rummy games. Then each player in turn, starting with the leader (or non-dealer if there are only two players), may take either the last discard or the top card of the stock, after which he must discard a card to reduce his hand. As in Gin Rummy, a player may not discard a card he picked up from the discard pile until his next turn of play.

Each player tries to build up the best possible five-card Poker hand from the cards he was previously dealt and the cards he takes from the discard pile and stock. The hands rank as in Draw Poker.

Whenever a player believes he has a good enough Poker hand, providing he holds jacks or better, he knocks (he merely says, "Knock"), but he may do so only after having made his discard to the discard pile. The knock means that the game will end after one more round. Each player has one more turn in which he may pick up the last discard or draw from the stock and then discard, until it comes to the knocker again, at which time the other players may decide either to drop out (fold) or stay. A player who drops out must immediately pay one chip to the knocker regardless of the outcome of the hand. The knocker does not have another play. He is stuck with the hand he had when he knocked, or as soon as any other player knocks. The betting in this game is unlike the usual Draw Poker betting. There is no betting during play. The pot consists of the antes plus an additional charge of one chip to the knocker from each of the players who dropped out.

At the end of the hand, the showdown takes place. If the knocker has the high hand he takes the pot, and in addition, all active players pay him two chips. However, if anyone beats the knocker, then the knocker must pay two chips to each active player and the winner takes the pot.

If the stock has been exhausted and no one has knocked, high hand wins on the showdown. At the showdown, if the winning player's hand is comprised of four of a kind or a straight flush, he receives a bonus award of four chips from each player. If he holds a royal flush he receives a bonus award of eight chips from each player. Only the winning player is entitled to a bonus award.

Strategy: A Poker player who already knows how to appraise the rank of a Poker hand must learn to readjust his Poker-hand values in this game. Be conservative in knocking. It pays to knock if you believe you will have the best hand even after each of your opponents has had his additional turn to draw. Any player who folds (drops out) must pay the knocker immediately and that's money that the knocker keeps whether he wins or loses. Aside from this, the knocker stands to win more than he can lose. His maximum loss can be no more than two chips per active player, while he can win two chips per active player plus the pot.

The man at the dealer's left possesses the best player position, and no matter who knocks, he will have as many draws as any other player. The dealer possesses the worst position. If he knocks, all other active players will have one more draw than he has prior to the showdown.

When to knock: Generally, the more players in the game the higher-rank hand you will need to knock. A player should abstain from knocking with a pair except when he happens to be the first or second man to play. Three of a kind warrants a knock on the second round, but the farther a player is from the dealer, the higher his three of a kind should be. Mathematically speaking, it's a fifty-fifty proposition in a seven-handed game that someone will possess a full house at the end of this third draw. So play it conservatively and keep track of the cards picked from the discard pile by your opponents.

52. *Knock Poker—Deuces Wild*

The rules that apply to Knock Poker apply to Knock Poker—Deuces Wild, with the following exception. A deuce may be counted as any card a player desires to call it. It may even be counted as a duplicate of a card already held by a player.

Bonus awards: Winning player holding five of a kind, a straight flush or a royal flush receives a bonus award of four chips. There are no bonus awards for four of a kind.

53. *Brag*

Great Britain's three-card representative of the Poker family. The rules of Draw Poker apply except as noted:

1. There are three wild cards: ace of diamonds, jack of clubs and nine of diamonds, ranking in that order and called "braggers."
2. The dealer antes an agreed amount into the pot (dealer's edge) and this ante is considered as an opening blind bet.
3. The dealer deals three cards face down to each player. This is followed by a betting round as in Draw Poker. Then each player in turn, beginning with the leader, may call the dealer's blind bet, raise

or drop out. If all players drop out, the dealer then retrieves his blind bet and the deal rotates to the player on his left.

4. After the betting round, if two or more active players remain, there is a showdown in which the highest-ranking hand—three of a kind, pair, or a high card—wins. In hands of equal rank, natural cards beat hands including wild cards. As between two hands both possessing wild cards, the highest-ranking wild card wins. If two players hold pairs of equal value, the highest-ranking odd card wins. If the odd cards are of the same value, high suit wins. The suits rank: spades (high), hearts, diamonds, and clubs (low).

There are many Brag variants, but the one just described is a good example of the basic game.

54. Pokino

This variant of standard Draw Poker, also known as Poke, is a game for two players only, using a standard 52-card deck. The object of the game is to score as many points as possible. Each hand is divided into two stages. First stage is played as in Five Card Draw Poker; in the second stage the cards are played out in the form of tricks.

The play of the hand: The players cut for high card. The player cutting the highest card becomes the first dealer. The deal alternates in subsequent hands.

First stage of play: Five cards are dealt to each player as in Draw Poker. The non-dealer plays first. He may stand pat or discard and draw from one to three cards. By drawing cards he doubles himself, that is, he is penalized doubly for each trick he loses in the play-out period. If, after his draw, he is still not satisfied, he may discard and draw a second time. This automatically redoubles him and he is penalized quadruply for each lost trick.

The dealer may stand pat, or he has the option (minus the penalty) of one free draw of one, two or three cards. This free draw may be followed by a double and a redouble, making three possible draws in all.

Second stage of play: The second stage of play begins with the non-dealer making the opening lead. The hands (five cards each) are played out in tricks, one card by each player. High card takes the trick regardless of suit, and a player does not have to follow suit. In case of two like-valued cards being played to the same trick, the first card led wins. The winner of a trick leads to the next. Each player retrieves his own card and faces it up to indicate a trick won, or down to indicate a trick lost.

A player may lead to two tricks at the same time by playing a pair (two of a kind). The opponent can win both tricks only by playing a larger pair. However, he does not have to respond with a larger or smaller pair; he may discard any two cards to the pair leads. In the same manner three or four of a kind can be played.

Scoring: In Pokino, as in Bridge, the score is kept in columns divided in the middle by a heavy line. Trick scores are entered below the line, while bonuses and honors are marked above the line. A player receives one point for each trick he wins, if opponent is not under penalty. If opponent is doubled, each trick is valued at two points, and if redoubled, four points.

After the last trick has been played and the score recorded, players show their Poker hands; the winning hand, in accordance with standard values of Poker hands, receives an honor score as shown in the table that follows. Both players may score trick points in the same hand, but only the winning hand gets an honor score.

If the player wins all five tricks, which is known as a "sweep," he receives a bonus of 250 points.

A game consists of 20 points below the line. The player making game receives a 100-point bonus above the line, and all partial trick scores of opponent below the line are canceled. If the same player wins his second game, he receives the 100-point bonus plus a rubber bonus of 750 points, provided his opponent has not won a game, or 500 points if his opponent has won a game.

Upon completion of a rubber, the player with the highest score is the winner.

TABLE OF HONORS

Pair	50 points
Two pairs	100 points
Three of a kind	200 points
Straight	300 points
Flush	400 points
Full house	500 points
Four of a kind	600 points
Straight flush	750 points
Royal flush	1,000 points

TABLE OF BONUS VALUES

Game bonus	100 points
Two-game rubber bonus	750 points
Three-game rubber bonus	500 points
Sweep bonus	250 points

55. *Red and Black*

In this game the cards of the deck are assigned an arbitrary numerical value as follows: king, queen, jack, ten, 10 points each; 1 point for the ace; and all other cards, their face or pip value. In figuring the value of the hand, the point counts of the cards are totaled. All cards in a red suit count their real value, but all cards in a black suit count a minus value. In a hand containing both red and black suits, one is subtracted from the other. Example: The point total for a hand containing king of clubs, jack of hearts, seven of spades, three of clubs, and two of diamonds would be a minus 8.

In actual play, after an agreed ante has been made by all players, each receives five cards, face down, one by one, in a clockwise rotation. There is an opening round of betting, followed by the draw. All active players have the option of taking one to three cards or not taking any cards at all. There is then a final round of betting and the showdown. The highest point count and the lowest point count divide the pot. It often happens that nobody in the game has a minus count; then the smallest number of plus points wins low, while the largest number of plus points wins high. Conversely, if nobody has a plus count, the smallest number of minus points wins high, and the largest minus figure wins low.

10

The Mathematics of Poker

HOW TO FIGURE POKER PROBABILITIES AND ODDS

The relative value of Poker hands was not just conjured up by some rulemaker or arbitrarily assigned by the first primitive Poker players. It was instead determined by counting the exact number of possible five-card Poker hands in a 52-card pack. The counting was under a mathematical formula based on the theory and doctrine of permutations and combinations, a formula used for calculating probabilities.

Making use of it, the exact total of possible five-card Poker hands was determined; this total was divided into groups or ranks—such as a pair, two pair, three of a kind, a straight, etc. These ranks were then arranged in relative value according to the frequency of their occurrence.

There are 2,598,960 possible Poker hands in a 52-card pack. This is the number of groups of five into which 52 different cards can be arranged, and is equal to the product of $52 \times 51 \times 50 \times 49 \times 48 = 311{,}875{,}200$ divided by the product of $5 \times 4 \times 3 \times 2 \times 1 = 120$, producing a final total of 2,598,960. A simplified method of calculation is to set up the permutations and arrangements as fractions and cancel them out:

$$\frac{52 \times 51 \times 50 \times 49 \times 48}{5 \times 4 \times 3 \times 2 \times 1} = 2{,}598{,}960$$

The above method of calculation, plus clear thinking and a knowledge of elementary arithmetic, determines the occurrence frequency of different five-card Poker hands.

Royal Flushes

There is only one royal flush in each suit; there are four suits, for a total of four royal flushes.

Straight Flushes

To calculate the number of straight flushes, first find the number of straight flushes in one suit. Let us take spades. Starting from the bottom and working up, we get nine straight flushes in spades: The ace, 2, 3, 4, 5, the 2, 3, 4, 5, 6, the 3, 4, 5, 6, 7, and so on. Since we have nine straight flushes in each suit, we get a total of 36 straight flushes for the four suits.

Four of a Kind

Though there are only 13 four-of-a-kind combinations (one for each denomination), there are 624 Poker hands containing four of a kind. With each of the 13 combinations, the fifth card could be any one of the other 48 cards. Therefore, we must multiply 13 by 48 to get the total possible hands containing the 13 four-of-a-kind combinations.

Full Houses

To calculate the number of possible full houses is easy—when you know how. Let's take three deuces as a starting point. There are four possible combinations of three deuces, since we are making use of only three deuces out of the four. But we have 13 different denominations from ace to king, and each of these has four possible combinations, for a total of 52 possible three-card combinations.

Now we must find the possible number of pairs to be matched with the three of a kind. Suppose we start with a pair of fours. The fours can be paired six ways. The same holds true for all the other denominations. But we cannot use the deuces; those have already been used to form the three of a kind. That leaves us with 12 different denominations. Multiplying, we get a total of 72 possible pairs to hold with our three deuces. To get the total number of full houses we multiply the 52 possible three of a kind by the 72 possible pairs, and get a total of 3,744 full houses.

Flushes

To find the number of possible flushes, we first must find the number of five-card arrangements that can be formed with 13 cards of the same suit. This we cancel out as follows:

$$\frac{13 \times 12 \times 11 \times 10 \times 9}{5 \times 4 \times 3 \times 2 \times 1} = 1{,}287 \text{ total}$$

But this total also includes one royal flush and nine straight flushes. Subtracting 10 from 1,287, we get 1,277 flushes in one suit. But we have four suits—hearts, clubs, spades, and diamonds—therefore we multiply the 1,277 by 4, and get a total of 5,108 flushes.

Straights

A simple method to calculate the number of possible straights is to start from the bottom and work up. For example, we use four aces, four deuces, four 3's, four 4's, and four 5's. Multiplying 4×4×4×4×4, we get 1,024 straights 5 high. We get a like number headed by each of the following high cards: 6, 7, 8, 9, 10, J, Q, K, and ace. Adding, we get a total of 10,240, from which we must discount four royal flushes and 36 straight flushes, leaving us a total of 10,200 straights.

Three of a Kind

We have already calculated the number of hands containing three of a kind at 52 (see Full Houses). But the two remaining cards in the hand must be odd cards. To prevent including the chances of making four of a kind or a full house when computing the chances solely for three of a kind, we must calculate that the first odd card must be one of 48 cards and the second odd card must be one of 44. Our complete figure is obtained thus:

$$\frac{52 \times 48 \times 44}{2 \times 1} = 54{,}912$$

—the number of hands containing three of a kind.

Two Pairs

We already have calculated the possible number of pairs with each denomination as six. (See Full Houses.) Multiplying six by 13 denominations, we get a total of 78 possible pairs. A player may hold any one of these 78 pairs plus another pair—but not of the same denomination —which total we arrive at by multiplying the 12 denominations by the six possible ways a pair can be in each denomination, for a total of 72 pairs.

Now, find the number of ways two pairs can be arranged, making use of the fifth, odd card; and our total figure is obtained thus:

$$\frac{78 \times 72 \times 44}{2 \times 1} = 123{,}552$$

One Pair

The total number of possible pairs is 78, as already calculated; therefore the player can hold any one of 78 pairs. But with this pair he must also hold three odd cards. Our total figure is obtained thus:

$$\frac{78 \times 48 \times 44 \times 40}{3 \times 2 \times 1} = 1{,}098{,}240$$

No Pairs

To obtain the total number of hands containing less than one pair, merely add all the hands containing a pair or better, and subtract that total from the total possible five-card hands, which we have already calculated at 2,598,960. It gives us a total of 1,302,540.

To ascertain the chances of being dealt any one of the above-ranking hands *pat* (in the first five cards dealt), divide the final total into 2,598,960, which again is the number of possible five-card Poker hands in a 52-card deck. *Example:* If you want to find your chances of getting a flush dealt pat you divide 5,108 (total number of flushes in a 52-card deck) into 2,598,960, and the result is 509.80. Our chance of drawing a pat flush is one in 509.80.

POKER PROBABILITIES

A good player must have a fair idea of Poker odds, percentages and probabilities. Without such knowledge he has no good way of deciding on his course of action in the various situations that arise, no way of making any mathematical analysis on which to base a decision. This information is given under the various game headings and in the Poker tables in this chapter. These same tables can also be used to prove the relative value of Poker hands and to settle disputes that arise regarding the chances of drawing certain valuable hands in Five Card Draw Poker, Five or Seven Card Stud Poker, or in the first five cards dealt in any other form of Poker.

It would be simple if all one had to do to become a winning player was to memorize the following Poker tables. But knowing the exact strength of your hand or the exact chances of bettering your hand on the draw will not always help you, because the playing habits of your opponents will often throw a monkey wrench into your best-laid mathematical plans. Example: A big raise by a habitually tight player means quite a different thing from the same big raise by a drunk who has already been caught trying to steal (bluff) the last half-dozen pots.

Although Poker is a game of skill, the judgments and decisions to be made by even the average Poker player involve a general knowledge of the game's probabilities. The chances of being dealt any certain pat hand are the same, regardless of the number of players in the game. The same holds true in drawing cards to try to improve a hand.

The following tables apply to Draw Poker, Five Card Stud Poker, Seven Card Stud Poker, and many of the Poker variants found in this book. The tables list the names of each different possible hand in order of rank, starting from the top, the possible number of ways each can be made, and the chance of being dealt such a hand in the first five cards dealt, such as the original five cards dealt in Five Card Stud or in Five Card Draw Poker before the draw.

The Poker odds, percentages and probabilities given in this book, including the following tables, are the most meaningful, informative and comprehensive found anywhere. They were worked out by me personally and are accurate beyond question (I hope).

POSSIBLE POKER HANDS IN A 52-CARD DECK

Ranking Order of Hands	Number of Possible Ways Hand Can Be Made	Chance of Being Dealt in Original 5 Cards
Royal flush	4	1 in 649,740
Straight flush	36	1 in 72,193
Four of a kind	624	1 in 4,165
Full house	3,744	1 in 694
Flush	5,108	1 in 509
Straight	10,200	1 in 255
Three of a kind	54,912	1 in 47
Two pairs	123,552	1 in 21
One pair	1,098,240	1 in 2⅖
No-pair hand	1,302,540	1 in 2
Total	2,598,960	

In the Chance column above, fractional figures have been rounded out to the nearest ⅖ or whole number. The probability of being dealt a pair or better in the first five cards dealt is almost even—and the probability of being dealt a no-pair hand is practically the same. So it's almost a three-to-one chance, when playing against two opponents, that one of them will hold a pair or better in the first five dealt cards. The probabilities vary slightly depending on what you hold.

The 1,302,540 possible five-card no-pair hands are divided as follows:

POSSIBLE POKER HANDS OF LESS VALUE THAN ONE PAIR IN A 52-CARD DECK

Ace Counting High	King Counting High Ace Low	Number of Possible No-Pair Hands
Ace high	King high	502,860
King high	Queen high	335,580
Queen high	Jack high	213,180
Jack high	Ten high	127,500
Ten high	Nine high	70,380
Nine high	Eight high	34,680
Eight high	Seven high	14,280
Seven high	Six high	4,080
Total		1,302,540

CHANCES OF HOLDING ANY PARTICULAR HAND OR BETTER IN FIRST FIVE CARDS DEALT

	Approximately Once in
Any pair or better	2 deals
Pair of jacks or better	5 deals
Pair of queens or better	6 deals
Pair of kings or better	7 deals
Pair of aces or better	9 deals
Two pairs or better	13 deals
Three of a kind or better	35 deals
Straight or better	132 deals
Flush or better	273 deals
Full house or better	590 deals
Four of a kind or better	3,914 deals
Straight flush or better	64,974 deals
Royal flush	649,740 deals

CHANCES (IN PERCENT) OF BEING HIGH WITH THE FIRST FIVE CARDS DEALT

	Number of Opponents							
Player's Hand	**1**	**2**	**3**	**4**	**5**	**6**	**7**	**8**
Three of a kind	98	94	92	89	87	84	82	80
Two pairs	93	86	80	74	68	63	59	53
Pairs:								
Aces	89	79	70	62	55	49	43	39
Kings	88	78	69	61	54	48	42	36
Queens	83	68	56	46	38	32	26	20
Jacks	79	63	50	40	32	25	20	15
Tens	76	58	44					
Nines	73	53	38					
Eights	70	49						
Sevens	66	43						
Sixes	63	40						
Fives	60	36						
Fours	57	32						
Threes	53	28						
Twos	51	25						

The above table presents the chances of a specific hand's being high at Five Card Draw Poker against one to eight opponents. This is expressed in percent; thus 98 means 98%, or, this will happen 98 times out of 100.

The lowest-ranking regular five-card Poker hand when an ace is both high and low is comprised of six, four, three, two, ace in mixed suits. The above table is particularly helpful to players who play high-low variants of Poker. In the short run, each additional active player in the game increases the odds against you on any particular hand. But in the long run, since all players have to put an equal sum into the pot, thus increasing the size of the pot in direct ratio to the increased odds, it doesn't make much difference, as far as odds are concerned, if you are bucking one or seven players. To simplify matters, the figures in the following tables have been rounded out when necessary to the nearest ¹⁄₁₀ or whole number.

Note that your chances of making four of a kind are three times as great when drawing to a pair minus a kicker than when holding a kicker. In fact, you have a better chance of improving your hand when drawing three cards to a pair than when drawing two cards to a pair plus a kicker. The tables above give ample proof of that. However, good Poker playing demands that you occasionally hold a kicker with a pair so as to keep your opponents in doubt as to your playing habits.

The chances of making a full house by drawing one card to two pairs are about 11 to 1.

ODDS AGAINST IMPROVING THE HAND IN DRAW POKER WHEN DRAWING THREE CARDS TO ONE PAIR

Odds against any improvement	2½ to 1
Odds against making two pairs	5 to 1
Odds against making three of a kind	8 to 1
Odds against making a full house	97 to 1
Odds against making four of a kind	359 to 1

ODDS AGAINST IMPROVING THE HAND IN DRAW POKER WHEN DRAWING TWO CARDS TO A PAIR AND A KICKER*

Odds against any improvement	3 to 1
Odds against making two pairs	5 to 1
Odds against making three of a kind	12 to 1
Odds against making a full house	119 to 1
Odds against making four of a kind	1,080 to 1

*An unmatched card held in the hand when drawing.

ODDS AGAINST CHANCES OF IMPROVING THE HAND IN DRAW POKER WHEN DRAWING TWO CARDS TO THREE OF A KIND

Odds against any improvement	8½ to 1
Odds against making a full house	15½ to 1
Odds against making four of a kind	22½ to 1

CHANCES OF IMPROVING THE HAND IN DRAW POKER WHEN DRAWING ONE CARD TO THREE OF A KIND PLUS A KICKER

Odds against any improvement	11 to 1
Odds against making a full house	15 to 1
Odds against making four of a kind	46 to 1

The two tables above show that the best chance for improvement with three of a kind is to draw cards and not hold a kicker. Holding a kicker increases the odds against the player for any improvement.

A very unusual mathematical situation arises in Deuces Wild and also in a 53-card deck with the joker wild regarding the relative value of three of a kind and two pairs. In Deuces Wild, as detailed in the

ODDS AGAINST FILLING IN A FOUR-CARD STRAIGHT IN DRAW POKER WHEN DRAWING ONE CARD

Odds against filling a straight open at one end	11 to 1
Odds against filling a straight open in the middle	11 to 1
Odds against filling a straight open at both ends	5 to 1

ODDS AGAINST FILLING A FOUR-CARD FLUSH IN DRAW POKER

The odds against making a flush by drawing one card of the same suit are about 4½ to 1. If you insist on drawing to a three-card flush, the odds against your catching two cards of the same suit are approximately 23 to 1.

ODDS AGAINST MAKING A STRAIGHT FLUSH IN DRAW POKER WHEN DRAWING ONE CARD

Odds against making a straight flush open at one end	46 to 1
Odds against making a straight flush open in the middle	46 to 1
Odds against making a straight flush open on both ends	22 to 1

CHANCES OF HOLDING VARIOUS POKER HANDS IN THE FIRST FIVE CARDS DEALT WHEN THE FOUR DEUCES ARE WILD

Rank of Hand	Number of Each	Chance
Five of a kind	672	1 in 3,868
Royal flush	484	1 in 5,370
Straight flush	4,072	1 in 638
Four of a kind	30,816	1 in 84
Full house	12,672	1 in 205
Flush	13,204	1 in 197
Straight	66,236	1 in 39
Three of a kind	355,056	1 in 7
Two pairs	95,040	1 in 27
One pair	1,222,048	1 in 2⅒
No-pair hand	798,660	1 in 3¼
Total	2,598,960	

CHANCES OF HOLDING VARIOUS POKER HANDS IN THE FIRST FIVE CARDS DEALT WHEN THE JOKER IS WILD (53-CARD PACK)

Rank of Hand	Number of Each	Chance
Five of a kind	13	1 in 220,745
Royal Flush	24	1 in 119,570
Straight flush	216	1 in 13,286
Four of a kind	3,120	1 in 920
Full house	6,552	1 in 438
Flush	7,768	1 in 369
Straight	20,532	1 in 140
Three of a kind	137,280	1 in 21
Two pairs	123,552	1 in 23
One pair	1,268,088	1 in 2½
No-pair hand	1,302,540	1 in 2
Total	2,869,685	

table on page 171, the chances of drawing three of a kind are one in 7 deals and the chances of drawing two pairs are one in 27 deals. In Joker Wild, you see that the chances of drawing three of a kind are one in 21 deals and the chances of drawing two pairs are one in 23 deals. This peculiar situation is caused by the fact that in one-pair hands the player holding a wild card will naturally call three of a kind instead of the lower-ranking two-pair hand.

Five Card Stud Poker Probabilities

The chances against holding a given hand in Five Card Stud are the same as in Five Card Draw. However, it must be noted that Stud players will drop out before receiving their fifth card if they have potentially weak hands. Therefore, the player who stays until the showdown in Five Card Stud has a higher average winning potential than those who remain until the showdown in Five Card Draw.

The following table gives the chances that a certain card (ace, king, queen, jack) is the high-hole (down) card, depending on the number of players. This table is expressed in percent.

CHANCES OF HOLDING VARIOUS HIGH-HOLE CARDS IN FIVE CARD STUD

Player's Hole Card	Number of Opponents 1	2	3	4	5	6	7	8
Ace	95	89	83	79	74	70	66	63
King	86	74	63	55	47	40	35	30
Queen	78	61	48	37	29	23	18	14
Jack	69	49	34	24	16	12	8	5

The following table gives the chances of pairing your hole card at Five Card Stud when each player has received two cards (one down and one up).

PAIRING YOUR HOLE CARD AT FIVE CARD STUD, THREE CARDS COMING

Number of Players	Approximate Chances of Pairing If Your Hole Card Is Unmatched on the Table	Approximate Chances of Pairing If Your Hole Card Is Matched Once on the Table
Five	Once in 6 deals	Once in 8 deals
Six	Once in 6 deals	Once in 8 deals
Seven	Once in 5 deals	Once in 7 deals
Eight	Once in 5 deals	Once in 7 deals
Nine	Once in 4 deals	Once in 6 deals
Ten	Once in 4 deals	Once in 6 deals

With your hole card matched twice in the upcards, the chance of catching that last hole-card match is about half that with one hold-card match showing. After being dealt your third card your chance of pairing your hole card on the last two cards is as follows:

PAIRING YOUR HOLE CARD AT FIVE CARD STUD, TWO CARDS COMING

Number of Players	Approximate Chances of Pairing If Your Hole Card Is Unmatched on the Table	Approximate Chances of Pairing If Your Hole Card Is Matched on the Table
Five	Once in 7 deals	Once in 11 deals
Six	Once in 7 deals	Once in 11 deals
Seven	Once in 6 deals	Once in 10 deals
Eight	Once in 6 deals	Once in 10 deals
Nine	Once in 5 deals	Once in 9 deals
Ten	Once in 5 deals	Once in 9 deals

Seven Card Stud Poker

The following tables give the approximate odds against making a straight, flush and full house when holding three or four particular cards in Seven Card Stud.

ODDS AGAINST MAKING A STRAIGHT IN SEVEN CARD STUD

Player's Hand	Odds Against Making a Straight
J-10-9	4⅕ to 1
J-10-9-4	8 to 1
J-10-9-4-3	21 to 1
Q-J-10-9	1 3/10 to 1
Q-J-10-9-2 (or A-Q-J-10-8)	2¼ to 1
Q-J-10-9-3-2 (or A-Q-J-10-8-3)	2 1/10 to 1
Q-J-10-8	2 7/10 to 1
Q-J-10-8-3	4½ to 1
Q-J-10-8-3-4	10½ to 1
K-Q-J (or 4-3-2)	6 3/10 to 1
K-Q-J-2 (or Q-4-3-2)	12 to 1
A-K-Q (or A-2-3)	12 6/7 to 1
A-K-Q-3 (or 3-2-A-J)	24 to 1

ODDS AGAINST MAKING A FLUSH IN SEVEN CARD STUD

Player's Hand	Odds Against Making a Flush
Three cards of the same suit	5½ to 1
Three cards of the same suit plus one odd card	9⅗ to 1
Three cards of the same suit plus two odd cards	23 to 1
Four cards of the same suit	1⅛ to 1
Four cards of the same suit plus one odd card	1⅘ to 1
Four cards of the same suit plus two odd cards	4 1/10 to 1

ODDS AGAINST MAKING A FULL HOUSE IN SEVEN CARD STUD POKER

Player's Hand	Odds Against Making a Full House
One pair and one odd card	13 to 1
One pair and two odd cards	19 to 1
One pair and three odd cards	39 to 1
Two pairs	4 to 1
Two pairs and one odd card	7 to 1
Two pairs and two odd cards	10 to 1
Three of a kind	1½ to 1
Three of a kind and one odd card	1½ to 1
Three of a kind and two odd cards	2 to 1
Three of a kind and three odd cards	4 to 1

Seven Card High-Low Stud Poker

The following table gives the approximate chances against filling in various low hands in Seven Card High-Low Stud governed by Scarne rules that state aces count both low and high and straights and flushes count only high. A cinch low hand is six, four, three, two, ace.

ODDS AGAINST MAKING A LOW HAND IN SEVEN CARD HIGH-LOW STUD

Hand	Odds Against Making a Six Low	Odds Against Making No Worse Than a Seven Low	Odds Against Making No Worse Than an Eight Low
6-2-A	4 to 1	2 to 1	Even
6-2-A-J	8 to 1	4 to 1	2 to 1
6-2-A-J-K	22 to 1	10 to 1	6 to 1
6-3-2-A	1⅓ to 1	2 to 3	1 to 3
6-3-2-A-J	2 to 1	1¼ to 1	2 to 3
6-3-2-A-J-K	5 to 1	3 to 1	2 to 1
3-2-A	6⅗ to 1	2¾ to 1	Even
3-2-A-J	12 to 1	5 to 1	2¼ to 1
4-3-2	12 to 1	3¼ to 1	1¼ to 1
4-3-2-J	24 to 1	6 to 1	2⅗ to 1

POSSIBLE POKER HANDS IN AN ITALIAN 40-CARD PACK
(stripped of eights, nines and tens)

Ranking Order of Hands	Number of Possible Ways Hand Can Be Made	Chance of Being Dealt in Original Five Cards
Straight flush	28	1 in 23,500
Four of a kind	360	1 in 1,828
Full house	2,160	1 in 305
Flush	980	1 in 670
Straight	7,140	1 in 92
Three of a kind	23,040	1 in 29
Two pairs	51,840	1 in 13
One pair	322,560	1 in 2⅓
No pair	249,900	1 in 2½
Total	658,008	

POSSIBLE POKER HANDS IN AN ENGLISH 32-CARD PACK
(stripped of twos, threes, fours, fives and sixes)

Ranking Order of Hands	Number of Possible Ways Hand Can Be Made	Chance of Being Dealt in Original Five Cards
Royal flush	4	1 in 50,344
Straight flush	16	1 in 12,586
Four of a kind	224	1 in 899
Full house	1,344	1 in 151
Flush	204	1 in 987
Straight	5,100	1 in 40
Three of a kind	10,752	1 in 19
Two pairs	24,192	1 in 8
One pair	107,520	1 in 2
No pair	52,020	1 in 4
Total	201,376	

11

Five Card Stud: The Daddy of All Stud or Open Poker Games

FIVE CARD STUD

Five Card Stud, also known as Five Card Open Poker, is the forerunner of all Stud or Open Poker variants. Five Card Stud differs from Five Card Draw in that four of the five cards dealt to each player are dealt face up and are seen by all the players in the game.

In the past twenty years, professional Five Card Stud has lost considerable popularity to Seven Card Stud, Seven Card High-Low Stud, Hold Em and various other Stud variations. In the legalized Poker rooms of the state of Nevada I've seen only one Five Card Stud game, as compared to hundreds of Seven Card Stud and Hold Em games. However, Five Card Stud is still a popular social game throughout America.

Five Card Stud, which has four betting intervals, allows for more strategy than Five Card Draw Poker, which has only two.

In Five Card Stud, the average rank of the winning hands is considerably lower than in Five Card Draw, since in Five Card Stud the maximum number of cards each player is dealt is five (one face down and four face up).

RULES OF PLAY

All the preliminaries before the actual play are as described under General Rules for Poker, such as the pack of cards, rank of cards, rank of hands, preparations for play, betting limit, time limit, royalties, selecting the dealer and establishing seating positions at the table, the shuffle and cut, and irregularities in cutting the cards. The number of players at Five Card Stud may range from two to ten. The better Poker players like best a game with eight, nine or ten players, on the theory that this allows more latitude for strategy.

Optional Betting Limits at Five Card Stud

There are numerous types of betting limits at Stud Poker, from among which the author has selected the most popular and most commonly used. Whatever the limits, the minimum and the maximum must be specified before the start of the game.

Betting Variation I

1. Players do not ante, nor does the dealer edge.
2. A minimum amount and a maximum amount are specified before the start of the game. *Example:* A penny and two, 5 to 10, 5 cents to 25 cents, 50 cents to $1, 25 cents to $2, or any two specified amounts.

A player may bet the minimum, the maximum, or any amount between limits at his turn.

Betting Variation II

In this betting variation only two different amounts may legally be wagered—no amount between limits. *Example:* 10 cents and 20 cents means a player cannot bet 15 cents, which would be between limits. Other limits: 5 cents and 10 cents, 25 cents and 50 cents, $1 and $2.

The maximum amount may be bet only on the following conditions:

1. If a player holds an open pair or better.
2. On the betting round prior to a player's being dealt his fifth or last card, and on the final betting round before the showdown.

Betting Variation III

Often *three* figures are mentioned in the limits—such as 5 cents, 10 cents, and 25 cents—meaning the player is permitted to bet the minimum amount or up to the second amount until the third and fourth betting round or until an open pair shows. Then he is permitted to bet up to the maximum.

Dealer's Edge (Variation IV)

Before the deal starts, the dealer edges into the pot an amount agreed upon, usually equal to the amount of the minimum limit.

PLAYER'S ANTE (VARIATION V)

Each player antes into the pot an amount equal to the minimum bet, or a larger amount agreed upon by mutual consent.

Jackpot

The following additional betting feature may be added to any of the above variations except Variations IV and V. When the opening bettor fails to have an active opponent on his first bet—that is, all the players have dropped out—the next deal is called a Jackpot. All the players must ante into the pot an amount equal to the bet made by the *lone active player* in the previous hand. After all the players have anted and a new hand is dealt, the opening bettor (in Jackpots, high or low card can check on the opening bet or thereafter as governed by the Stud Poker rules) is permitted to bet an amount equal to the total amount anted into the pot. In other words, if that amount is in excess of the maximum limit, the new maximum limit for that Jackpot is the amount anted into the pot before the opening bet is made.

Open Blind Betting

Each player antes a stipulated amount into the pot. Then the leader (player to the left of the dealer) opens blind or "force in" as it is sometimes called. In other words, the leader must open and bet before receiving his first two cards. The amount of the blind bet is usually the minimum bet permitted. Sometimes the game is played so that not only does the leader open blind but the second position (player to the left of the leader) raises blind. And occasionally this blind-betting procedure is carried through to the third position and becomes open blind, raise blind, and reraise blind. This type of betting is favored in Nevada casino Poker rooms with high stakes and in most of California's licensed Draw Poker clubs, where only Draw Poker is allowed by law. The purpose of this open blind betting is to increase the action and at the same time put the tight player at a disadvantage—rather than an advantage as he is in most Poker games.

Pot Limit

At his betting turn, a player is permitted to make a bet or raise by an amount equal to the size of the pot. To keep such bets from getting too big, a maximum limit is usually agreed upon.

Table Stakes

Each player puts up on the table in front of himself before the start of the game the amount of cash or chips he wishes to set as his own limit; this is known as a "table stake." Each player's table stake may be decided by a fixed minimum amount, but with no special maximum limit set. Or it may be agreed before the start of the game that each player must begin with an equal table stake.

A player is not permitted to make a bet that exceeds his table stake, nor is he forced to meet any other player's bet that is greater than his table stake. A player is not permitted to add to his table stake during the play of a hand. However, he may add to it between hands, but only in amounts not below the minimum set at the start of the game.

A player is permitted to continue play until all his table-stake amount is gone, regardless of how little of it remains in front of him. If he wants to continue play after his original table stake is exhausted, he must start with a new table stake equal to his original, but this is only permitted between hands.

Should a player fail to have enough money or chips to cover other player's bets, he is permitted to play for the pot (see Tapping Out under Additional Rules at Five Card Stud that follow).

Freeze-out

At the beginning of the game, each player puts up an equal amount of cash or chips on the table before him. He is not permitted to add to this amount, take any of it off the table or lend any part of it to any other player at any time. As soon as a player loses the original amount placed on the table, he must withdraw from the game entirely. The surviving players continue play until one player has won all the cash or chips on the table.

The Beginning of the Deal

The dealer deals each player face down one card (which is known as the hole card), starting with the player to the dealer's left and rotating clockwise, dealing the last card to himself (the dealer), then one card face up to each player in the same order. Then he places the pack face down on the table in front of himself so that the cards are handy for the following part of the deal. The hole card is very carefully protected by each player to keep it hidden from his opponents. The hole card is the only card in Stud Poker that is unknown to the other players, and on the rank of this card depends the betting and the outcome of the hand.

Each card that is face up on the table shall be known as an *upcard*, after the expression I coined for the American servicemen during World War II.

First Round of Betting

The players having carefully examined their hole cards, the player holding the highest-ranking upcard must make the opening bet (first bet). It may be a specified amount agreed on, or any amount within the limit. (Some players, to speed the betting, rule that the lowest-ranking card must make the opening bet.) Should two or more players hold matching high-ranking or low-ranking cards (whichever rule is adopted), the player nearest to the dealer's left must make the opening bet. Thereafter each player in turn, starting with the player to the bettor's left and rotating clockwise, must make one of the following plays:

1. He may fold up or drop out, which means he does not want to continue playing his hand. This is indicated by his saying, "Out," and putting his two cards face down on the discard pile on the table.
2. Or he accepts the bet, and says, "I'll play," or "Stay," and puts into the pot an amount of money equal to the opening bettor's.
3. Or he *raises the pot*, and this is done by putting into the pot an amount of money equal to the previous bettor's plus an additional amount within the limit.
4. Or he *reraises* (if a previous player has raised) by putting into the pot an amount equal to the raiser's plus an additional amount. Any active player can reraise the reraiser by putting into the pot an amount equal to the reraiser's plus an additional amount, etc. Each player in proper turn must follower this procedure until:
   - A. Only one player remains in the game; he wins the pot. Should all the other players drop out and only one player remain, he does not have to expose his hole card.
   - B. Or until two or more players have put an equal amount of money into the pot, which means that the opening bet, raise or reraise, if any, has been *met* by all the active players.

If two or more active players are still in the game and all bets have been met by these players, the dealer continues the deal by dealing each player one card (their third card) face up in the same rotation as before, except that from now until each active player has been dealt a complete hand, or if only one player is active, the cards must be dealt in the following manner: The dealer cannot pick up the remaining stock, but must leave the stock resting on the table. Dealing must be done with one hand, picking one card at a time off the top of the stock.

This rule is highly recommended to minimize dealer mistakes and to help eliminate cheating on the deal. This method of dealing is used in most of the high-stake games the author has witnessed.

To lessen the possibility of cheating with marked cards, do as the Nevada Poker rooms do—burn (discard) the top card of the deck at the start of each dealt round of cards.

Second Round of Betting

The player holding the highest-ranking hand with the two upcards has the option of making the first play, which consists of:

1. *Dropping out* of the pot; and this he signifies by saying "Out," and throwing his hand face down into the discard pile.
2. *Checking*, which he signifies by saying "Check"—which means he desires to play but does not desire to make a bet at present.
3. *Betting*, which he signifies by putting an amount of money into the pot, within the limit.

If the player who has the option of betting does not bet, the turn to check, bet or drop out passes to the player on his left. This procedure continues until all players have had their turn of play.

Should all the players *fail to bet* and there are two or more remaining players in the game, which means they have *checked*, the dealer deals each player one card (his fourth card) face up in the same rotation as before.

But should a player make a bet, each player in turn, starting with the player to that player's left, must:

1. *Play* or *stay*, by putting into the pot an amount equal to the previous bettor's.
2. *Drop, fold up*, or *go out*, by throwing the three cards he is holding face down into the discard pile.
3. *Raise*, by putting into the pot an amount equal to the previous bettor's plus an additional amount within the limit.
4. *Reraise*, provided a previous player has raised. This is done by putting into the pot an amount to equal the raiser's plus an additional amount. Any active player can reraise the reraiser by putting into the pot an amount equal to the reraiser's plus an additional amount, etc.

A player cannot check after a bet has been made. Any player who had previously checked must abide by the above four rules.

This procedure is followed until only one player is left in the game and he wins the pot, or two or more active players remain in the game and all bets have been met by the remaining players.

The dealer then deals each player another card face up in the proper rotation for a total of three upcards plus a hole card, and the third round of betting takes place under the same rules as for the second round.

On completion of that betting round, if there are still active players, the dealer deals each player one upcard in proper turn for a total of five cards to each player.

Fourth and Final Round of Betting

This is the final round of betting. The same rules govern this play as are stipulated for the second round of betting, except that a play hand is now called a *call hand.* If at any time before the hand is called only one player remains in the game, he wins the pot and does not have to expose his hole card. The only time the players must expose their hole cards is when a call is made after each player has been dealt five cards.

A *call* is similar to a *play* or *stay* in Round 2, but it completes the hand. The dealer must call attention to the highest-ranking hand at each turn of play by announcing it orally. Should any player hold a hand comprised of a pair or better, he must call it so that all players can hear. He must also call possible flushes or straights, and must announce the last round of cards being dealt.

Showdown

When the final betting round is over, all active players, starting with the player who is being called, and rotating to the left clockwise, must turn their hole card face up on the table for all the players to see. The player holding the highest-ranking hand wins the pot. For further rules on tied hands, see "Object of the Game" under General Rules for Poker.

On completion of each showdown the game continues in the same manner with a new deal.

ADDITIONAL RULES AT FIVE CARD STUD

Misdeals

Whenever a misdeal occurs, there must be a new shuffle and cut. The same dealer deals again. Should the same dealer make a second misdeal, the deal passes to the player to the dealer's left.

Misdeals—Yes or No?

1. If one or more cards are exposed in cutting or reuniting the cut packets, there is a misdeal.
2. If the pack has not been offered to the proper player to cut and the betting has not started, there is a misdeal.
3. If the pack has not been cut and the betting has not started, there is a misdeal.
4. If one or more cards are observed face up in the pack and the betting has not started, there is a misdeal.
5. If the dealer exposes his own or a player's hole card while dealing it, or a card is found face up while dealing a player a hole card, there is a misdeal.
6. If a player exposes his hole card after it is dealt face down, it is *not a misdeal.* Nor can a player call for a face-down card to be his new hole card. He must face down the exposed card, and it continues to be his hole card. A player must protect his hole card at all times.
7. If an imperfect pack is found being used containing fewer cards than the standard pack or duplicate cards, the play must stop immediately on its discovery, and the players take out of the pot the money they put into it. If it is discovered after a pot has been collected, the previous hands stand, and are legitimate.
8. If any player has been dealt out, or an extra hand has been dealt in, there is a misdeal.
9. If a player (or players) has been dealt too many or too few cards before the betting has started, there is a misdeal.
10. If the dealer has dealt a player a hole card out of turn and that player has looked at it, there is a misdeal.

Passing the Deal

A dealer cannot pass his deal in his turn to deal unless incompetent to deal the cards.

Dead Hands

If a player holds too few or too many cards during the betting interval or at the showdown, his hand is foul or dead. But should this be discovered after that player has collected the pot, it stands as a legitimate hand.

On Being Dealt an Exposed Card

If a card is found face up in the pack and the betting has started, the player must take that card in his turn of play, except if it is the first card to be dealt of a new round. That card is immediately *burned* (put aside, onto the discard pile), and after the betting has been completed on that round, the dealer must burn enough other cards from the top of the pack so that the total number of burned cards equals the active number of players in the game.

Dealing in More or Fewer Players

If a dealer deals a player out or deals an extra hand in, and it is discovered before the players have looked at their hole cards, and if the error can be corrected so that each player receives his proper cards (by shifting a card from one player to another and placing the extra card or cards back on top of the pack or dealing one or more cards from the pack *without any of the cards being exposed to any player*), there is not a misdeal.

Exposing the First Card of a Round

If the dealer exposes the top card of the pack before the betting has been completed on the previous round, he leaves the card face up on the pack until the betting on that round is completed. After the betting has been completed on that round, the dealer must burn, or bury, from the top of the pack as many cards (including the exposed card) as there are active players in the game. Under no conditions are the players permitted to look at the burned cards. Thereafter the play continues according to the rules.

Improper Dealing

A dealer is not permitted to deal the first card face up and the second card face down. The first card must be dealt face down, becoming the player's hole card.

Protecting a Hole Card

A player must protect his hole card at all times. Protecting a hole card is to permit no other player to know its identity, regardless of whether the player is active or dead.

A player is not permitted at any time to turn up his hole card and call for his next card face down.

A player, when folding up, is not permitted to expose his hole card to any of the players or to mention its identity.

Checking on the Last Round

If a player checks on the last round, all other players, in order to check too, must be able to beat the checking player's four open cards. Otherwise a check is not permitted. Example: A player who has checked has a pair of open aces. The next and following players *cannot check* unless they can beat the open pair, although they may bet if the situation permits. This rule is incorporated to protect a player's hand against another player who calls an impossible hand, although there is no penalty that could be imposed on a player for failure to comply.

Betting out of Turn

The following rules apply to staying, calling or raising out of turn. A player making a bet out of turn must leave the bet in the pot. He cannot take it back, and the play reverts to the proper player. When it is the proper turn of the player who bet out of turn, he must do one of the following:

1. If no bet has been made by any preceding player, the bet stands as is.
2. If a bet has been made by a previous player smaller than the bet made out of turn, it stands as a raise.
3. If a bet has been made by a previous player equal to the bet out of turn, it stands as a stay or call. The player who bet out of turn cannot raise.
4. If a previous bet was raised by another player and the bet is in excess of the amount bet by the out-of-turn player, the out-of-turn player may drop out of the pot, stay or call by equaling the bet made by the previous bettors, or reraise the pot after equaling the bet.

Verbal Betting

If a player in his turn of play announces orally that he is making a bet, he must abide by the announcement. He cannot increase or decrease the bet. Should a player make an announcement not in his proper turn of play and has not placed any money in the pot, it should be disregarded and considered a joke or an attempted bluff.

Tapping Out

If a player has put all his money into the pot and no longer can bet, and when that player is permitted to play for the size of the pot up to the time he no longer has money, this is called a tap-out. If the other players keep betting, they put their bets to one side, as the tapping-out player has no interest in that side pot. The tapping-out player receives cards until the hand is completed, and, should he have the highest-ranking hand on the showdown, he wins only the pot, not the side pot; that is won by the player having the highest-ranking cards among the remaining bettors. A player is permitted only one tap-out during a Poker session.

A player when tapping out can raise only if he still has an amount equal to the maximum limit, so in case of a reraise he can call the bet. A player cannot tap out with money on the table.

Improper Fold-up

If a player decides to drop out of the pot or fold up, he cannot give an indication, verbal or otherwise, until it is his proper turn of play. Strict observance of this rule will make for a better game. Should he fold up out of turn his hand is dead.

Dealer Errs in Calling Highest Open Hand

When the dealer errs in calling the highest open hand, and as a result the wrong player bets (if it is discovered before the betting is completed on that round), the dealer must correct the play by giving back out of the pot the money that was improperly bet. This is the only time a player is permitted to take money out of the pot.

Going Through the Discards

In no circumstances is a player permitted to look at the discards either before or after the showdown. Nor is a nonactive player permitted to look at an active player's hole card before or after the showdown, unless a bet has been called and the player is compelled to expose his hole card.

Looking at Undealt Cards

Looking at the top card or any of the undealt cards while a hand is in progress, regardless of whether the player is out of that pot, is not permitted.

Lending Money or Chips

Under no circumstances is a player allowed to borrow money or chips from another player during the play. If a player desires to borrow money from another player, it must be done before the cards are dealt. Passing money or chips from one player to another during the play is not permitted.

Betting for Another Player

Under no circumstances is a player permitted to bet for another player.

Angling

Angling is positively prohibited—for example, discussion among two or more players about splitting the pot regardless of the winner or giving back part of the money, asking for a free ride or call, or any conspiracy toward violation of the Poker rules.

Overs in the Pot

No money or chips may be taken out of the pot, except that a player may take out his proper change after placing a bet in his turn of play (it must be observed by all the players that the proper change is taken), or as specified under the infraction when the dealer errs. Should a player put into the pot a larger amount than required and should another player make a bet, change may not be taken out of the pot.

Exposed Hands on Showdown

All players, active or nonactive, are entitled to see all active players' hole cards on the showdown, provided a bet has been called.

Illegal Cutting of Cards

Under no circumstances may a player ask to cut the cards after a bet has been made. I must stress particularly that cards cannot be cut *after* the deal has started or for that matter at any other time except *before* the start of the deal.

Man and Wife

Most of the Nevada casinos forbid man and wife to play Stud Poker at the same table. This is a sound ruling, and I incorporate it into my rules. The exception is when they play in a small-limit game primarily for pastime.

Criticism

A player is not permitted in any circumstances to criticize another player's methods. Stud Poker is a game in which each player plays his own hand at his own risk as he desires. No consideration should be expected by one player from another.

THE MOST HIGHLY PUBLICIZED STUD POKER GAME IN HISTORY

During the Roaring Twenties (1923–1928), I made it a habit whenever in New York City to visit world-famous Lindy's Restaurant, situated on the east side of Broadway at Forty-ninth Street, to partake of a portion of cheesecake and a cup of coffee. At the time I lived in Fairview, New Jersey, directly across the Hudson River from New York City. I was a practicing young card-trick magician specializing in entertaining at private functions.

This was part of the period when Prohibition laws caused the greatest upsurge in criminal activity in the history of the country. And, as it developed, this was the period that was to become known as the Roaring Twenties—those reckless, flamboyant years when millions of otherwise law-abiding citizens entered into a joint conspiracy to break the unpopular Prohibition laws, in spite of the fact that in doing so these respectable citizens were contributing hundreds of millions of dollars yearly to the underworld.

In those days, bootlegging, nightclubs and speakeasies were the underworld's biggest sources of revenue. Bootleggers, racketeers and big-time gamblers were powerful figures on the American scene. Those were the years when Five Card Stud Poker games flourished all over the country, and when racketeers and bootleggers controlled the fight racket and had also taken over the night-life and show-business industry. Every town and city had at least one speakeasy or nightclub. New York City boasted of Lucky Luciano's House of Morgan, Bill Duffy's Silver Slipper, Larry Fay's El Fay Club, Dutch Schultz's Embassy Club, Jack "Legs" Diamond's Hotsy Totsy Club, Owney Madden's Cotton Club, the 300 Club, run by Texas Guinan, who greeted her customers with the words, "Hello, Sucker," and others too numerous to mention.

Therefore it was inevitable that millionaires, politicians, show people, socialites, businessmen and plain Joe Doakes and John Scarne should rub elbows with gamblers, racketeers, bootleggers and other members of the underworld.

This was the era of high living and low morals. Gamblers, bootleggers and racketeers were glorified, accepted socially and paid homage to by the millions of Americans who believed that Prohibition was a joke. Anyone who made the newspaper headlines was looked up to. The top bootleggers and mobsters were on the same celebrity scale as Jack Dempsey, the heavyweight champion, or Babe Ruth, the Home Run King, and they mingled with the outstanding citizens of that era.

In those days many were prouder to shake hands with Arnold Rothstein, America's kingpin gambler, or Al Capone, the Chicago racket boss, than with Calvin Coolidge, the President of the United States.

It was during this same period that a few outstanding individuals became better known by their nicknames than by their real monickers. These were the days of Babe Ruth, the Bambino; Jack Dempsey, the Manassa Mauler; Al Capone, Scarface; Arnold Rothstein, the Brain; Jesse L. Livermore, the Boy Wonder of Wall Street; William J. Fallon, the Mouthpiece; Ivar Krueger, the Match King; and William V. Dwyer or Big Bill Dwyer, the Bootleg King.

During this period of American history, New York City, like the rest of the country, was a gambler's paradise. The center of the gambling action was on and off Broadway from Forty-second Street to Sixtieth Street. Five Card Stud games were found in every pool hall and private and social club, as well as in countless private dwellings.

It was at Lindy's, however, that the most prominent members of the gambling fraternity were found—gamblers, Poker-game operators, card and dice cheats, racetrack touts, race and sports bookies, bootleggers, mobsters and their bodyguards. Famous syndicated columnists such as Walter Winchell, Damon Runyon, O.O. McIntyre, and other writers would nightly join the colorful crowd at Lindy's to see and be seen, eat, and talk shop.

Arnold Rothstein, whom I had entertained professionally with my card trick act on many an occasion over a five-year span, used Lindy's Restaurant as a kind of second office. He was given his telephone messages by the night cashier, and he held discussions with his friends and business associates there.

Arnold Rothstein was the most notorious big-time gambler in the country. His high-stakes Poker games with Nick "The Greek" Dandolos were legendary. Rothstein had won $500,000 on the first Dempsey-Tunney fight in 1926; in 1921 he had won $850,000 on a colt named Sidereal at Aqueduct. To millions he was the man who fixed the 1919 World Series. To most political observers he was the political boss of New York City. To the men who wrote the headlines for the tabloids, he was "King of Gamblers." To Damon Runyon, celebrated newspaper columnist, he was "The Brain," and F. Scott Fitzgerald based Wolfsheim, his gambler in *The Great Gatsby,* on Rothstein.

To impress the reader with the enormity of Rothstein's gambling winnings during the Roaring Twenties, let me state that at the time a two-room suite at a top New York City hotel was priced at $14 a day, and a steak dinner with all the trimmings would set you back $1.50. The $500,000 that Rothstein won on the first Dempsey-Tunney fight would amount to about $5,000,000 in today's dollar market, and Rothstein's $850,000 win on Sidereal would be equal to $8,500,000.

Whenever Rothstein spotted me in Lindy's he would ask me to perform a card trick or two for him and his friends. It wasn't long before I got to meet many of the nation's most famous and infamous people. Some of the gamblers and race and sports bookies Rothstein introduced me to were George McManus (alias Humphreys), who was the big-time dice book at Warren's, which operated a $2,000-limit Open Craps game in a West Side warehouse several blocks from Lindy's; Meyer and Sam Boston, two brothers who operated Darnell and Company, a Wall Street brokerage firm that was actually a front for their big-time race and sports book; Martin Bowe, a big-time race bookmaker, Poker player and close friend of Jimmy Meehan, a gambler who ran a Poker game in his apartment.

As a result of my conversations with Rothstein and the above mentioned gamblers I learned of Meehan's nightly Poker game, which was patronized by many Broadway gamblers, journalists, show people and businessmen. Meehan ran his Poker games in his three-room apartment situated in the Congress Building on the corner of Fifty-fourth Street and Seventh Avenue.

The most memorable Five Card Stud Poker game in history started there at 11 P.M. on September 8, 1928, and continued until mid-afternoon on September 9, when most of the players had reached the end of physical endurance and the game ended. It was a $100- and $200-limit game, but the big-money bets were placed on high spades. Eight players participated in the game. They included Arnold Rothstein, George McManus, Meyer and Sam Boston, Martin Bowe, and three West Coast gamblers who were playing in the game for the first time —Joe Bernstein, "Nigger" Nate Raymond and Alvin C. Thompson, alias Titanic Thompson.

At the end of the game, Rothstein, the big loser, offered to cut Raymond high card for $40,000. Raymond accepted and cut first. He cut a king, Rothstein a ten. Raymond won the $40,000 bet, the biggest single wager on a high-card cut in history.

Since Poker at the time was played with cash (Poker chips were unknown then), at the end of the game no settlements were required, winners taking their Poker winnings and losers lamenting their losses. That is, with the exception of marker side bets placed on high spades, which is betting to see who was dealt the highest-rank spade card on the first dealt upcard of the Stud hand. This wagering began at a hundred dollars a hand and rose rapidly to five and ten thousand a hand. The principals involved in the spade side bets were Rothstein, McManus, Thompson, Raymond and Bernstein.

When it came time to settle the spade-bet markers on September 9 at the game's end, Rothstein owed Nigger Nate Raymond $219,000, $70,000 to Joe Bernstein and $30,000 to Titanic Thompson. Meyer and Sam Boston played only for an hour or so and left the game a couple of hundred dollars winners. George McManus, who stayed to the end, claimed he had lost $51,000 in cash, and Martin Bowe, who went broke after a couple hours of play, maintained he had lost $5,700 in cash.

After the game had ended Rothstein asked Meehan to total his high spade markers. Meehan tallied the markers and said, "Arnold, your markers total $319,000."

Arnold Rothstein collected the markers from Meehan, totaled them again, called out the amount owed to each winner and then tore them up and put a match to the torn scraps of paper. All the winners now had was Rothstein's word that he owed them $319,000.

Rothstein walked out that morning a $60,000 cash winner—money that he had exchanged for markers during the game. As Rothstein left the game, he was quoted by George McManus as saying that the winners would be paid within a couple of days.

However, a few days later, according to McManus, Rothstein had a change of heart and refused to pay off. He insisted that the game was crooked and that McManus had brought three card cheats to the game to fleece him.

I first learned of this memorable Poker game on a visit to Lindy's in the middle of October. As I was munching on a pastrami sandwich, Rothstein, accompanied by Jimmy Meehan, entered and sat down at his favorite table. Minutes later when he spotted me, he motioned to me to come over to his table. Once I was seated at Rothstein's table, he said, "Johnny, have you heard about the crooked game that took place in Meehan's apartment?"

"No, Mr. Rothstein. I have no idea what you're talking about."

"Well, Johnny, you know George McManus. I introduced you to him at one of my parties when you entertained with your card tricks."

"Sure, I remember him, Mr. Rothstein. He's the dice bookie at Warren's crap game," I replied.

"Well, Johnny, McManus brought three stranger card cheats to Meehan's card game just to cheat me with marked cards. Now George McManus has been calling me several times a day for the past couple of weeks asking me to pay at least part of the $319,000 in markers that I was supposed to owe those three stranger card cheats. I told him that's none of his business and that if the three card cheats want to give me their sad tale, they can find me here at Lindy's any night in the week."

On Sunday, November 4, 1928—only weeks after that infamous Poker game—Arnold Rothstein was shot in Room 349 of New York City's Park Central Hotel, and he died two days later in Polyclinic Hospital of the gunshot wounds.

Three weeks later McManus was arrested and charged with Rothstein's murder. Thompson, Raymond, Bowe and Meehan were arrested and each was held in $100,000 bail as a material witness. Joe Bernstein had fled the state and could not be located.

A year later McManus was brought to trial for the murder of Rothstein. Titanic Thompson and Nigger Nate Raymond as the defense's star witnesses told the judge that George McManus was a "square and honest guy" and that the high-card spade game had been entirely on the level. The judge seemed satisfied with Thompson's and Raymond's testimony, so much so, in fact, that when the defense asked for a directed verdict of acquittal, it was granted by the judge.

During one of my many visits to the Sands Hotel Casino in the late fifties, Aaron Weisberg, a Sands casino executive, introduced me to Joe Bernstein, the same Joe Bernstein who had taken part in Meehan's Poker game back in 1928. I asked Bernstein if he would agree to my interviewing him with regard to gambling in Las Vegas. The following morning found Bernstein in my Sands Hotel suite being interviewed by me. Toward the end of the interview, with tongue in cheek, I asked Bernstein if the Rothstein card game was crooked and what part he played in it. He smiled and said, "You don't expect me to answer that question, do you?"

"Yes, if you care to," I replied.

"Scarne, I won't answer that question, but I'll tell you what happened the night Rothstein was shot. As you already know, McManus had brought Titanic Thompson, Nigger Nate Raymond and me to Meehan's game that night. So, when we heard Rothstein wasn't going to honor his $319,000 in markers, Nigger Nate told McManus he was responsible for the marker collection. When Rothstein told McManus he wasn't going to honor the markers because he said he was cheated, McManus became worried and he began to drink. He drank a lot. He telephoned Lindy's that fatal night and asked Rothstein to meet him at the Park Central Hotel, where he had rented a suite. When Rothstein arrived, McManus was drunk, and he had a gun which I guess he hoped would frighten Rothstein into paying off at least part of the markers. He pointed the gun at Rothstein, who was sitting down. Rothstein pushed the gun away and accidentally it went off. McManus panicked and threw the gun out the window and ran from the room, forgetting that his overcoat was left in the room. It was an accident, no doubt about it, but it screwed me out of seventy grand."

After Bernstein finished relating his views on the night of the murder, I said, "Mr. Bernstein, why was McManus so intent on collecting the $319,000 in markers, which did not involve him at all? One of the card game principals once told me that the game was rigged, that McManus was the ringleader, and that he brought you, Titanic and Nigger Nate to Meehan's Poker game to cheat Arnold Rothstein."

"Mr. Scarne, that ends this interview. I told you at the start, I would not discuss the card game. So—I'm leaving. Goodbye, Mr. Scarne."

Several months later, at the same Sands Hotel Casino in Las Vegas, I met up with Titanic Thompson accompanied by Nigger Nate Raymond. Following is the story Titanic Thompson told in answer to my question about whether they had cheated Rothstein during that infamous 1928 Poker game.

"Before that game of high spades began that night, Rothstein took me [Thompson] aside and suggested that we play partners, and I agreed. However, later in the evening, when Raymond and Bernstein entered the game, I decided to end the partnership in order to work with Raymond and Bernstein. We knew each other real well, having participated in many swindles together. We had worked together in many Poker games in Texas and California. We knew all the Poker cheating methods such as signaling and playing the best hand, fixing the high spades, using strippers and marked cards. Raymond and Bernstein were two of the best Poker cheaters and connivers, and I thought we might do a little business together that night. Sure, we cheated Rothstein out of the $319,000 in markers, and if it wasn't for that drunk McManus shooting Rothstein we might have collected our money."

When I asked Titanic Thompson how come that when he was arrested as a material witness to the Rothstein shooting he told the New York City Police that McManus had taken him, Raymond and Bernstein to the Poker game that night and that the game started about ten minutes before Rothstein's arrival, Titanic Thompson replied, "That game took place more than thirty years ago. How do you expect me to remember everything?"

To summarize: After reading the court records of the McManus trial and all the front-page testimony carried by *The New York Times* concerning the game and the Rothstein shooting, plus my conversations with four of the principals who were involved, I'm of the firm opinion that George McManus, Titanic Thompson, Nigger Nate Raymond and Joe Bernstein as a team had set out to fleece Arnold Rothstein at Poker with marked cards and stripper decks.

Strategy for Five Card Stud Poker

The traditional theory of Five Card Stud is not to play unless you can "beat the board"—that is, you should drop out unless you have a better hand showing at the time you make your bet. I regret to say that this idea is almost entirely true. Tight players eventually are bound to win the money. In this game there is only one hole card; thus the game has little chance for bluffing and hiding the strength of one's hand.

The real Poker hustler prefers Five Card Stud to any other game in the Poker family. He shuns such games as Draw Poker, Lowball, Seven Card Stud or any other Poker variations wherein wild cards are used. Five Card Stud Poker permits a player to use much more strategy than any of the variations. When wild cards are added, the element of skill is greatly diminished, and the element of chance is greatly increased.

The best game of Stud—looking at it from a smart gambler's viewpoint—is without an ante or dealer's edge, but if the dealer does edge, the amount must be comparatively small. For example, in a $2-limit game, the dealer edges 25 cents. The reason is that the gambler likes to have some information to guide him before betting. Gamblers don't like to put money into the pot without seeing at least part of their hand; therefore the first two cards dealt in Stud (the hole card and the first upcard) are the cards that are valued by the gambler and determine the betting.

Getting back to the reader (whom we might as well call the player), let us assume he has been dealt a hole card and his first upcard. This is the most important part in any Stud game. The player must decide the value of those two cards, which is done by considering the value of his two cards and the value of every other player's upcard. To give you a general rule to cover this situation is impossible; so instead I am going to discuss what one of the smartest gamblers in the business does under any conditions.

First, if his hole card is lower than a ten-spot, he folds up (provided he does not hold a pair back to back), regardless of the value of his upcard. If it is an ace or a high card and he is compelled to make the opening bet, he bets the minimum amount permitted.

The player must bear in mind that the chances of being dealt a pair or better in five cards are approximately one in two. Therefore, if three or four players remain until the showdown, almost invariably the winning hand will hold a pair or better. With this thought in mind, the smart gambler, failing to hold a pair, always has to have a higher-ranking card in the hole than any other player's upcard. He bases his calculations on the theory that if he holds two cards lower than the upcard of one or more players and he has the possibility of pairing one of his low cards, each of his opponents also has the same possibility. And, if he and one of his opponents each pair a card, his hand is valueless, because his opponent paired a higher card. This gambler uses sound judgment.

So much for the first two cards. Now the first betting round has ended, and each player has received his second upcard.

This gambler, should he see any other player's two upcards paired, and if he fails to hold a pair, will at his proper turn of play fold up. His theory, which is sound, is "Never play a hand at the start which you know is lower than your opponents'." In other words, don't chase a pair or a higher hand when the pot is small; because if you did play for the third upcard, you might be tempted to chase your money which you have in the pot, and that is not good Poker playing.

The substance of the above boils down to this: You must play them tight, at least up until you receive your third upcard.

Let us go back to the hole card and the first upcard. When your hole card has a ranking value of a jack or better and your upcard is a ten or lower, it is worth a reasonable bet. That is, provided a jack is not showing as one of your opponent's upcards. Should this be the case, fold up at your turn, because your chances of pairing that jack have been reduced 33⅓%.

The player must always bear in mind that an upcard paired has much less value than a hole card paired; and the smart player will consider playing the hand in an attempt to pair his hole card rather than an open card or upcard.

It is also advisable for a player to know that the chances of pairing a hole card with a second upcard (provided no player holds a card of the same denomination as his upcard) are deduced by checking the number of upcards. Example: The game is seven-handed; a player sees seven upcards, none of which can pair up his hole card. The computation is as follows: The player's chances of being dealt a card to pair his hole card are 3 in 44, or 13⅔ to 1 against pairing his hole card. And the chances of pairing either his hole card or his upcard, provided the upcards showing are not of the same denomination, are exactly 7 to 1 against. So if the pot holds eight or more times the amount it will cost you to put in and draw that second upcard, it is worth the gamble. If the pot has much less, it is not worth the risk.

One thing a player must not be afraid to do is to fold up. Sure, you like action; that is why you play Stud. But I still have to find the Stud player who enjoys losing money. And if you are afraid to fold up, and crave action when your hand doesn't merit your playing, you must eventually lose.

A player must also realize that should he fold up his first two or three cards, he will lose little or nothing, because rarely is the big betting under way at this part of the game. As a rule, a player holding a big pair back to back won't raise at that time for fear of causing the other players to fold up. And a player holding a weak hand doesn't raise, because he is trying to better his hand with the second upcard.

Should a player reraise before drawing his second upcard, he must first analyze the player who made the raise as well as the upcard he is holding. Is he a winner up to this time? If he is, the chances are better than even that he is bluffing; a big winning player frequently seems to go on a betting spree. Or is he a heavy loser? If he is, maybe he is trying to steal the pot or might be trying to change his streak of bad luck. If you hold a good hand at this time, it is advisable to play for that second upcard and not reraise.

Whenever a player has his hole card paired with one of his two upcards and another player has an open pair showing of a lower rank than the first player's, it is worth a raise for two reasons: (a) to attempt to drive out the other players and possibly the holder of the pair; (b) the holder of the lower hand must intimate the value of his hand by either dropping or raising. But the main reason is to get the most money possible into the pot with the fewest players.

One of the most stupid plays at Stud is to play for a flush when holding only three cards of a flush. The chances of making it by drawing two cards depends on the number of cards of the same suit in the upcards. For example, with three cards of the same suit showing in the other players' upcards, the chances against making the flush are approximately 24 to 1.

When you are in a pot and have drawn your third upcard, with one more to go—should a player have you beaten with his upcards, and if the pot is not especially big, fold up. But should the pot be extra big and a merely reasonable amount be required of you to bet to receive that last card, and if you believe your chances of winning that hand are good should you draw a certain card (and the card is still alive), then by all means play.

If you do not hold a cinch hand and are in doubt about your holding the winning hand, a check is the proper play. You must think about trying to save money on an uncertain hand, and by checking you won't play into a trap and give your opponent a chance to raise should *he* hold a cinch hand.

After you have received your last card at Stud, odds should no longer be considered. By this time you know whether you have a cinch hand or not. If you have a cinch hand, bet the limit; don't check in the hope that your opponent will bet and you can raise him. If he has a raise in mind the chances are that he will raise anyway, should you bet. If not, he probably will check also, and you are out money.

Never give an opponent an opportunity to see your hole card free when holding a cinch hand.

Probabilities of Five Card Stud

The probabilities of holding any specific five-card combination in Five Card Stud are the same as in Five Card Draw minus the draw. The following table lists the odds against a player pairing his hole card at Five Card Stud. Obviously all Stud probabilities are affected mathematically by exactly what face-up (exposed) cards are shown on the table.

First, let us consider the situation when the player has an ace in the hole and an odd card shows, and he wants to know exactly what his chances of pairing that ace on the end of the hand are. Here are the odds against the player eventually pairing his hole card.

Number of Active Players	No Exposed Aces Showing Odds Against	One Exposed Ace Showing Odds Against
Eight	4.00 to 1	6.35 to 1
Seven	4.12 to 1	6.51 to 1
Six	4.23 to 1	6.69 to 1
Five	4.34 to 1	6.81 to 1

When two aces are exposed, the odds against catching that last ace are about doubled those with one exposed ace. The same odds listed above hold true for the pairing of a king, queen, jack, etc.

The following table gives the chance against the player of pairing his ace (hole card) after the third card has been dealt and there are two cards to be dealt.

Number of Cards Exposed by Other Players	No Exposed Aces Showing Odds Against	One Exposed Ace Showing Odds Against
12	5.32 to 1	8.34 to 1
10	5.66 to 1	8.90 to 1
8	5.99 to 1	9.41 to 1
6	6.35 to 1	9.86 to 1

The two tables above are approximations. Surely, the odds against pairing a hole card will vary slightly with the exact number of cards exposed. Such precise odds against figures, however, are unlikely to help the player in actual competition.

56. *Five Card Stud (Low)*

This form of Poker is quite different from most other forms of Stud in that no player can conceal his hand's strength; a player can only conceal his hand's weakness. A player is dealt only five cards, and any one of them can destroy his hand. He may buy a pair of high cards and there's nothing he can do to conceal it unless he pairs a low upcard with his hole card. Example: An opponent shows X-5-4-J-2—his hand cannot be better than jack high, though it might be considerably worse.

The game is played exactly the same as Five Card Stud (High) with two major exceptions. First, the lowest hand wins, 6-4-3-2-A being the best low hand. Second, straights and flushes don't count, and aces count low.

Strategy: The average winning hand in this form of Low Stud is jack high. With nothing higher than a jack, or if you can beat everything in sight, stay for a third or fourth card.

If you can beat everything showing on the board, bet the limit. Don't be scared off by the large number of active competitors. You are the favorite for winning the pot, and the more money you can get into it the better.

In this game, you have to go in with a low card no higher than a nine. On the next card, bet the limit to try to drive your opponents out. Or try to force your opponents to stay as long as you are top man showing.

If you yourself have the best hand showing on the five cards dealt, but you have been destroyed by matching your hole card, the only way you can possibly win the pot is by bluffing. However, you should always know your opponents when trying a bluff. And it's not worth trying against a player who calls constantly. Since the brutal fact of this Low Five Card Stud is that one card can destroy your hand, many Las Vegas professionals shun the game, saying that it's the only Stud game where luck outclasses skill.

57. *High-Low Five Card Stud*

This game is rarely played today although it's quite an interesting one. In High-Low Five Card Stud, the hands players are going for, either high or low, are quite obvious. In this variation there are no declarations prior to the showdown. "Cards speak" (see General Rules for Poker concerning high-low games).

When playing this game, play for either a high or a low hand, not for both, because both hardly ever develop. When going for high, play more or less as in Five Card Stud (High) making due allowance for active opponents who appear to be going for low. These are not always easy to spot. Several low upcards may be accompanied by an ace in the hole or the upcard may pair the hole card. And keep in mind that a perfect three-card low can be turned into a strong high hand by the fourth and fifth drawn cards.

When going for low, play more freely than in Five Card Stud (Low), since there is always the chance that an opponent, although holding a strong-looking low hand, may in fact be going for high.

This game is often played with the option of turning up the hole card and taking the last dealt card face down (as a hole card). This style game has several added strategic features. Example: A player with four fair low cards will often do this, for it gives him an opportunity to win the pot by a bluff if his fifth dealt card has wrecked his hand.

A player holding three low upcards showing, who takes his last dealt card face up, may be presumed to be holding a high hole card or a pair. No doubt a good player varies such strategic plays from time to time in order to befuddle his opponents.

12

America's Seven Most Popular Seven Card Stud Games

FACTS ABOUT AMERICA'S SEVEN BEST POKER GAMES

As mentioned earlier, Five Card Stud as a gambling Poker game has lost considerable popularity during the past two decades. This is due mostly to the advent of the following seven Poker games. 1. Seven Card Stud High; 2. Razz (Las Vegas Low Seven Card Stud); 3. Seven Card Stud Low; 4. Seven Card High-Low Stud; 5. Seven Card High-Low Split Cards Speak; 6. Hold Em Club and Home Game; 7. Hold Em Las Vegas Style. A game that I believe equals any of these seven Stud games in both skill and entertainment is English Stud. For this reason I have included it in this chapter as well.

Results of my latest national Poker survey of hundreds of legal and illegal professional Poker rooms and clubs all over America (except those 400-odd Poker clubs situated in California, where only Draw Poker is permitted by law) revealed that Seven Card Stud games are the most popular private and professional money Poker games currently being played in America.

The seven Stud Poker games that follow are far superior to Five Card Stud and its variants for several basic reasons. First, each player is dealt seven cards from which he selects the five best to use on the showdown. Second, in these Seven Card Stud games there are three hole cards (face-down cards) dealt to each player instead of the one dealt in Five Card Stud. These two factors lead to a more scientific and interesting game with considerably more betting and bluffing, and much bigger pots—all because of the nature of the game. In most

Seven Card Stud games there are five betting rounds, and each player who stays until the showdown will be dealt seven cards, four face up and three face down.

The reader will find the general rules and strategy pertaining to Seven Card Stud in Chapters 3, 4 and 11 and under each of the specific Seven Card Stud games that follow.

58. *Seven Card Stud: America's Most Popular Poker Game*

In the past two decades, Seven Card Stud, also known as Seven Card Stud High, and Down the River, has become the most popular gambling Poker game in the United States. My survey of Nevada Poker rooms revealed that Seven Card Stud has a 2 to 1 popularity edge over all other forms of Poker combined. As a matter of fact, several Las Vegas Strip casinos such as the M-G-M Grand Hotel Casino permit only Seven Card Stud in their Poker rooms. Untold billions of dollars are won and lost yearly at the tens of thousands of Seven Card Stud games that take place throughout the country.

The first two cards are dealt face down and the next four cards are dealt face up. A round of betting takes place after the dealing of each face-up card. The best hand showing, as in Five Card Stud, is first to act, and checking is usually allowed in all but the first betting round. The seventh and last card is dealt face down and is followed by the fifth and final betting round. At the showdown, any active player may use any five cards of his dealt seven to make up his best possible Poker hand.

The playing of Seven Card Stud is completely different from Five Card Stud. There is considerably less information to be analyzed from the four upcards of opponents, who may at the showdown hold four of a kind without even a pair showing among their face-up cards.

In this game the average winning hands have more in common with those in Draw Poker for the values of the hands are about the same. A fairly high three of a kind is an average winning hand with four or more active players at showdown. Two pairs wins the average pot when two or three active players remain at the showdown. However, when five or more players remain to the end, straights, flushes and full houses are so common that a player can't bet on anything less, provided that the face-up cards of the opponents (plus their previous betting) would justify any possibility that opponents hold higher hands.

The tactics of betting and raising in Seven Card Stud are almost the same as in Five Card Stud. The only difference is that the players can seldom be certain of holding the winning hand because, with three face-down cards at the end, the possible five-card Poker hands that can be made with the three face-down cards and the four face-up cards total the gigantic number of 133,784,560 as compared to the 2,598,960 in Five Card Stud.

One of the most common mistakes made by the average player in Seven Card Stud is that when he believes he has the best hand, he tries to build up the pot by letting his opponents remain in the pot rather than by attempting to get his opponents to fold (drop out of the pot). The above reasoning holds true only when the player holds an exceptionally strong hand.

Strategy at Seven Card Stud

Most of the tips covered in Chapter 4, General Strategy, plus much of the strategy in Chapter 11, Five Card Stud, apply to Seven Card Stud, in addition to the strategy that follows.

The most important decision that a player can make in Seven Card Stud is what he does with his first three dealt cards. This decision will determine whether or not he is a winner or loser at this game over the long run. If the player stays in with weak cards, he'll usually emerge a loser. If he stays in with three strong cards, he'll usually emerge a winner regardless of how he plays the remaining four cards to be dealt. The player who plays with three first dealt strong cards will find that he'll win more pots and bigger pots than the player who plays with three first dealt weak cards.

Good plays in this game on the first three cards (two face down and one face up) are roughly as follows. However, before we discuss the initial three-card strong hands, I will point out the difference between holding a hidden pair or a split pair: a hidden pair is, for example, two face-down jacks and a king up; a split pair is jack and king face down and a jack face up. The probability of improving with the following one, two, three, or four cards is the same in both cases, but the player's chance of winning a big pot is much better with the hidden pair.

As mentioned earlier, it is possible to have four of a kind with no pairs showing, and when a player has such a hand, an opponent holding a full house, flush or straight is very likely to raise or reraise the hidden four of a kind, making for a big pot.

Strong plays in this game with the first three dealt cards are roughly as follows. Three of a kind, a holding such as 9-9-9, or any three of a kind, will usually end up a winning hand even if you don't better them. Any three cards in sequence as good as 8-9-10; any high pair, tens or better; any high concealed pair such as aces, kings, queens or jacks—all are strong. At times an ace or king in the hole, provided that one or more of the same rank is not shown in the opponent's face-up card, is strong.

Should the player go in with the above-described three-card hands, he will in the long run beat the player or players who start with three bad cards.

After the fourth card has been dealt and the second betting interval is to begin, you should fold if you fail to hold at least a high pair or a four-card straight or flush or a three-card straight flush. You may lessen these requirements if you can string along with a small call bet.

It may appear unusually tight for a player not to stay for a fifth card when holding a three-card straight or flush in his first four dealt cards, but the probabilities of the situation are against staying. The odds against the player ending up with a four-card straight or flush are about 8 to 1. Naturally, a player who always plays to the end in such circumstances will eventually fill in his straight or flush, but it's a sure bet that his gains will not cover the money lost in the process.

After the fifth card, the player should fold if he does not have at least a pair of queens or a four-card straight or flush. By this time the player should have some idea of the strength of the opponents' hands by the betting and the face-up cards shown on the table.

If no serious betting is taking place, a player's high pair is worth playing, provided that no card of that denomination has appeared face up. If it has, the player's chances of making three of a kind are so reduced that they aren't worth taking. A four-card straight or flush is usually worth staying for the sixth card, and generally for a seventh, especially if you have two or more opponents. However, there are two exceptions. One is when it appears that even if the player does make the straight or flush, his opponents may hold a higher-ranking hand —a seventh card is not worth the price of another card. The other exception is when odds against filling do not warrant the money contained in the pot.

Probabilities in Seven Card Stud

The following table gives the odds against being dealt various combinations with the first three dealt cards, plus the odds against improving various dealt combinations in Seven Card Stud (High) Poker. For strategic reasons many of these figures are somewhat deceptive—a player with only a potential hand may be forced to fold before he has received his complete hand.

THE ODDS AGAINST BEING DEALT A THREE-CARD STARTING HAND IN SEVEN CARD STUD

Chances of Being Dealt the Following on the First Three Cards	Number of Possible Combinations	Odds Against
Any three of a kind	52	424 to 1
Three aces	4	5,524 to 1
Three jacks, three queens or three kings	12	1,840 to 1
Three fives, three sixes, three sevens or three eights	16	1,380 to 1
Three twos, three threes, three fours, three fives, or three sixes	20	1,104 to 1
Any pair plus one odd card	3,744	4.90 to 1
A pair of aces and one odd card	288	75.7 to 1
A pair of jacks, queens or kings plus one odd card	864	24.5 to 1
A pair of twos, threes, fours, or fives plus one odd card	1,152	18.1 to 1
A pair of fives, sixes, sevens, eights, or nines plus one odd card	1,440	14.3 to 1
Three-card* straight flush	256	85.3 to 1
Three-card flush	888	23.8 to 1
Three-card straight	3,840	4.7 to 1

*There are 22,100 possible three-card combinations.

59. *Razz, Las Vegas Low Seven Card Stud*

Razz, one of the popular forms of Poker played in Nevada Poker rooms and in club games west of the Mississippi River, is far superior to the low five-card form of Stud Poker because each player is dealt seven cards and uses the best five of seven to form his hand. Razz is played in the same manner as Seven Card Stud High with two basic exceptions. First, the winning hand is the one which would be the lowest (worst) ranking hand in a game of Seven Card Stud High. Second, straights and flushes don't count and are eliminated from consideration. Aces count only as low. This game is played on the ace-to-five scale, where a 5-4-3-2-A is the best hand—no hand can be better. It is called a "wheel" or "bicycle."

In Razz, as in other forms of Poker, suits have no relative value, and if two players have the same valued hands they split the pot.

For the twenty best-ranking hands in this game, see California Lowball Ace to Five, page 132. Next in ranking come the pairs—the lower the pair the better the hand. If both players have identical pairs, then the highest-ranked odd card is lowest of the remaining cards. On the showdown, the best five-card low hand out of seven is the best hand and wins the pot.

A curious feature of Razz as played in Nevada is that the high upcard has to bet first in each betting interval. This means a player is throwing $3, $10, $20, $30, $100 into the pot, depending on the game limits, on a king, queen or jack. Normally someone showing a low upcard is going to raise the opening bet, and the opener usually throws in his hand without further play. After the first betting interval the best low hand starts each of the succeeding betting intervals.

This game is a much easier game to play strategically than Seven Card Stud High because here we're concerned with low cards only, whereas in Seven Card Stud High, those hole cards can hide all kinds of big, strong hands.

I wholeheartedly agree with Joey Hawthorne, one of America's best Lowball experts, who remarked that Razz contained 95% luck and only 5% skill.

Strategy in Razz

Here are some tips about the more strategic aspects of the game.

1. The first and most important thing to remember about Razz is that your starting hand is based principally on your first three dealt cards (two hole cards and one upcard) and what upcards your opponents have showing. Table position is most important in this game: Even though a player may alter his betting position on the next round, try to sit behind a player or players who call and raise more often, simply because they put their bets in the pot before it becomes your turn to bet.

2. It's important to remember as many opponents' exposed upcards as possible because that's the basis of expert play.

3. In this form of Seven Card Stud, the best strategy is to start with three odd good cards before the first betting interval. An excellent play is to begin the first round of play with three odd cards of which the highest is a seven. This is the recommendation of Johnny Moss, the dean of the Las Vegas Poker professionals, and I entirely agree with his Poker philosophy.

4. The minimum three-card hand you should hold against a raise at the start should be, at its worst, an 8-5-4.

5. As a rule, the higher an active opponent's upcard, the greater the possibility that he holds real good cards in the hole.

6. When you possess what you believe to be the best hand, you

must make your opponents pay big to call your hand on the showdown. Your raising should begin, if possible, with the first betting interval.

7. To prevent yourself from being labeled as a super-rock, you should occasionally go in with an eight high—otherwise you'll be playing about one in ten hands if you insist on not playing without a 7-6-5 or better in the first three dealt cards.

8. If you hold a 9-3-A and all your opponents show upcards higher than nines, you're in the driver's seat and you should make your opponents pay dearly.

9. So, to sum up—play with three odd cards, the highest being a seven. Bet big when you think you hold the best hand, and fold when you hold bad cards.

60. Seven Card Stud Low

This is a very popular private and club game throughout the South and the West. It is played for low, moderate and high stakes.

The main difference between Razz, the Nevada casino game, and this private and club-style game is that in this version of Low Poker, low card is forced to open the betting at each betting interval.

The strategy listed under Razz also applies for this Seven Card Stud Low.

61. Seven Card High-Low Stud (Declare)

Seven Card High-Low Stud with a Simultaneous Declaration rivals Seven Card Stud High as the most popular Poker gambling game in America. This version of Seven Card Stud is also known as Seven Card High-Low Split, and, as the name implies, the highest and the lowest hands split the pot.

Seven Card High-Low Stud Declare is the favorite gambling game of millions of small-time and moderate bettors comprised of women and men who meet once a week to play Poker. Big-time professional Poker players in Las Vegas and elsewhere refuse to play this Declare version of Seven Card High-Low Stud because it is a perfect game for cheating at the showdown by two signaling confederates, and it is most difficult to prove that signaling has taken place.

Most people who play this game regularly for small or moderate stakes agree that it is the best of all Poker games. It is remarkable that this is the only Poker game at which bad and good players are happy to play together continuously and exclusively; this is because of the action generated and the chance to share part of the pot by winning either high or low.

The game is played the same as Seven Card Stud, with the following exceptions and additional rules: The number of raises permitted in any particular round is three except when only two active players are involved. Then they can raise to their heart's content. In this variant, each active player is required to declare, after the last betting interval but before the showdown, whether he is going for high, for low or for both. At the showdown, each player's best five cards out of his seven may be used to form either a high or a low Poker hand, or he may also use his two best groups of five cards out of his seven to form both a high and a low Poker hand.

The rank or value of high hands is the same as in any Poker game; however, low hands are the reverse. The Scarne rule that follows is to count aces as both high and low. Therefore, the cinch or perfect low hand is 6-4-3-2-A of mixed suits. If they are all of the same suit it counts as a flush and in effect becomes a disaster when playing for low. Similarly, straights, including A-2-3-4-5, are considered high and disastrous for the low player. Treating the aces as either high or low adds extra zip and skill to Seven Card High-Low Stud Poker.

For detailed information on simultaneous declarations before the showdown and High-Low betting restrictions, see General Rules for Poker.

Strategy at Seven Card High-Low Stud

Most of the tips, hints, and strategies listed under Five Card Stud, Seven Card Stud and Razz are applicable to Seven Card High-Low Stud Declare, plus the following. The accepted strategy rule in this version of High-Low Stud is to start off by playing for low. If your first dealt cards are queen, queen, and a two, you are destined for a high declaration. However, at the showdown, you may find a starting low hand ending up with three of a kind or two big pairs and beating you for high. Consequently, to give your playing the flexibility of making either a low or high hand or both, it is best to start out playing for low.

A low three of a kind (aces, twos, threes, fours, fives or sixes) is an excellent starting hand because it will usually win for high with or without improvement and may also win the low. A pair of aces plus a low card is also an excellent three-card opening hand. A hidden low pair plus a low upcard is not really a good hand but it is worth a one- or two-card draw, provided that the cost of playing is not too excessive.

Naturally, if you sit there and wait for three low cards before entering the pot, you'll be playing very few hands and your opponents will consider you a rock, causing you to lose the element of deception which is essential to playing a winning game.

Following are the various starting three-card hands that I recommend.

1. Any three low cards (ace to seven).
2. Any low pair with an ace hidden.
3. A pair of aces plus a low card.
4. Any three of a kind.
5. Three-card flush with a low upcard.
6. Three cards in sequence no higher than 8-7-6.

To become a consistent winner at this game, at times you must do many things to deceive your opponents; these include changing your betting style and mannerisms in order to win pots. Expert players win many a pot with a weak hand simply by befuddling their opponents by raising just after being dealt a high card (king or queen) when they hold a cinch low hand. This kind of betting is done to get an opponent to declare low so that the expert may win the entire pot by his deceptive betting. This deceptive type of betting will often win a player many a big pot that his hand did not call to win.

Being able to read your opponents' hands is more important in becoming a winner in this version of Poker than in any other. Knowledge as to whether or not an opponent will declare either high or low makes an expert a sure winner at this game. Not too often does a player's opponent possess a hand that will permit him to declare both ways.

Anytime you can read an opponent's hand with a high degree of accuracy you take many pots or half pots even if you don't fill in your hand. To achieve this goal you simply declare the opposite way you believe your opponent will.

Contrary to what most Seven Card Stud Poker players believe, simultaneous declaration is a less mathematical game than most other forms of Poker. It is also more psychological. Expert players at Seven Card High-Low Stud Declare steal many more pots by deceptive declarations than an expert bluffer wins at Seven Card Stud High.

62. *Seven Card High-Low Split (Cards Speak)*

This version of High-Low Split is popular in our Western states, especially in Nevada's legalized Poker rooms, where it is the only high-low form of Poker played. The rules for Seven Card High-Low Stud Poker Declare apply with the following exceptions. 1. The game is played without a declaration prior to the showdown. The principal reason why the game is played without a declaration in Nevada's Poker rooms is that it is next to impossible for the Poker-room personnel to protect the game against cheating partners who specialize in signaling each other how to declare prior to the showdown. Also, the game is very difficult for the dealer to recall who declared high, low or both, thereby leading to continuous arguments. 2. In order to force the betting, on the first round the high upcard must bet first. Thereafter the low card is considered high and must act first (bet or check) in the four succeeding betting rounds. 3. Whenever there are more than two active players competing, there is a limit of one bet and three raises on each betting round. The three-raise limit is to prevent cheating partners from whipsawing other players.

Since this game is more streamlined than other high-low games, it's a much faster game than Declare, making it the perfect high-low casino game. This in turn lends itself particularly to the scientific and analytical-minded Poker player.

Generally speaking, in Nevada's Poker rooms, the ante runs from 10% to 15% of the minimum bet, but in many casinos the ante is much higher. Example: In Nevada's Poker rooms the antes average $10 in a $50 and $100 limit game, $15 in a $100 and $200 limit game, and $100 in a $300 and $600 limit game.

For detailed information on Cards Speak, see General Rules for Poker.

Strategy at Seven Card High-Low Split (Cards Speak)

Much of the strategy discussed under General Strategy (Chapter 4), Seven Card Stud High, and Seven Card Stud Low applies to this Cards Speak version of High-Low Split, in addition to the strategy that follows.

The basic strategy rule for most high-low games including this one is to play only low hands with the first three cards. The reason why I recommend such a rule is because a starting three-card hand can very often work itself into a two-way hand, whereas, with few exceptions, it is very unlikely that a three-card high hand will work itself into a low hand.

Top Las Vegas Poker pros, more often than not, fold a starting three-card high hand unless it's an exceptionally high strong hand such as three of a kind, etc. They claim there's no money in it when playing one-way hands, and that's what most high hands are—just one way.

But what one must remember is that there are also many low starting hands that cannot develop into two-way hands and should be folded as quickly as a starting high hand. Starting hands such as 7-3-2-K-5 and 6-6-4-3-Q with no flush possibilities should be folded, since their chances of a scoop both ways are quite remote.

Another important thing to remember is that whenever you catch a "paint" (jack, queen or king) as your fourth card and you are holding an average three-card low starting hand—fold, don't hesitate.

Following are listed several best two-way hands: A-A and 5 or lower, A-A-6 or lower, A-A-7 or lower and A-A-8 or lower, three small cards 5 or below, three small cards 6 or below.

Following are just a few of the countless unplayable starting hands found in High-Low Split. Any three-card starting hand that possesses two paints should not be played even if all three cards are suited. Whenever you play a hand with a paint in it, more often than not you'll be playing a six-card hand against your opponents' seven. If you follow the strategy rules listed above, your High-Low Split game will be greatly improved.

63. Hold Em Seven Card Stud, Club and Home Game

Hold Em, also known as Texas Hold Em and Texas Seven Card Stud, is one of the most popular commercial Poker games played in the Southwestern part of the United States. However, Hold Em's greatest popularity is found in Las Vegas Poker rooms, where it runs second to Seven Card Stud in popularity. In the legal and illegal Poker rooms throughout the Southwest, Hold Em is a big-money gambling game with plenty of action, excitement, skill and luck to keep any Poker player interested.

Due to the continuous national and international publicity on television and in the news media given the yearly Las Vegas World Series Hold Em Tournament, I've received many requests from club and home Poker players for a set of Hold Em rules to suit their game. However, the Hold Em rules of play as used in Nevada's legalized Poker rooms and the countless illegal Poker clubs throughout the Southwest pertain only to commercialized Poker—therefore these requests could not be fulfilled.

During the writing of this book I decided to remedy this situation by taking the liberty of changing the Las Vegas Hold Em rules of play to conform with club and home Poker. I take great pride in announcing that here for the first time in print are the playing rules for club and home Hold Em Poker.

All the preliminaries before the actual deal are as described under the General Rules for Poker, such as the pack of cards, rank of cards, rank of hands, preparations for play, betting limit, time limit, royalties, selecting the dealer and establishing seating positions at the table, the shuffle and cut, irregularities in cutting the cards, etc.

The advantage claimed for this game is that as many as twenty-three players can take part. The disadvantage is that more than nine players destroys the tempo of the game. The best game is played with two to nine players.

After the deck has been shuffled and cut, each player, before the cards are dealt out, antes an equal number of chips into the pot. All players must ante in turn, starting with the leader (player to the dealer's left) and rotating clockwise.

Next, each player, in clockwise fashion starting with the leader, is dealt two face-down (hole) cards, one at a time. After each player has received his two hole cards, the first betting interval takes place, the leader acting first. There are four betting intervals altogether. After the first betting interval, the dealer then deals three consecutive cards face up in the center of the table. These three cards are called "the flop." They are community cards used in common by every active player. This is followed by a second betting interval. After that, a fourth card is dealt face up and placed alongside the flop cards resting in the center of the table. This is followed by a third betting interval. A fifth and final card is dealt face up onto the center of the table, and a last interval of betting takes place.

If there are two or more active players left in the game at the end, the pot is won by the player with the best five-card hand made with either one or both of his hole cards combined with either three or four of the community cards resting on the center of the table. Sometimes the pot is split by two players holding identical hands (usually straights).

Strategy at Hold Em Poker

In low-limit games you must play good starting hands because it's most difficult to chase anybody out of a pot. But in high-limit Hold Em Poker, you very often can compel your opponents to drop out of the pot by taking advantage of position play and big betting.

A very important fact one must take into consideration to play a good game of Hold Em is to remember that each active player may make use of either three or four of the five community cards resting in the center of the table to complete his hand. With this in mind, it is important when playing a low-limit game to stay in with two good hole cards on the first betting round prior to the flop, so that when the flop is dealt, your superior hole cards will more often than not give you the edge and an opportunity to control the game.

Control of a small-limit game can only be had by holding superior hole cards. What hole cards does one stay in with is easier said than decided upon. If you're the leader (first to bet) you need better cards than if you were last to bet.

Two aces in the hole are naturally the best hand. They are considerably stronger with only one active opponent on the showdown, but no other two hole cards will win more pots, regardless of the number of active players.

Following are the ten best-rated two-card hands held by a player with his first two dealt cards and the odds against such an occurrence.

Player's Hand	Odds Against
1. A pair of aces	220 to 1
2. A pair of kings	220 to 1
3. Ace and king of the same suit	331 to 1
4. A pair of queens	220 to 1
5. Ace and king of different suits	110 to 1
6. Ace and queen of the same suit	331 to 1
7. Ace and queen of different suits	110 to 1
8. King and queen of the same suit	331 to 1
9. King and queen of different suits	110 to 1
10. A pair of jacks	220 to 1

The total number of two-card hands before the flop is 1,326, and the odds against a player holding any pair in the hole are 16 to 1. The odds against a player holding any two cards suited in the hole are 3.24 to 1.

The ten ranked hands, but not their probabilities, however, are based on a full game comprised of six to nine players with an average of four or five players staying for the flop. Some of these hands become more valuable with fewer players, others with more players. Example: Low pairs, possible straights and flushes become more valuable with four or five players; high-valued pairs become less valuable. The ace and king predominate in the above-listed hands and are more powerful if they are of the same suit in a hand. A player holding ace and king of the same suit not only has a possibility of making the highest pairs, but also for a straight or flush ace high.

A pair of aces, kings, queens, or ace, king of the same suit deserve a raise before the flop, and the reasons are as follows. First, you tend to narrow down the number of active opponents, thereby improving your chances of winning the pot. Second, you increase the money in the pot with a good hand.

Once the flop has dropped, there are two things you need to be aware of in every pot in which you're involved. First, how much money is in the pot and do the odds against your winning the pot warrant your bet? Second, who, if anyone, has raised and how many players behind you are still to act?

Probably the most important thing to remember in Hold Em is that it is a seven-card game, and after the flop two cards are still to come. That's where luck takes over.

64. Hold Em, Las Vegas Style

All the rules of Hold Em, Club and Home Game apply to Hold Em, Las Vegas Style with the following exceptions.

1. Limit-Hold Em is rarely played with more than eleven players, and table stakes Hold Em is most often played with nine or fewer players.

2. The dealer is a house employee at all times. He runs the game, handles the antes and bets, and deals the game. The house dealer also shuffles the cards and cuts them (one straight cut).

Because the last player in Hold Em to act (bet, raise or fold) has a decided advantage (and to make things equal for each player), the theoretical deal moves around the table clockwise from player to player. A rotating button is placed in front of a player to signify that he is the dealer in terms of betting and acting last.

3. The house charge (rake) depends on the particular Poker room and the size of the limits. In the low-limit games, the charge is higher in terms of percentage and can run as high as 25%. In the very high-limit games the charge varies from Poker room to Poker room and is usually based on the hour.

4. The ante also varies, but for a $1 and $3 game it is usually 10 cents, 25 cents, or 50 cents and goes up in proportion to the betting limits.

5. After the cards have been shuffled and cut by the house dealer, he "burns" the top card of the deck by dealing it face down in front of him, out of play. He then proceeds to deal each player two face-down cards, one at a time in clockwise fashion beginning with the leader (player on the left of the button), who is the first player to bet and thus is under the gun. In most Hold Em high-limit games the dealer burns the top card of the deck before dealing each additional round of cards.

In high-limit and table stakes Hold Em, the game is usually played with a blind. The leader is said to be "in the blind" and must make a forced bet to start the action. The blind is also "live," permitting the leader the option of raising when the turn of play gets back to him—or he can play (call) without putting any more chips into the pot provided his blind bet has not been raised. In low-limit Hold Em there is usually an opening blind preceded by an ante from each player. Often the high-limit version is played with multiple blinds and no ante.

If you are seriously thinking of plunking down $10,000 to qualify as a contestant in the Horseshoe Club's yearly Las Vegas World Series Hold Em Championship, I would suggest that you first visit the Poker room in the Golden Nugget Casino in downtown Las Vegas and sit yourself down at the $10 and $20 limit Hold Em table. Should you spend eight hours or so a day for several days gambling at that table, and should you come out a winner, you are prepared to enter the World Series Hold Em Championship, because that table is patronized by the best Hold Em players available in Las Vegas at the time. It is the toughest public Poker game anywhere, and a win there after several days' play qualifies you as a topnotch Hold Em player and ready to take on the best in the nation.

This $10 and $20 limit Hold Em table is in session almost every day of the year. This game is usually dealt to a full table of eleven with a small 50-cent ante. The leader to the left of the button (theoretical dealer) must make an opening blind bet of $5. Thereafter, each player at his proper turn of play may fold, call the $5 blind bet, or increase it to $10. This bet is not considered a raise, but a completion of the $5 blind bet, making for a $10-unit bet. Players to follow may now call the $10 bet or raise it to $20. However, if the $5 blind bet is not raised by the time it gets back to the blind, he has the right to increase his $5 blind bet to $10—or he may merely let it ride. Should the blind increase the bet to $10, players may now call the $10 bet or raise it to $20.

All bets after the flop, be they call bets, raises or reraises, must be made in units of $10. The bets and raises or reraises after the sixth and seventh cards have been dealt must be in units of $20.

The tips, hints and strategy described under Hold Em, Club and Home Game also apply to this version of Hold Em.

65. English Stud Poker

This is the standard Stud game played in the English-speaking countries, especially England, Australia and South Africa. In most

London gaming clubs it is usually the only kind of Stud Poker permitted. English Stud is a fascinating and exciting game that combines the best features of Draw Poker and Seven Card Stud.

Terence Reese, England's top Bridge and Poker expert, once wrote, "English Stud is a highly skilled game, perhaps one of the four most difficult Poker games to play well." I wholeheartedly agree with this statement.

The rules for Five Card Stud apply, with the following exceptions and additional rules.

Each player's first two dealt cards are dealt face down and the third card face up. Then the first betting interval takes place. When the first betting interval has been completed, a fourth card, face up, is dealt to each active player, followed by a second betting interval. Then a fifth card, face up, is dealt to each active player followed by a third betting interval.

Now each active player has the option to discard a face-up card or a face-down card or stand pat (refuse to draw). If a player discards a face-up card, he is dealt a face-up card. If he discards a face-down card, he is dealt a face-down card.

Upon the completion of the first discard and replacement, the fourth betting interval takes place, followed by a second and last discard and replacement (same as the first), and the fifth and final betting interval takes place.

Strategy: The rank of winning hands is much greater than in Five Card Stud because of the two discards and replacements. The most common mistakes made by the average player are staying with a low pair or staying after the third betting interval with a three-card straight or flush.

The rank of final hands is slightly lower in this English Stud variation than those found in Seven Card Stud High, merely because the two discards and draws make it considerably more difficult to improve the first five dealt cards. In this game the average winning hands are a low three of a kind, such as three fives or lower, or a high two pairs. There are fewer flushes and straights made than in regular Seven Card Stud.

Good plays in this English Stud game on the first three dealt cards (two hole cards and the third card face up) are roughly as follows: Any three cards in sequence are good, as a jack-ten-nine, or any three cards of the same suit; any high pair, eights or better; any pair in the hole; and ace-king in the hole, provided that opponents' face-up cards do not reveal one or more aces or kings.

The tactics of betting and raising in this Stud variation are almost identical to those in Five Card Stud. The one difference is that in English Stud one can seldom be nearly so sure of possessing the winning hand, because the discard and draw of the last two cards may play havoc with your hand. Early raises are about the same in one game as in the other. However, bets and raises in the fourth and fifth betting intervals in English Stud are in a class by themselves. The opponents' bets, discards, draws, stand pats and upcards must now be taken into consideration. Example: If your most serious betting opponent shows three cards of different numerical value which cannot be made into a straight or flush, he cannot possibly have better than three of a kind of his highest upcard. However, if you can account for two cards of that rank, then his best three-of-a-kind hand will be three of a kind of one of the two next remaining face cards shown. As in all Stud games, you must be careful of betting into a possible cinch hand.

66. *English Low Stud Poker*

This is one of the best Low Stud Poker games found anywhere. The rules of play are exactly the same as those governing English Stud Poker, described above, with one notable exception. The winning hand is the one that would be the "worst," that is, the lowest-ranking, in a game of English Stud Poker. In addition, aces count low, straights and flushes count high, and the best possible low cinch hand is 6-4-3-2-A.

The game requires less concentration than California Lowball because the information gathered from active opponents' discards is more revealing. Generally speaking, the rank of hands on the showdown is higher than in California Lowball, due to the two single card draws after the fifth card has been dealt. The average winning hand in a six-or-more-handed game is an eight high or better.

Strategy: After three or four cards have been dealt to each player, play if you have (1) the best showing hand; (2) you hold only one card higher than a nine; (3) should a good one card draw give you a better hand showing than any of your opponents. Raise if you hold three good low cards in the first three or four dealt cards and no one has previously raised.

After each player has received his fifth card, play with a three-card eight, if no raises have preceeded. If no raises have occurred, raise with a four-card high nine.

After the second discard and draw, the player who has the best hand showing and acts first will usually have the edge and should raise. On the showdown, you will often be able to judge that an opponent is not so strong as he pretends by recalling his betting style on earlier betting intervals, and which cards the opponent had discarded and replaced.

THE ACCUSATION THAT ROCKED THE BRIDGE WORLD

The mention of Terence Reese's name in connection with English Stud Poker brings back memories of the Bridge accusation that rocked the Bridge world. It was the year 1965 when the American Bridge team entry of B. Jay Becker and Dorothy Hayden, playing in the World's Duplicate Bridge Championship Tournament held in Buenos Aires, Argentina, accused Terence Reese and Boris Shapiro, members of the British team, of cheating by supposedly making use of illegal finger signals. Alan Truscott, the Bridge columnist for *The New York Times*, who at the time was covering the tournament for his paper, joined Becker and Hayden in accusing Reese and Shapiro of cheating.

The Reese and Shapiro case led to several lawsuits and a full-length inquiry by the British Bridge League. The inquiry included the examination and cross-examination of dozens of witnesses including the accused and the accusers. The verdict: Reese and Shapiro were acquitted of cheating. The World Bridge Federation, however, had previously ruled that Reese and Shapiro were guilty of using illegal finger signals.

Sometime after the Buenos Aires Bridge debacle, I received a phone call from Alan Truscott (now married to Dorothy Hayden) inquiring if I would write the introduction to an upcoming book supporting charges that Reese and Shapiro cheated in the Buenos Aires Championship Bridge Tournament.

Truscott apparently thought the validity of the cheating accusations leveled against Reese and Shapiro needed further affirmation, so he dreamed up the idea that John Scarne (famous for his card-cheating exposés during World War II) should write the introduction supporting the accusations, thereby strengthening the cheating charges.

Truscott later forwarded to me a set of the page proofs to read. I don't recall if the book was authored by Truscott, Hayden, or both. What I do remember, however, is that after reading the page proofs I concluded they failed miserably to substantiate the serious cheating accusations leveled at Reese and Shapiro. Hence, I refused to write the introduction. Reese and Shapiro had been accused of cheating by supposedly making use of the most childish and ludicrous code of finger suit signals that has ever come to my attention.

I recognize Terence Reese as one of the world's top Bridge and Poker experts and therefore it's beyond my comprehension that if Reese wanted to cheat he would resort to this childish and readily detectable signal code that he and Shapiro were accused of using. Particularly so when I considered the countless number of undetectable signaling codes used by various Bridge experts at championship tournaments.

A detailed explanation of the finger-signaling code supposedly used by Reese and Shapiro to cheat at the World's Duplicate Bridge Championship Tournament in Buenos Aires as described by Truscott, Hayden, Becker and others follows. The code allegedly worked in this way: Whenever Reese or Shapiro held one, two, three or four fingers on the back of their thirteen-card hand prior to the bidding, it meant that the holding in the heart suit was one, two, three or four hearts respectively. When two fingers were spread apart, this meant a holding of five hearts. Three fingers spread apart meant a holding of six hearts. Truscott, Hayden or Becker failed to mention the finger signal code for a void or seven or more hearts.

If you want absolute proof of the detectability of this childish finger-signaling code, place a Bridge hand of thirteen cards on the table. Next, pick up the cards and hold them in your normal manner. Then, after looking at your Bridge hand, readjust your fingers on the back of your hand to hold the cards in each of the finger positions described above. If this finger-movement adjustment is not detected by the lowliest Bridge player after one session of play, my name is not John Scarne.

I have no doubt that if Reese really wanted to cheat in that tournament, he would have made use of one of the countless undetectable suit signal methods used by various international Bridge experts, which I'm sure he is familiar with.

My comments concerning the Buenos Aires Bridge accusation should not be construed to mean that cheating does not take place in national and international championship tournaments. As a matter of fact, of the more than three thousand Bridge tournaments played annually in this country and abroad, few, if any, are completed without one or more incidents in which a team appeals to the tournament directors for redress from some cheating practice committed by an opposing team. And much more tournament cheating takes place that goes undetected by the players. I know because I've seen it.

Of the hundreds of card games being played today, Poker, Rummy and Bridge are responsible for the most crookedness. Bridge, because of its partnership play, offers more opportunities for both the amateur and skilled card cheat than any other card game. The most common cheating method in Bridge is illegal signaling (during the bidding and the play of the hand) by facial gestures, hand or foot signals, vocal hesitations, or body movements. A pair of cheats trained in the art of signaling can get away with murder even among top Bridge masters.

The World Bridge Federation (WBF) tried to remedy the situation in early 1975 at the World Team Championship of Contract Bridge held in Bermuda. In an effort to prevent partners from illegally conveying the strength of their suit hands to each other, the WBF installed a large opaque wooden screen (three feet high and five feet wide) diagonally across the table so that the partners would not be visible to one another. In addition, bidding boxes were installed to receive written bids so that partners could not hear one another. The two bids from one side of the screen were called aloud to the players by a tournament official. After the bidding ended and the opening lead had been made, the screen was lifted from the table and normal play proceeded. To eliminate foot signals a screen was also installed under the table. The WBF, however, failed to take into account that considerable signal cheating among partners takes place during the actual play of the hand. In 1978 the American Contract Bridge League, in an attempt to eliminate the possibility of partners' signaling one another during the bidding and play of the hand installed a hanging curtain over the table. After the bidding, this curtain is raised just enough for the players to see the playing surface of the table. Sorry to say, neither the wooden screen nor the curtain eliminates signal cheating. At the time of writing a number of illegal suit-bidding codes have made their appearances in Bridge tournaments, thereby making the large opaque wooden screen and the curtain separating the partners worthless.

It's my opinion that the introduction by the World Bridge Federation of the opaque screen and the American Contract Bridge League's curtain, with all their so-called precautionary anticheating devices, will do more harm to Bridge in the future than all the notoriety given the actual or imaginary cheating that takes place in Bridge, be it in private, club or tournament play.

13

Five Card Stud Poker Variations

FACTS ABOUT STUD POKER VARIATIONS

In the following selection of the miscellaneous Stud Poker variations, there are many which appear in print for the first time. The variants are of Five Card Stud, unless otherwise specified. These games have been collected from years of watching various kinds of Stud Poker being played in cardrooms, Poker clubs and casinos here and abroad. I have divided the Stud, or Open, Poker variants into two general categories: Basic Variations of Stud Poker and Miscellaneous Stud Poker Variants. The player will find the rules governing these games under General Rules for Poker, under Five, Six and Seven Card Stud Poker Rules, and in the text that follows.

BASIC VARIATIONS OF STUD POKER

67. Five Card Stud—Deuces Wild

Played exactly as is Five Card Stud, except that the deuces are wild, and on the showdown cards do not speak for themselves; a player must announce the value of his hand in his proper turn of play. Announcement cannot be changed after a player's turn of play has passed on the showdown. Often the joker is added as an extra wild card.

Strategy in the private game of Five Card Stud, Deuces Wild: You must remember that there are four wild cards, and when the joker is added that makes five wild cards. Therefore hands such as two pairs and three of a kind, which would ordinarily be winning hands in regular Five Card Stud, will most often become losers when an opponent's hand is comprised of one or more wild cards.

To win, you have to reevaluate your playing hand much higher. If a pair of jacks was a raising hand in regular Five Card Stud, increase it to three of a kind in this variant. When you do this, you'll come out all right. Wild cards shouldn't deter the tight, strong player because players loosen up and more players stay to the showdown, making for bigger pots.

68. *Five Card Stud with the Bug*

Played exactly as Five Card Stud except that the joker is added, making a 53-card deck, and the joker is used only as the "bug" (only as an ace or a wild card to fill a straight or flush).

In this game, beware of aces, which assume great importance when the bug is in play. There are now five aces that can be made and many more straights and flushes. For complete strategy in making use of the bug, see California Draw Poker with the Bug (pages 106–108).

69. *Five Card Stud—Joker Wild*

Played the same as Five Card Stud except that the joker as a wild card is added to the standard 52-card deck. A player may count the joker as any card he wishes. Should a player hold four of a kind and the joker, he has five of a kind, which beats a royal flush. The reason for playing with a joker is to loosen the game and increase the action. In Draw Poker it seems to work that way, but in Five Card Stud, strangely enough, the added joker decreases the action because if the joker appears as an upcard in a player's hand, opponents who do not hold a good hand immediately drop out. Furthermore, any player who raises is usually suspected of having the joker in the hole.

70. *Five Card Stud—Last Card Down*

A fascinating variation of Five Card Stud. This game is very popular in my neck of the woods, northern New Jersey. This variation is played the same as Five Card Stud except that the last card (fifth) is dealt face down giving each active player two hole cards and three upcards.

Dealing the last card down makes for a good game. All the strategy and mathematics described under Five Card Stud apply to this variation. Furthermore, due to the second hole card, much more bluffing takes place.

In this variant it is best to be more conservative than in Five Card Stud.

71. Five Card Stud—Five Bets

This game, which is also known as Pistol Pete, Hole Card Stud, and John's Poker, is played as is Five Card Stud Poker, except that there is an extra betting round that occurs after the hole cards have been dealt to each player and before any upcards are dealt.

On the first betting round the leader must make the first bet. He cannot check nor drop out. Thereafter, on each betting interval, high card or high hand bets first.

The only difference from regular Five Card Stud is the additional round of betting after each player has received his hole card. This game, rather than increasing the action of regular Stud, does just the opposite, since Poker hustlers and tight players fold on the first dealt hole card unless they get a high card (ace, king, queen, jack). In social or friendly games, however, the game is fun, since most players stay in the pot with any kind of hole card. However, even in social or friendly games, this game possesses a great weakness—namely, that the Poker hustler or the tight player who plays only with an ace or king in the hole will eventually win all the money.

72. New York Five Card Stud

This variation of regular Five Card Stud is very popular with big-time gamblers in the state of New York, where it has become known as New York Poker. In this variant a four flush (a four-card flush) beats a single pair but loses to two pairs or higher. In the final betting round a player with a four flush showing bets first, as compared to a player with a high card or any single pair showing.

While regular Five Card Stud is the tightest of all Poker games, the introduction of the four-card flush transforms it into a fine and looser game. And it appears that the only time a player folds early is when he holds two low cards of different suits.

Actually the only real skill in this game consists of betting a good opening hand to the maximum limit. Let's suppose you have a high pair back to back, and some other active player made the opening bet, raise when it comes your turn to bet. Should your first three cards be of the same suit, the odds against making your four flush are about 1½ to 1 against. Accordingly, if the pot odds are good, it is well worth a couple of raises. In short, if you hold a three-card flush in the first three cards, you are in the driver's seat.

But don't think that being dealt a four flush in your five dealt cards is any easy matter. As a matter of fact, probabilities inform us that there are 115,540 possible four flushes that you can draw from. But since the total five-card combinations (hands) in a 52-card deck are 2,598,960, we divide this total by 115,540 (four-card flushes) and learn that the chances of being dealt a four flush is 1 in 22.49 deals. And the chances of being dealt two pairs is 1 in 21.03 deals. This proves that a four flush should not only beat a single pair but two pairs as well—but that's not the way this game is played. However, I'm sure this knowledge will serve you well.

73. *Spanish Stud Poker*

This variation is played the same as is Five Card Stud Poker, and the same rules apply, with the following exception—a 32-card deck is used, made up by stripping out all the twos, threes, fours, fives and sixes.

74. *Canadian Five Card Stud*

Canadian Five Card Stud is played the same as New York Five Card Stud, in which a four-card flush beats a pair, but in this game a four-card straight beats a pair and a four-card flush beats a four-card straight. Skill is even more important here than in regular Five Card Stud and New York Stud.

As mentioned earlier, there are 115,540 five-card combinations in a 52-card deck that make a four-card flush. The chances of catching a four-card flush in a five-card hand are 1 in 22.49 deals. Furthermore, there are 408,576 possible five-card combinations that contain four-card straights, and the chances of catching one of these is 1 in 6.36 deals.

The strategy in New York Five Card Stud shown above also applies to this variation, except that the player requires more analytical observation in deducing the opponents' possibilities in making four-card straights.

75. *Five Card Double-Handed High-Low Stud*

In this game, which is also called Bimbo High-Low, the play is the same as Five Card Stud except for the following:

1. Each player is dealt two hands of five cards each. Each hand is dealt separately in turn and is bet as a different hand.
2. When a player bets on one of his hands, his other hand must call the bet, along with the opponents, or fold.
3. A player may fold one hand at any time and stay with the other.
4. Before showdown, each player announces what he is going to do with each hand—go low, or high, or high-low.

76. *Five Card Stud with Spit Cards*

Played the same as Five Card Stud except that at the dealer's option after each round of betting the dealer calls "Spit" and deals a face-up spit card in the center, which may be used by all players in making their best hand. This is followed by a round of betting. The dealer has the option of refusing to deal a spit card in the center—whenever he chooses. This game slightly favors the dealer because, should he hold a valuable hand, he may not spit. However, with each player having a turn at dealing, the odds are equalized.

77. *Three Card Substitution*

Also known as Three Card Buy, this game is a high-low variation of Five Card Stud, but after each player's fifth card has been dealt and its betting round is completed, the dealer calls "Buy one," or "Substitution one." Then, each player in turn is permitted to discard and draw a card. Players may discard an upcard or a hole card. If an upcard is discarded, the player receives an upcard. If a hole card is discarded, the player receives a face-down card. After the first substitution, or "buy-in," there is a round of betting. Dealer then calls "Substitution two," and there is another substitution followed by another round of betting. Then the dealer calls "Substitution three," followed by a discard and draw and a final betting round. A player may reject the opportunity to substitute any time he wishes. The substitutions, or buy-ins, are not free; they must be paid for. In a one-, two-, and three-unit-limit game, the first buy-in costs three units, the second costs six units, and third costs nine units.

78. *Two Card Buy or Substitution*

Played the same as Three Card Substitution except that only two substitutions, or buy-ins, are permitted.

79. *One Card Buy or Substitution*

Played the same as Three Card Substitution except that only one buy-in is permitted.

80. *Crazy Five Card High-Low Stud*

This unusual type of Stud Poker, also called Shove 'Em Along, Forward Pass, Take It or Leave It, Push, and Rothschild, is played the same as Five Card Stud, with the following exceptions and additional rules:

1. Crazy Five Card High-Low Stud begins with each player receiving a hole card. The dealer then deals an upcard to the leader (player at his left). The leader has two alternatives: He may keep the upcard or pass it on to the player on his left. If he passes it on, he receives another dealt upcard, which he must keep. However, if he decides to keep the original dealt card, the dealer deals an upcard for the next player in turn. This player also has the option of keeping the upcard or passing it to the next rightful player.

2. The procedure continues clockwise around the table with each player either accepting a passed upcard or passing it on to the player on his left and having the dealer deal him an upcard in its place, which he must keep; or if he has not been passed a card, the dealer must deal him an upcard, and he has the option of keeping the upcard or passing it to the player on his left, in which case he will be dealt a second upcard, which he must keep. In any event, a player is not permitted to accept a passed card and have an upcard dealt to him too.

3. The above procedure continues until the dealer's turn of play, when he is bound by the following rules: He may accept a passed card or refuse it and burn it (place it face up) on the bottom of the deck. If he refuses it, he deals himself an upcard, which he must keep. If a passed card has not been offered to him, he may keep his first dealt upcard, or burn it and deal himself a second upcard, which he must keep.

4. When each player has received a hole card and his first upcard, a betting interval takes place. After the betting, the dealer deals a second round of upcards and the play continues as before. This deal is again followed by a betting interval, and this procedure of play and betting continues until each remaining player has a hole card and four upcards and the fourth betting interval takes place.

5. And now comes another unusual aspect of this fascinating game:

a delayed showdown. Each remaining player in turn may discard his hole card or any upcard and be dealt another card in its place. If a hole card is discarded, a face-down card is dealt in its place. If an upcard is discarded, a face-up card is dealt in its place.

6. The fifth and final round of betting then takes place, followed by a high-low showdown. At the showdown, the highest and the lowest hands divide the pot equally.

81. *Five Card Turn-Up Stud*

This game is also known as Mexican Stud, Peep-and-Turn, and Flip Poker, and is played the same as Five Card Stud, with the following exceptions and additional rules:

The first two cards are dealt face down to each player, and he has the option of turning up whichever one he chooses. This is followed by a betting interval in which high hand bets first. The third card is also dealt face down, and again the player has the option of turning up either card. This is followed by another betting interval. Each player's fourth and fifth (last) cards are also dealt face down, and another betting interval takes place after each player turns up his optional card. A player may turn up either his previous hole card or the one just dealt, but he must always have only one card in the hole.

The strategy for Five Card Stud applies to this fascinating variant.

82. *Shifting Sands*

This game is played the same as Five Card Turn-Up Stud except that the first card that a player turns up and every other card of the same rank in his hand at the showdown are wild.

83. *Monterey*

Played like Five Card Turn-Up Stud, except that in this game, which has been called Rickey de Laet by some, every player's hole card and every other card of the same rank in his hand are wild.

84. *Blind Five Card Stud*

Played like Five Card Stud, with the following exceptions and additional rules:

One card is dealt each player face down followed by a betting round started by the leader. A second face-down card is dealt each player, followed by a second betting round. The leader starts the betting each time a card is dealt. The same procedure of being dealt face-down cards and betting is followed until five cards have been dealt face down. No player may check; he must either bet, raise or get out. This game may also be played with deuces wild or with the added joker as wild card.

85. Pig Five Card Stud

This is a variation of Five Card Stud and Five Card Draw Poker combined. The rules are as follows:

1. The player whose turn it is to deal antes an agreed amount into the pot.
2. Each player is dealt three face-down cards, one at a time, in rotation.
3. The leader, as in Stud Poker, makes the first bet, followed by each player in rotation, and each player at his turn of play may check, bet, raise or drop out.
4. After this betting round is completed, a fourth card face up is dealt to each player and another betting round takes place, with high card betting first. The fifth card dealt, also an upcard, is followed by a betting interval.
5. The player now has five cards, three face down and two face up. He picks up the two upcards and places them face down among the three face-down cards; he then plays it out as in Five Card Draw Poker by discarding and drawing to his hand, or by standing pat.

Pig Five Card Stud Poker is considerably more interesting, incidentally, when played deuces wild and joker wild.

86. Six Card Stud

This is a fascinating version of Five Card Stud and it possesses an additional betting round for a total of five. Played the same as Five Card Stud with the above exception plus the two rules that follow.

1. A player is dealt his sixth card face down to give him two hole cards and four upcards.
2. The best five cards out of six may be used to form a Poker hand. In staying in the early rounds, all you have to do is follow the same strategy as you would in Five Card Stud.

This is an additional Six Card Stud variation: To start the game each player is dealt two hole cards and one upcard, as in Seven Card Stud. After the first betting round, another upcard is dealt, followed by a second betting round. Then a third and fourth upcard are dealt each player, followed by a third and fourth betting round.

Follow the same strategy in this game as that described under Seven Card Stud (page 204). However, a player must remember that good hands are considerably more difficult to come by in this game than they are in Seven Card Stud.

87. *Six Card High-Low Stud*

Played the same as Six Card Stud, in which the player gets his sixth card in the hole, plus the following additional rule: Any player may go for high or low, or both, according to rules governing high-low declarations as found under General Rules for Poker, page 45. As in Seven Card High-Low, the best starting high hand is three of a kind, and the best low hand is three very low cards. However, in this six-card game, three of a kind wins many a hand, and two pairs follow right behind.

88. *Seven Card Stud—Deuces Wild Plus the Joker*

Played exactly like Seven Card Stud, except that a joker is added as a wild card and the deuces are wild. In this variation of Stud, cards shown do not speak; player must call or announce his hand. Once called, hand must stand; it cannot be changed.

Strategy: Because of the deuces and joker wild, there are frequent two-way hands. Thus the game is often referred to as Hog It. Anything can happen in this game, such as four or five of a kind, and even royal flushes. The high is rarely won with less than four of a kind. In fact, a low four of a kind often loses the pot. Anything other than a sixty-five in the low department is usually a loser.

Following are playable hands for your first dealt three cards: six or lower, low hole card paired, a pair of aces, kings, queens or jacks, and a three-card straight or flush.

89. *Seven Card Stud—Low Hole Card Wild*

This is one of the few Poker games with wild cards that I have seen played high-limit table stakes by professional gamblers—in Hot Springs, Arkansas, a while back. During my observance I witnessed a number of pots that each totaled $10,000 and better.

This game is played like Seven Card Stud, except that the lowest-ranking card in the hole is wild, and all in the hand of the same denomination are also wild. Example: Suppose in your first three dealt cards you have a six and an ace in the hole and a six up. You now have two wild cards, or, if you wish, three aces. However, this is a game that can easily backfire on you. You must always bear in mind that Low Hole Card Wild is the name of the game. In the above example, you hold two sixes and an ace, or, to repeat, three aces. However, your final seventh card is dealt face down (hole card), and it turns out to be a deuce—you no longer hold three aces, but two aces instead.

Even a backed-up pair of jacks in the hole is worth nothing because you have to catch a king or queen on the seventh card (third hole card) to still have two wild cards—three jacks.

On the showdown, if you don't have two or more wild cards, you've got a losing hand. Suppose you have a seven and a queen in the hole and your first upcard is a king and your second upcard is an eight. Your seven is wild and all you possess is a pair of kings. It's almost a sure bet that in a seven-handed game at least several of your active opponents can beat a pair of kings on their first four dealt cards.

This is one of a very few Poker games where you may hold four of a kind with your sixth dealt card. Then you are dealt your seventh and last card (hole card) and bango, you now possess a low-high full house.

90. Seven Card High-Low Progressive Stud

Played the same as Seven Card High-Low Stud, with the following exceptions and additional progressive betting rules: The first player to the dealer's left starts the first round of betting, and he must bet one unit (10 cents) or drop out. On the second round of betting the second player on the dealer's left must start the betting with two units (20 cents) or drop out. On the third round of betting the third player to the dealer's left starts the betting with three units (30 cents) or drops out. The fourth player on the dealer's left starts the fourth round of betting with four units (40 cents) or drops out. On the fifth and final round the fifth player on the dealer's left starts the betting with five units (50 cents) or drops out. Should a player whose turn it is to bet drop out, the turn to bet rotates to the next active player, and so on.

The strategy is identical to that of Seven Card High-Low Stud, (pages 209–10).

91. Seven Card High-Low Stud with a Joker

This game is played like a Seven Card High-Low Stud as described earlier, but it is played with 52 cards plus a joker. The joker is called the "bug" and may be used as an ace or as a wild card in a straight or flush.

To play to win you must play a tighter game than in regular Seven Card High-Low. Two pairs is a relatively good hand in Seven Card High-Low, but not in this variation, due to the easier chances of filling a straight or flush. Conversely, a better low hand is required because of the fifth wild ace. High-Low hands are more common in this variation of Seven Card High-Low, since the wild joker in a low hand can more easily include a low straight. Example: a hand comprised of joker, 6,2,4,5,K,J is a sixty-five low and a straight.

If you lack the joker with your first three dealt cards, stay only on a strong three-card low or a three-card high. An eight or nine low should never be your goal, since the joker plays havoc with low hands.

92. *Flip Seven Card Stud*

In this variation of Seven Card Stud, four face-down cards are dealt to each player. After examining them he may turn up any two. There is a betting interval, then play proceeds as in regular Seven Card Stud, with three more cards dealt, two up and one down, a betting interval following each.

In another variation, each player first receives two cards, one up and one down, followed by a betting interval; then another two cards, one up and one down, and another betting interval; then two cards, one up and one down, a third time, and a betting interval; then a seventh card face down. Each player then discards one of his face-down cards and one of his face-up cards, leaving himself with three concealed cards and two exposed cards. The final betting interval and showdown follow.

93. *Kankakee Seven Card Stud*

In this Seven Card Stud variation, there is a betting round after two hole cards are dealt, beginning with the player at the dealer's left. Then, the first face-up card to each player is wild and all like it are wild to that player only. After the wild cards are given there is a betting interval, starting with the player at dealer's left. Three more face-up cards and one final face-down card are then dealt to each active player, with a betting interval after each.

94. Seven Card Stud Rollover

This game, which is also called Beat Your Neighbor, Beat It, No Peekie, and No Lookie, is similar to Seven Card Stud except for the following:

1. Seven face-down cards are dealt, one at a time, to each player, moving clockwise from the dealer's left. Keeping their hands concealed, even to themselves, the players arrange them into a pack, which is placed face down on the table. Then the player to the left of the dealer rolls over (turns face up) one card and bets on it. After the betting round, the player to the leader's left rolls over cards until he beats the card turned over by the leader. There is another betting round. Play continues in this way with each remaining player.
2. This procedure of rolling over cards until the player beats the card turned over by the player before him, followed by a betting round, continues around the table.
3. When a player runs out of cards without beating the preceding player, he is out of the game.
4. Play continues around the table until one player presents an unbeatable hand and wins the pot.

95. Anaconda Seven Card Stud

This game is played like Seven Card Stud except for the following:

1. Seven cards are dealt, face down, one at a time to each player. A single betting round follows, beginning with the person on the dealer's left.
2. After the close of the betting round, each player passes three cards of his choosing, face down, to the player on his left. The pass is made simultaneously by all players on a signal from the dealer. Following the pass, a betting round commences with the player to the dealer's left.
3. On completion of the second betting round, each player passes two cards, face down, to the player on his left, and a betting round follows in the same manner as before.
4. After the third betting round, each player passes one card, face down, to the player on his left, and a betting round follows in the same manner as in rule 2.
5. After the betting has stopped, each player selects his best five cards and places them, face down, in a pack before him on the table.
6. On signal from the dealer, each player rolls the top card of his

pack. When everyone has one card exposed on the table, a betting round opens, starting with the player exhibiting the highest card. Then another card is simultaneously rolled over by all active players, and another round of betting follows, and so forth. The game can be played either as a high game or as a high-low game. In the latter case players must declare low or high hands at the end of the betting round when only one card remains, face down, in front of each player. This last card is then rolled for the showdown, and low and high hands divide the pot.

Note: Frequently Anaconda Seven Card Stud is played with only one passing phase. That is, rules 3 and 4 are omitted.

96. *Screwy Louis Seven Card Stud*

This game is played the same as Anaconda Seven Card Stud except that each player passes two discards to the active player nearest his left. On receipt of these discards the player may use either or both of the cards in his hand. But before the game rolling begins, he must place two discards in the center of the table, face down.

In a variation of Screwy Louis, instead of passing two cards, you pass three to your left and discard two from your new seven cards. This feature of one additional card to pass can be most frustrating, especially when you have to break up a ready-made straight, flush or full house.

97. *Eight Card Stud*

The same as Seven Card Stud except that each active player receives an eighth card dealt either up or down as the players have decided in advance.

MISCELLANEOUS STUD POKER VARIANTS

98. *Fairview High-Low Stud*

This game is a two-card High-Low Stud game that has three buy-ins, or substitutions. Each player is dealt a downcard after which a three-raise-limit betting round takes place. Then an upcard is dealt and another betting round takes place. This is followed by three separate buy-ins, with a betting round after each trade. Ace is a high card only. A pair of aces is a perfect high hand and a three and a deuce is a perfect low. However, a pair of sevens always takes the whole pot.

99. Five and Ten Stud Poker

In this variation, which can be used in any type of Five, Six or Seven Card Stud, mixed fives and tens are wild, but you must have at least one of each. Example: If you hold one five or more, and no ten, the fives are not wild. The same holds true if you hold one or more tens and no five. However, if you hold one or more fives and one or more tens, all fives and tens are wild. Deuces and threes may be used instead of fives and tens if desired. Four of a kind are common in this variation.

100. Two-Leg Stud

In this variation, which can be used in any Stud game, no player may rake in the pot until he has won two hands. These need not be won consecutively. This is an exciting and thrilling gimmick for building big pots.

101. Baseball Stud

This is dealt like Seven Card Stud with the first two and the last card dealt face down. A three-spot upcard strikes a player out, and out he goes—no matter how much he has contributed to the pot, and regardless of how good his hand may be. The nines are wild, whether face up or face down, and a four dealt face up to a player gives him an extra face-up card. The holder of the four-spot receives his extra card after all the players have been dealt their upcards for that round. A three or a four in the hole has no special significance; it is played the same as other nonvalued cards. The betting is the same as any Seven Card Stud variation. After the first upcard is dealt, and every round thereafter, a betting round takes place. It usually takes a flush or better to win a pot, but a straight will occasionally stand up.

102. Football

This game is the same as Baseball except that all sixes and fours are wild, a four requires a player to match the pot or drop out, and a deuce entitles a player to an extra hole card.

103. Woolworth

In this Seven Card Stud game, fives and tens are wild. A player dealt a five face up must pay five chips to the pot or drop out, and a player dealt a ten face up must pay ten chips to the pot or drop out. Note: Woolworth is sometimes played so that a player is knocked out (must drop out of the game) if a ten is dealt face up. In this version, the holder of the five does not have to ante extra chips to the pot.

104. Heinz

This Seven Card Stud game is played with fives and sevens wild, but a player dealt one of these cards face up must match the pot or drop.

105. Dr. Pepper

This Seven Card Stud game is played with all tens, fours and twos wild. There is no penalty and no extra chips are required when they are exposed. Note: Some play so that when a deuce is exposed as an upcard the player must put two chips in the pot or drop; if a four is dealt up, four chips must be put in the pot or the player must drop; and when a ten is exposed, the player must pay ten chips to the pot or drop.

106. Four Forty-four

This is an Eight Card Stud game in which four cards are dealt face down, one at a time, in clockwise rotation. Then one card is dealt face up and there is a betting round. Then three more upcards are given, with a betting interval after each. All fours are wild.

107. Three Forty-five

Similar to Four Forty-four except that only three cards are dealt face down at the start. There is a betting round after each of the next four upcards is dealt. Then the eighth card is dealt face down and there is a final betting interval. All fives are wild.

108. Night Baseball

This game, which is also called No-Peekie Baseball, is a combination of Rollover and Baseball Stud. That is, the threes and nines are wild, but when a three comes up, the player must drop or pay a penalty. Any four rolled up entitles the recipient to an additional card, which the dealer immediately gives him, face up, from the top of the pack. In the play of the game, each player in rotation turns up his cards, one by one, until his showing combination beats any cards previously turned, after which there is a betting interval. Remember that no one can look at his cards until they are exposed to all. The penalty for peeking should be stiff, say five chips for each card that is face down, or, at the beginning of the game, twenty-five chips.

109. Pass the Garbage

This game, which is also called Screw Your Neighbor, is a Stud game in which seven cards are dealt to each player face down. This is followed by a round of betting. After the bet, each player passes three cards to the individual on his left. After another betting round, each player discards two cards, making his best high hand, or his best low hand, if high-low is played. Then four cards are turned up, one at a time, with a bet after each card. After the final betting interval there is a showdown.

If your memory is bad and you cannot recall the cards you passed and the cards you received, you'd better pass this baby by. The hands run very strong on the showdown and the action is usually good. Average winning hands on the showdown are as follows—a full house for high, and a sixty-five for low.

110. Basketball

Basketball is played the same as Pass the Garbage except that an extra passing round is added. After the first betting interval, each player passes three cards to the player on his left. There is a betting period, after which each player passes two cards to the person on his left. (The game can also be played where the players first pass three cards to the right and then on the next round pass two to the left.) Then each player discards two cards, and after a final betting round, there is a showdown, at which the high hand takes the pot. This game can also be played high-low.

111. Follow the Queen

In this game, which is also called Follow the Lady, the card following the last queen turned face up on the table is wild, as are all of the same rank. If the last card turned up to an active player is a queen, then nothing is wild. The cards may be dealt as in Seven Card Stud: three down, four up; or the first two cards may be dealt down and the remaining five may be turned face up. The latter method is usually preferred, and there is a betting interval after each face-up card round. This game is most interesting since the wild card may change several times during the game, each time a queen is turned up, and there is always a possibility that nothing will be wild, should a queen be exposed on the last card dealt. In this game there can never be more than four wild cards in play.

112. Follow the King

Also called Follow the Cowboy, this game is played in the same manner as Follow the Queen, except that the card following the last exposed king is wild, as are all of the same rank. If the last card exposed to an active player is a king, then nothing is wild.

113. Follow Mary

This game is played like Follow the Queen except that all queens are wild cards. In other words, the queen, whether in hole or face up, is always wild; also, the card following the last exposed queen, and all cards of the same denomination, are wild. This means that there could be a total of eight wild cards in play. Of course, if the last card exposed to an active player is a queen, then only queens are wild.

114. Curaçao Stud

Curaçao Stud, or Dutch Stud, is a very unusual form of Stud which is most popular in the Netherlands and the Dutch West Indies. It is played as follows:

Each player is dealt a face-up card. If two or more players receive cards of the same denomination, the cards are dead and placed at the bottom of the deck by the dealer. The dealer continues dealing a card to each player until each has a card of a different denomination. When this occurs, the dealer reshuffles the remainder of the deck, and after the cut, continues dealing cards face up onto the center of the table until a card is dealt whose denomination matches a card in a player's hand. The player whose card it matches, says, "Give it to me." Each time a matching card is dealt, a round of betting takes place, and the player who has received that matched card starts the betting. As in Five Card Stud, a player at his turn of play may check, raise, call or fold. When a betting interval is ended, the deal continues. Play continues in this manner until some player has been dealt four of a kind, whereupon he takes half the pot. The other half goes to the low hand. Since not all players have the same number of cards, low hand is ranked as follows: low single card, low pair, and low three of a kind.

115. Put-and-Take Stud Poker

Put-and-Take Stud is one of the few banking games in the Poker family. As in most banking games, the dealer banks the game and players bet against the dealer. Two to eight players may participate, but five or six make the best game. The game is played like Five Card Stud, with the following exceptions and additional rules:

1. Each player except the dealer antes a chip into the pot.
2. The dealer deals each player (except himself) five face-up cards, one at a time, in Stud Poker fashion.
3. The dealer then deals himself five face-up cards (called put cards) one at a time. As the first put card is turned up, any player who has a card or cards of the same denomination antes to the pot one chip. For the second put card, the rate goes up to two chips, four if it is the third, eight if it is the fourth, and sixteen chips if the player matches the fifth put card. After the dealer's fifth upcard has been dealt and the holders of matching cards have contributed to the pot, the dealer places his five face-up cards on the bottom of the deck.
4. Now comes the payoff to the players by way of a second deal of cards, and these cards are called take cards. The dealer again deals himself five cards, one at a time, but this time the holders of matching take cards collect from the pot at the same rate that governed the put-card contributions.
5. If there are any chips left after the dealer's fifth take card has been turned up, the dealer takes them. But if the pot does not have enough chips to pay the winners, the dealer must make good.

The dealer has a chip advantage equal to the original antes. However, with a rotating deal, this advantage is equalized.

116. Acey-Deucey

This is a form of two-card Poker popular in the United States Army. Each player is dealt two cards, one up and one down. He may stand on the cards he is dealt, or at any later time, or he may draw by discarding one of his cards and being dealt a replacement (when his turn comes). If he discards a face-down card, the replacement is dealt face down; if he discards a face-up card, the replacement is face up. If he draws one card, he pays the pot one chip; for a second card he pays two chips, and for a third card five chips. Betting begins when all hands have stood. High card bets, as in Stud Poker. The game is usually played high-low. Only pairs and high cards count. Highest hand is two aces; lowest hand is ace and deuce, since the ace is treated as low when the player tries for low (but a pair of aces is never a low pair). Winners split the total pot, including bets and chips paid to draw cards.

117. Checkerboard High-Low Draw

I've decided to end this series of Stud Poker variations with Checkerboard High-Low Draw, a fascinating and skillful Draw Poker variant. This game is also known as Black and Red and Colors. It's the favorite game among the ladies at their weekly social Poker games.

The game is played the same as Five Card High-Low Draw Poker (simultaneous declaration) with the following exceptions and additional rules.

1. Clockwise, starting with the leader (player on dealer's left), the dealer deals a card to each player until each player has five cards. The dealer gets the last card.

2. The dealer continues the deal by placing six face-down community cards into two adjacent vertical rows of three cards each in the center of the table (see chart below). The row to the dealer's left is called the black row and the one to his right the red row.

Black	Red
1	2
3	4
5	6

Six Possible Community Cards

3. Once the players have studied their hands, the dealer turns up the top card of the black row. If the turned-up card is black, it remains on the table and in play. If it is red, it is discarded and put to one side out of play. Next—beginning with the leader each time—the first of six betting rounds takes place. Next, the dealer turns up the top card of the red row. If the turned-up card is red, it remains on the table in play. If it turns out to be black, it is discarded and put out of play. The same procedure is followed with the four remaining face-down cards followed by a betting interval.

4. Once the sixth betting round has been completed and if there is more than one player remaining, the player with the best five-card Poker hand comprised of the remaining community cards and his own

dealt hand wins the pot. However, each player's hand on the showdown must possess at least one card from his original five-card hand.

Variations: This game can also be played as high only or as low only.

14

Protection Against Poker Cheats

FACTS ABOUT POKER CHEATS

Though I should have preferred to spare you the reading of this chapter, we had better face the facts about playing Poker for money. And one of these facts is that more cheating takes place at illegally operated private Poker games than at all other forms of private card games combined. In fact, the Poker-playing fraternity is cheated out of untold billions of dollars each year. The first reason, of course, is that more money is gambled at Poker than at all other private card games combined, and secondly, the average Poker player knows little or nothing about Poker-cheating techniques, hence is easily victimized. The legalized Nevada and California Poker rooms and clubs are exempted from this discussion since their operators take anti-cheating precautions to try to protect their customers from being cheated. This, however, is not meant to imply that cheating does not take place in these two areas. It does, but not as often as in unprotected Poker games.

Of the hundred-odd private Poker games that my aides and I scouted during my Poker survey, we found that cheating in one form or another took place in one out of ten games. My male and female helpers detected three decks of marked cards in use and spotted cheating in one form or another taking place in seven other Poker games. Most of these male and female cheats spotted in action were very amateurish and it was sometimes difficult for my survey helpers to distinguish between the amateur cheat and the thoroughgoing, no-holds barred, honest Poker player.

The one-in-ten ratio varies from Poker game to Poker game and town to town, depending on the players' ability to detect cheating. A knowledge of cheating methods and the ability to detect them is your best protection against dishonest players in private games. It is for this reason that the most ethical, fastidiously honest Poker games are those in which players are top-notch gamblers, gambling operators, gambling-house employees—and card cheats. When they play together, the game is *nearly* always honest. It has to be because they play in an atmosphere of total and icy distrust and their exhaustive knowledge of the mechanics of cheating makes using the knowledge much too dangerous. They do not cheat because they fear detection and its consequences. But there are times when a new cheating method or device comes into possession of a big-time gambling cheat, and if he believes it will not be detected by other sophisticated gamblers, he certainly will not hesitate to put it to use in any kind of Poker game. For example, in the early sixties the late "Nick the Greek" Dandolos, the most famous gambler of this era, was cheated out of $500,000 with a radio cue prompter (which was new at the time) during a two weeks' session of Poker and Gin Rummy. The game took place at a famous Las Vegas Strip hotel casino. Nick and the cheat who fleeced him were attired in bathing suits, and the cheat's accomplice with telescope and radio cue prompter operated from a hotel room overlooking the pool. The player cheat's radio receiver was hidden under his bathing suit. Incidentally, the table and chairs were fastened to the pool's concrete floor to prevent Nick the Greek from moving his cards out of range of the telescope.

I ran into Nick at the Flamingo Hotel Casino bar soon after the cheating incident and it was he who told me how he was cheated of $500,000. Nick's legal difficulties arose still later when several of his friends, knowing that he was broke at the time, took it upon themselves to try to recoup part of his losses from the cheat. The cheat had them arrested for attempted extortion. They were found guilty and each received ten years in prison. Recently the cheat met an untimely death when a hidden bomb in his automobile exploded, sending him to kingdom come.

Some writers of Poker books contend that explanation of card cheating has no legitimate place in the proper study of Poker games. They claim that exposure of cheating methods may teach readers to do a bit of cheating on their own. This is possible, but the disadvantage is far outweighed by the protection such exposure gives to the many thousands of honest players, and by the fact that widespread exposure makes the practice of cheating at Poker more difficult for the cheat to get away with. The writers making these objections also have another reason for not discussing cheating methods in detail. They don't do so because they can't—they know so little about the subject themselves that when they copy the cheating material from *Scarne on Cards* or *Scarne's New Complete Guide to Gambling,* they garble it so badly that it misleads rather than enlightens the reader.

I am proud (not vain, I hope) to repeat what many experts on gambling and top-flight card magicians have been saying for the past forty years: "John Scarne is the greatest card manipulator who ever lived and knows more about cheating at cards than any other living person." Furthermore, I must add that I can flawlessly execute every cheating Poker technique described in this chapter, plus hundreds of others that space does not permit me to dwell on here.

POKER CHEATS

There are three kinds of Poker cheats: the amateur, the semiprofessional and the professional. I call the amateur that not because he doesn't win money cheating but because he is a brazen and unskilled cheat. The semipro is one who earns part of his living by cheating but lacks the manipulative skills of the real card sharp, and who, when he is working single-o, has to depend upon marked cards and other gaffed gambling equipment. The professional card sharp is the skilled sleight-of-hand expert who has spent many hours in practice to gain the necessary proficiency in crooked card manipulation. He is called a "card mechanic," and he usually travels a lot, seldom staying in one spot too long.

Cheats working together are known as a "card mob." The mob is usually made up of a card mechanic, a bankroll man who supplies the necessary money to finance the operation, a couple of shills and several steerers. The latter are often good-looking girls who pick up victims on the pretense of taking them to their hotel rooms, and steer them instead into the crooked game.

The semipro who works with a card sharp helps by misdirecting attention away from the cards at the moment the sharper makes his crooked move, by signaling the value of his hand, by making the right kind of cut when given the deck by the sharper, etc.

The honest player's best protection against these crooks is to learn enough about their methods so that he can spot the most common cheating moves when they occur. The crooked angles, ruses, subterfuges, sleights and mechanical methods are so many and so varied that a detailed description of them all would more than fill this book. The most common methods can, however, be spotted when you know what to look for. Most of them require unnatural moves or actions on the part of the cheat. You may never be able to catch the expert card sharp's bottom or second deal at the split second that it is made, but there is a way of recognizing the expert card mechanic for what he is by the way in which he holds the deck. For a detailed description of the "mechanic's grip," see How to Spot a Skilled Poker Cheat, page 248.

Amateur Poker Cheats

These are some of the ways you can spot an amateur cheat.

1. The amateur Poker cheat will just forget to ante and then will swear earnestly that someone else is shy.
2. The amateur Poker cheat will announce he is changing a $10 bill in the pot and take an extra buck out of the pot and considers the feat an act of skill.
3. The amateur Poker cheat will connive with another player and each will give the other some sort of signal when he has a good hand and wants his friend to drop out. For every dozen crooked moves made by the agate-eyed professional card sharp, the amateur will blandly and brazenly attempt a hundred swindles.

What do you do when you suspect a friend or acquaintance of cheating? This is a department of etiquette that Emily Post doesn't mention. It can develop very easily into a sticky situation because it is possible that an honest player may unconsciously do some of the things that amateur cheaters do and your suspicions may be unjustified. There is no need to raise a hue and cry. Your best bet is to demand quietly and graciously that the rules of the form of Poker being played be strictly followed. This should in most cases remedy what is wrong or looks wrong. If not, then make some polite excuse and leave the game. This will give no offense and do no harm to anyone's sensibilities or reputation, or to your pocketbook.

Professional and Semiprofessional Poker Cheats

The gambling world has many names for various types of professional Poker cheats. A person who manipulates cards for cheating purposes is referred to as a "card mechanic." In the western part of the United States, Nevada included, a professional card cheat who travels over the country seeking Poker games to ply his trade is called a "crossroader." A cheat who specializes in palming cards is referred to in the trade as a "hand mucker" or "holdout artist." A cheat who deals from the bottom of the deck is a "base dealer" or "subway dealer." Two or more cheats working as a team are known as a "card mob." Two or more Poker sharps who make use of signals to cheat are referred to as "office men" or "wire men." A cheat who specializes in the use of marked cards is called a "paper man." A cheat who deals the second card from the deck when he appears to be dealing the top card is referred to as a "second dealer" or "number two man."

The surreptitious manipulation of cards by card mechanics, hand muckers, holdout men, crossroaders, card sharks, base dealers or other card cheats requires considerable skill and practice, plus the courage of a thief. A top-notch card mechanic must be considerably more adept with a deck of cards than a first-rate magician. The magician is free to use a great deal of conversation and misdirection to fool his audience, but the card cheat is limited by the game's regulations. As a matter of fact, most present-day magicians—including most of those who advertise their act as an exposé of crooked gambling tricks—know little about the operation of the modern card sharper. They themselves are as easily fleeced by a good card mechanic as the average layman. Much of the sleight of hand and nearly all of the mechanical gadgets they expose were discarded by the cheats decades ago.

There is a popular delusion that card cheats and magicians can take a well-mixed deck of cards, riffle and shuffle the pack several times and then deal each player in the game a good hand—in Poker, for example, four jacks to one player, four kings to another and four aces to himself.

The truth of the matter is that no card sharper or magician can take a deck honestly shuffled by someone else, shuffle it two or three times and arrange more than a couple of cards in two different hands without previous sight of, or prearrangement of, the deck. Whenever you see any sleight-of-hand expert claim to do this and deal out a perfect Bridge hand of thirteen cards of one suit, or four or five pat Poker hands, you can be sure that the cards were previously stacked.

Actually the cheat doesn't need to do anything so spectacular. It doesn't matter whether the game is Draw Poker or Stud Poker in some gin mill or the most recondite Poker game at a Park Avenue club—a cheater can take all the chumps in the game simply by knowing the approximate location of a very few cards. If he knows the exact position of only one of the 52 cards, he will eventually win all the money in sight.

Never overestimate a Poker cheat. Don't expect him to work miracles. Just expect him to win the money. If luck favors him, he may not have to make a crooked move all night, or he may make only one crooked move in the whole card session. But that one move always comes at just the right time to get the money. In most games the move can even be executed clumsily and get by; the average player almost never spots it because he seldom suspects the people with whom he plays, and because, even if he did suspect them, he lacks the necessary knowledge to know what to look for and wouldn't recognize it if he did happen to be looking in the right place at the right time.

Believe it or not, most sharpers are poor card players on the square (playing honestly). A good card mechanic spends so much of his time practicing cheating moves and concentrating in play on watching for the right opportunity to use his skill that he seldom develops a good sense of card strategy.

During one of my recent gambling lecture demonstrations at the Eastman Kodak convention hall in Rochester, New York, a member of the audience asked me, "Isn't the old rule, 'Never play cards with strangers,' about the best protection one can have against Poker cheats?"

"That rule," I replied, "gives the average Poker player as much protection as a broken umbrella in a rainstorm." The card cheat has had the answer to it for years. Suppose that Harry, the card mechanic, discovers there's a big and neighborly Poker game every Friday night in the back room at Joe's cigar store. He also learns, for instance, the name of a doctor who is one of the players. Harry simply puts in a phone call and makes an appointment to have a physical checkup. During the examination Harry steers the conversation around to Poker and manages to get an invite to the game. It's easy; he's done it a good many times before. And when Doc introduces him to the other players as one of his patients, no one thinks of him as a stranger; he's already one of the boys. After several Poker sessions, Harry, who is no longer a stranger, brings Ed, his confederate, to the game, and that's when they go to work making use of their cheating specialty, be it signaling, cold-decking, stacking, second dealing, bottom dealing, etc.

It is much easier for a card sharp to cheat at Draw Poker than at Stud Poker for the relatively simple reason that the player at Draw holds his cards closed in his hand, while his hand at Stud remains in full view of the other players on the table before him at all times.

All the crooked moves in the cheat's armory such as stacking, false cutting, second dealing, cold deck switching, and palming in particular, are used to cheat in Draw Poker. But sharpers have found that the most consistently profitable way to cheat at Draw Poker is to work in a team with a confederate.

The same crooked moves and artifices used at Draw are also used by the cheat at Stud. However, the number one cheating specialty used to cheat at Stud is marked cards, because each player's hand is spread out on the table in view of all players, thereby making it easy for the cheat to read the backs of each opponent's face-down marked cards. Draw and Stud Poker variants that make use of face-down "community cards" are the favorite cheating games for marked-card Poker cheats. Signaling between two confederates is most rampant at Stud and more so at High-Low Stud Declare, where knowledge of each confederate's hand wins many a pot from the rightful winner. Signaling and whipsawing also go together. Signaling between confederates at table stakes or high-limit games is the least detectable cheating practice that takes place among top-notch Las Vegas Poker professionals. Hole card switching, although dangerous and requiring considerable skill, is also to be guarded against.

I repeat: The best protection against Poker cheats is the knowledge of how they operate and some ability at recognizing their slick sleight of hand and other crooked ruses. Most cheating moves, fortunately, have one or more giveaway signals, usually an unnatural action, either in preparation for the move or in executing it. If after learning how to spot these clues to trickery you still think you are being cheated at cards, your best bet is to take up some non-card game, preferably a game that can't be cheated at. Since I invented it, naturally I hope you'll pick Teeko.

How to Spot a Skilled Poker Cheat

Most top-notch Poker cheats announce the fact that they are skilled mechanics long before they make a crooked move. They do it as soon as they begin to deal. The giveaway is the peculiar manner in which they hold the deck, known as the "mechanic's grip."

The skilled Poker cheat holds the deck in either the right or left hand (we will assume from here on that it's the left hand). Three fingers are on the edge of the long side of the deck and the index finger at the outer right corner. Some mechanics keep two fingers on the side of the deck and two at the outer corner.

Most professional dealers in Nevada's and California's legalized Poker rooms and those working in illegal commercialized Poker rooms throughout the country also hold the deck in this manner, but for a different reason—they do it to prevent players from glimpsing the bottom card. But when you spot a player using the mechanic's grip in a private friendly game, find yourself another game. The odds are that the player who holds the deck this way is doing so because peeking at the top card, second dealing, bottom dealing and other cheating moves require this grip. The index-finger position at the outer corner of the deck acts as a stop when the cheat is second dealing and peeking and also helps conceal a card when it comes from the bottom of the deck. It is possible that an honest, even innocent, player might accidentally hold the deck this way, but it is highly unlikely because it takes considerable practice. The only reason anyone would practice this grip is because he intends to cheat. There's one other exception: card magicians also use the mechanic's grip, but not many of them play Poker for money, for the same reason I usually give: "If I win I am accused of cheating; if I lose they think I am a lousy Poker player."

Protection Against a Second Deal

One of the most common cheating moves used by both the top-notch card mechanic and the would-be card sharp is the second deal. This consists, as the name implies, of dealing the second card from the top rather than the first. Any good second dealer will clip the best of players in any card game. He is known to ordinary gamblers and to magicians as a second dealer; the underworld knows him as a number two man.

Dealing seconds is the move most often used in Stud Poker when the cheats have had no opportunity to stack the cards. This time the cheating is done during the deal rather than earlier. The time-honored mechanic's grip is again used. When the left hand holds the pack, the thumb pushes the top card over the side of the deck in the usual fashion so that it can be gripped and taken by the right thumb and forefinger. As the second card leaves the pack, the right thumb pulls the top card back to its starting position, the curled index finger of the mechanic's grip acting as a stop for the swinging top card. When expertly done, the sleight is a split-second, beautifully coordinated move that is exceedingly difficult to detect even by the most observant players, and it will deceive the average player if done merely competently.

When playing Stud Poker or one of its variants some cheats deal with one hand only, turning the deck over as the card is dealt so that it comes out face up. Don't let this one-hand action convince you that everything must be on the up and up; a good mechanic can and does deal seconds with one hand just as neatly as with two.

Second dealing isn't worth a plugged nickel unless the cheat knows what the top card is and wants to save it for himself or a confederate, or give it to the player who doesn't want it. It is, for this reason, mostly employed with marked cards although it is also used with a peek, which is explained below.

If you suspect a second dealer is at work, look for the mechanic's grip; they nearly all use it. The best protection against the second deal in Stud Poker is to insist that after the first round of betting has been completed the dealer cannot pick up the remaining stock (undealt portion of the deck) but must leave the stock resting on the table. Dealing for each succeeding round must be done with one hand, picking one card at a time off the top of the deck. This method of dealing is recommended especially for high-stake Stud games and their variations.

How to Spot the Peek at Stud Poker

Peeking is the art of secretly glimpsing the top card of the deck. This is one of the most useful and valuable dodges in the Stud Poker cheat's repertoire. When the peek is used in conjunction with the second deal, a good peeker is poison in any Poker game. It is especially useful in Stud Poker and its variants.

The move, a simple one, consists in exerting pressure on the top card with the thumb and pushing it against the fingers on the opposite outer corner of the deck. This causes the card to buckle or bend upward near the index corner just enough so that the cheat can look into the opening thus formed and glimpse the index. He gives it a careless glance at the right moment, releases the pressure of his thumb, and the top card flattens out again.

Some cheats peek while dealing one-handed. Others pretend to look at the face-down card in their Stud Poker hand and peek the top card at the same time.

Eye with suspicion the player who uses the mechanic's grip and looks too often at his face-down (hole) card or cards. However, to prevent peeking, it is better still to insist that after the first betting round has been completed the stock must remain in the center of the table and all further dealing be done with one hand. For further details see Protection Against a Second Deal, above.

Shifting the Cut

The greatest challenge to the card cheat who works alone is to overcome the cut. If the rules did not ask for a cut, gambling with cards would have long ago become obsolete and playing cards would now be used only for Solitaire. Stacking, false shuffling and a confederate's false cutting are moves not too difficult for the average sharper to master, but the dealer-cheat's shifting the cut (secretly returning the cut deck to its original order) without detection under the pressure of the game and under the watchful and observant eyes of experienced card players requires the skill of a master cheater. Since most card players are chumps who can't spot crooked card moves even when sloppily executed, some cheaters still manage to get away with it. Professional cheats manage to avoid the cut altogether by working with a confederate who false-cuts the deck.

Ordinarily, when the deck is cut, the dealer pushes it toward you and says, "Cut, Mac?" You take a block of cards off the top, put them on the table, and the dealer completes the cut. He picks up the bottom block and places it on the top block you cut off. This buries the cards the dealer-cheat is trying to control; he must undo the cut and return the deck to its precut position for the move to be effective. It must be done swiftly and without causing any suspicion.

There are dozens of different methods of shifting the cut used by various card mechanics. Following are the most popular crooked cut shifts in use today.

1. One-handed shift cut: Here the two portions of the deck are shifted back to their original positions with one hand only. It is deceptive because the chumps don't suspect that such a complex maneuver can be done with one hand and do not, therefore, watch closely when the deck is held this way. Since the other hand is away from the deck, some other type of cover must be used. The usual practice is to reach across the body with the free hand to take a cigar or cigarette from an ashtray which has been purposely left at that side. The reaching arm covers the hand holding the deck for a brief moment and the shift takes place unseen.

2. One-handed table cut shift: After an honest cut, while the two blocks of cards are still on the table, the cheater completes, or rather pretends to complete, the cut. He picks up the cards originally on the bottom and appears to place them on the top block. Actually the bottom block passes above and a bit beyond the top block, comes quickly back and slides in under the top block. This is a very deceptive shift provided that it is done with lightning speed and a single, unhesitating sweep of the hand.

3. Two-handed cut shift: Magicians, who call this "the pass," have used this shift for many years; it is still used by some sharpers. After the cards have been cut by another player, the cheat replaces the lower block on the upper one, but not squarely; it projects slightly at the inner end, leaving what is called a step. He scoops up the cards

and inserts his little finger into the deck at the step. In the act of apparently squaring the deck and under cover of the hand above the deck, the lower half of the deck is pivoted upward. It pushes against the upper half, which swings aside as though hinged, and is deposited again on top, where it was before the cut was made. This is accomplished in a split second.

There is a foolproof defense against shifting the cut, and that is the Scarne Cut (see page 257).

Protection Against the Bottom Deal

Ordinary gamblers call the cheat who deals cards from the bottom of the deck a bottom dealer; the inner circle—the boys in the know—refer to him as a base dealer or subway dealer.

The bottom deal is considerably more difficult to execute without detection than the second deal—hence very few card mechanics can deal a perfect bottom. However, good or bad as they may be, there are countless Poker game crossroaders who favor the bottom deal as their cheating ace in the hole.

The bottom dealer, like the second dealer, uses the mechnic's grip. His left thumb pushes the top card over as the right hand comes up to take it, but the right hand has other instructions. Instead, its forefinger moves in under the deck at the outer right corner and pulls out the bottom card while the left thumb is engaged in pulling back the top card. The index finger of the left hand in the mechanic's grip position covers much of the front edge of the deck, making it difficult for an observer to see whether the card comes from top or bottom. The movement, naturally, must be fast and smooth and must follow the same rhythm as when the top card is taken legitimately.

The subway dealer saves time because he doesn't have to fuss around stacking cards. He or his confederate usually picks up the cards after the previous hand and places the previous deal's winning hand or some useful discards on the bottom of the deck. He retains them there during a phony shuffle and deals them off the bottom as needed.

This is easier said than done—much easier. It takes years of practice to become a good bottom dealer, and the chances that you will find yourself in a game with a cheater who can bottom-deal cards from a full deck noiselessly and undetectably are roughly about 100,000 to 1. There is another character, however, whom you might meet oftener. Since it is easier to deal a respectable bottom from half a deck of cards, there are mechanics who have the nerve to pick up the bottom half of the deck after the cut, skip putting them on the top half, and begin dealing. When this happens, ask that the cut be completed in the usual manner; then keep your ears open. If he attempts a bottom deal with a full deck you may hear it—when badly executed, it is noisy.

There's a foolproof defense against the bottom dealer—the Scarne Cut (see page 257). This is guaranteed to lose the cheat's carefully iced cards in the deck and make him an honest man.

How to Spot a False Shuffle

The ability to appear to be shuffling a deck while keeping some or all of the cards in their original positions is an absolutely essential weapon in the arsenal of the accomplished card sharp. The most popular and most deceptive of the false shuffles is the "pull through," a dazzling and completely crooked shuffle which doesn't alter the position of a single card.

When a hand of cards has been completed, the cheat scoops up the tabled cards, taking special care not to disturb hands or discards which he wants and which he places on either the top or bottom of the pack. This shuffle is also used when a cold (stacked) deck has been switched into the game which must be shuffled without disturbing its prearrangement.

The deck is cut into two blocks and their ends riffled together quite honestly. The move comes during the split second that the cards are pushed together and reassembled into a single pack. The cheat pushes the two blocks of interwoven cards into each other at an angle, an action that is covered by the manner in which he holds his hands. Then, without any hesitation, he gives the cards a fast cut—or that is what seems to happen. Actually, he takes a new grip on the cards, grabs the right-hand block with the left fingers, the left-hand block with the right fingers, pulls the interwoven blocks through each other, slaps the block originally on top back on top, and squares the deck fairly as he should have done but didn't do immediately after the riffle. The pull-through action is done so smoothly and so fast that as far as the average chump is concerned it is quicker than the eye can follow.

Although the cards were fairly riffled and the action had the appearance and sound of a legitimate shuffle not a single card has changed position.

You have only one small clue here—that fast "cut" following so closely on the heels of the shuffle.

Protection Against False Cuts

Like the false shuffle, a false cut, when well executed, appears to transpose the two halves of the deck but actually leaves them just as they were. When the other players are in the habit of letting the dealer do his own cutting, he executes the false cut. Otherwise, a confederate at his right does the dirty work. This last is the most effective method because suspicion is much less likely to fall on the dealer.

In games involving more than two players, particularly Poker, most cheating is done by two cheats who pretend to be strangers to each other. This partnership in crime is more dangerous to your bankroll than any other kind of cheating.

False cuts are employed not only when the cheat is the dealer but also when it is your deal. How? Most players are honest and awkward. When they shuffle, they often fail to mix the bottom cards of the deck thoroughly. The cheater detects something down there he wants, or he may glimpse the bottom card during the shuffle and see that it could be useful.

The most popular, the most effective and the least suspicious-looking false cut is the "running false cut." The reason that this false cut is next to impossible to detect when expertly done is that it resembles an honest series of running cuts. The honest running cut is used by house dealers in legalized Las Vegas Poker rooms to prevent the players from tracking the positions of certain cards during the shuffle. However, the last cut prior to the deal used by all Las Vegas dealers is the regular and plain one-handed cut.

The running false cut is executed as follows: the sharper, instead of making use of the regular one-handed single cut, makes a false series of single cuts using both hands. The sharper pulls a small block of cards off the bottom, slaps it on top and leaves a step. He repeats the action with the opposite hand, and continues until the block originally on top has gone down through the deck and, on the last cut, comes back once more to the top. It looks good, but nothing was changed; all the cards are in their original order. Many honest players make running cuts like this—but eye anyone closely who does so. Watch for a step in the deck, although the whole action is done so fast that your chance of spotting it is slim.

Regarding the question of cutting the cards prior to the deal, I agree with the statement of "Amarillo Slim" Preston, Las Vegas Poker expert, that "the last and final cut prior to the deal should be a plain and simple one-handed cut by the player immediately to the dealer's right. A one-handed cut always is best because that way there cannot be any hocus-pocus. If I were in a game and a player was cutting those cards two or three times with both hands, I'd be pretty wary of that cat because he's either locating some cards on you or else he's not cutting the deck at all."

The above advice offered by Amarillo Slim is good, but it possesses one major loophole. It does not prevent an unsuspecting player or the cheat's confederate from cutting into a "crimp," which serves the same purpose as a false cut. A crimp is a bend placed in the deck by the cheat. When the crimp is placed in the middle of the deck it causes a small break or opening in the deck's edge which can be felt and easily cut to by the dealer's confederate.

There's a foolproof defense against the two-handed running false cut and the crimp—the Scarne Cut (see page 257). This is guaranteed to force the cheats to find themselves another game where the Scarne Cut is not employed.

How to Spot Stacking the Deck

There are various methods of stacking Poker hands during the shuffle. The "riffle shuffle stack" is the most difficult of all card-stacking methods, but the sharper who has perfected it is capable of fleecing the most seasoned Poker players. If, at Draw, Stud, or any of their variants you detect an opponent using this cheating method, beware: you are up against a practiced, unscrupulous and perhaps even dangerous card mechanic.

The sharper, let us say, has three kings on top of the deck. He cuts the deck into two blocks and shuffles them together. It looks like an ordinary standard shuffle, but during the action he puts just the right number of cards between the kings so that in the deal, which will be on the level, his opponents get cards at random and he gets the kings. It may take him four or five riffles to arrange the kings as he wants them, but if the riffle is his specialty, he can and will do it in two or three riffles. He gets the same result as in the pickup stack, but this sleight-of-hand method will take the smart boys who would spot the overhand stack and the pickup stack (both explained below).

Cleverly executed, this stack is almost detection-proof, but there is one way of spotting it, and then, if you can't correct the matter by forcing the cheat out of the game, the only safe thing to do is force yourself out. Most riffle-stack sharpers riffle the first cards fast and slow up perceptibly near the top, where they must count the cards as they riffle. They also watch the deck carefully as they count the cards into place. Riffling in this fast-slow tempo and watching the deck too intently during the shuffle are the danger signals. The player may not be a riffle-stack expert, but he's acting like one. Look out!

The semiprofessional sharper who is unable to execute the riffle shuffle stack makes use of the "overhand shuffle stack." It involves considerably less skill than the riffle shuffle stack, and will not pass in fast company. However, there are plenty of chump games available that will stand for this nonsense.

The sharper puts the cards to be stacked on the bottom of the deck. During his shuffle he milks the deck, pulling down one card from the bottom and one card from the top at the same time. On these two cards he shuffles off two cards fewer than the number of players in the game. He repeats this maneuver once for each card he wants to stack. He lets the next card project slightly from the deck, shuffles the remaining cards on top. He is now set for the deal. The wanted cards are spaced out so that they will fall to the dealer, or perhaps to a confederate, during the deal. The cut is then canceled or avoided as explained in the section on the pickup stack.

The giveaway signal here is the unusual sound of the shuffle caused by having to run off so many cards singly. A second clue is the fact that this shuffling sound is interrupted slightly at regular rhythmic intervals each time another bottom card is pulled down. The smart card player keeps his ears open as well as his eyes.

Following is the most commonly used method of stacking cards. It is called the "pickup stack" and is used by professional, semiprofessional and amateur cheats alike. It requires no special manipulative skill and it rarely fails. Its cleverness lies in its simplicity. Suppose you are a cheater in a five-handed Stud Poker game. The next deal is yours, and two hands were exposed in the hand just completed. In each hand you spot one card you'd like to get for yourself the next time around. Let's say these are two aces.

You simply stack the deck in such a way that you deal the two aces to yourself. You do it in full view, and it's ridiculously easy. As dealer, you pick up the cards, taking them a hand at a time. You pick up the cards lying above the first ace, then use these cards to scoop up the remainder of the hand. Place these cards on top of the deck. This puts the ace fifth from the top. Repeat the action with the remaining hand. That's all there is to it. The deck is stacked, ready for the deal, and you will get the fifth and tenth cards—the two aces—back to back. If you have a fair memory and can remember the other cards and their order in the first hand you picked up, you will also know your opponents' hole cards, which can be an equally lucrative advantage.

Yes, you must shuffle before the deal, but that's not difficult either. You only need to riffle and let the top ten or so cards fall last, thus keeping them on top. As for the cut, the cheat has many ways of taking care of that without even resorting to sleight of hand. He may simply deal without offering the cards to be cut, he may cut and then pick up the two packs incorrectly, or he may have a confederate on his right who refuses the cut, saying, "Run them." That's darned near all there is to stacking as it is generally practiced by the professional, the semi-professional, or the amateur cheat. When the cut is omitted, insist that some other player or yourself be allowed to cut. The dealer may feel insulted but he can't object; the rules give you this right.

There's a foolproof defense, however, against all stacked decks—this is the Scarne Cut, which follows.

THE WORLD-FAMOUS SCARNE CUT

While acting as gambling consultant to the United States Armed Forces and *Yank: The Army Weekly* during World War II, I devised the Scarne Cut to protect servicemen against the skilled Poker sharp who employs sleight of hand to cheat the GI and deal himself or his confederate the winning Poker hand. When the Scarne Cut is put into use, it will protect the Poker player against most of the sharp's crooked moves described in this chapter. As to the effectiveness of the Scarne Cut and my exposures of gambling cheats in *Yank* and national periodicals during World War II, I will simply quote General Hap Arnold, Commanding General of the U.S. Army Air Force. He said, "John Scarne's one-man crusade against crooked gambling in the Armed Forces during World War II saved servicemen tens of millions of dollars a month in potential gambling losses when he practically cleaned up crooked gambling in the Armed Forces singlehanded."

Over the years I have appeared as guest star on hundreds of national television shows on which I demonstrated the Scarne Cut during my gambling exposés to untold millions of viewers. Among the many national TV shows that I have appeared on are those of Jack Paar, Tom Snyder, Mike Douglas, Joe Franklin, Merv Griffin, Johnny Carson and countless others.

The use of the Scarne Cut eliminates in one stroke most of the card sharp's best crooked moves. The Scarne Cut is accomplished as follows.

1. Pull out a block of cards from the center of the 52-card deck.
2. Place them on top of the deck and square it up.

3. Then cut the deck in the regular one-handed manner.

4. Next, pick up the former bottom block of the deck and place it on top of the cut block, and finally, square up the 52-card deck. Get into the habit of using the Scarne Cut and you won't need to worry about nearly all cut shifts, bottom deals, stacked decks, crimps, false shuffles, cold decks, false cuts, etc. At the very least, it will give any Poker cheat enough headaches to cut his cheating close to the vanishing point. It may frighten him out of the game entirely, or even into playing honestly.

Protection Against Steer Joints and Cold Decks

This concerns a special breed of Poker mob that operates steer joints. Such a Poker mob specializes in switching the deck in play for a prearranged deck known in the trade as a "cold deck," "cooler," or "package." These Poker mobs go out after the high-rolling Poker-playing suckers and steer them to a specially arranged Poker game setup in which the victim hasn't a ghost of a chance. These mobs usually work in teams of four. Their crooked games may be found in any big city and around famous resort areas such as Miami Beach, Las Vegas, Puerto Rico and Atlantic City. The mob usually rents a hotel suite or apartment for its cheating operation, covering its tracks with a phony hotel or apartment name registration.

Sometimes when the mob hears of an unsophisticated high-rolling Poker player who looks like a promising victim, they travel thousands of miles to set up their joint for this lone prospect. I know of one New York Poker mob that once fleeced a number of Hollywood moguls in California of a cool one million dollars in a week's play, after which its members vanished into thin air.

Most of these mobs employ "steerers," whose job it is to locate prospective victims and bring them to their crooked Poker game. Sometimes the steerers are not regular members of the Poker mob but merely gamblers who steer in their best friends. Anyone with larceny in his heart will fill the bill as long as he listens and gives a nod to the proposition "Bring your friend around and we'll cut you in on his losses."

These Poker cheats specialize in switching the deck in play for a stacked or prearranged deck. The mob's style of Poker is mostly Draw, since all the players' cards in Draw are hidden from view and the mark (victim) has no idea what his opponents may be holding.

The actual swindle is accomplished as follows. The four player cheats, having picked their intended victim, play honest for an hour or so, then have a cold deck ready for the moment when the victim agrees to play pot limit on the suggestion of one of the cheats. He never realizes that in a game where each player antes $1 he is to lose $20,000 or $30,000 in one hand, and on probably not more than six raises in all.

One of the most common methods used by the mob's card mechanic of switching the deck in play for a cold deck follows: When the mark has completed the shuffle and offers the deck to be cut by the player to his right (who happens to be the mob's card mechanic), the cheat at his left asks the victim to change a large bill. While he is busy being helpful and making change, the cheat who should be cutting the deck is switching it. He takes his handkerchief out, blows into it and lets it cover the shuffled deck momentarily on the way back to his pocket. As the shuffled deck leaves the table under the handkerchief, the cheat's left hand replaces it with the cold deck. And when the mark turns back to take the deck for the deal, the cheat executes a false cut to put him at his ease. The mark is now ready to deal himself to the cleaner's.

The mark deals the cards, and when he picks up his hand and examines the cards, he is speechless because he has dealt himself a straight flush (king high in hearts)—and only one hand, a royal flush, can beat it.

The cheat to the mark's left holds the ace, king, and queen of spades plus two low cards. The next two players usually hold three of a kind, and one of them opens the pot. After the pot is opened, the discard and the draw take place, and the cheat to the mark's left draws the jack and ten of spades for a royal flush. The other cheats also draw cards. The mark stands pat with his straight flush.

Then the whipsawing begins, one confederate betting the entire pot, another doing the same. After this has gone on for about six raises, IOU's and checks come into play. The mark will usually bet very big because he rarely if ever suspects cheating while he is dealing. Millions of dollars annually are won by sharps with cold decks.

Just to prove to the reader that it is possible for a mark caught by one of these Poker mobs to lose $30,000 in one pot when playing $1 ante and pot limit—naturally with the use of a cold deck—I give you the following example:

Suppose four Poker cheats plus a mark are playing pot limit. The ante is $1. Each of the five players antes $1 for a total pot of $5 before the cards are dealt. The cheater to the mark's left we will call Pete, the cheater to Pete's left is Joe. The other two players' names are irrelevant. The mark will be known as—Mr. Mark.

The pot is opened by Pete for $5. All the players stay, and each puts $5 into the pot, making a total of $30 in the pot. The draw now takes place. After the draw Pete bets the pot limit, which is $30, making a total of $60 in the pot. Joe calls Pete's $30 bet, and raises it $5, making a total of $95 in the pot. The other two cheaters drop out. Mr. Mark calls the raise by putting $35 into the pot. The pot now holds $130. Pete calls Joe's $5 raise, and reraises the pot limit, which is $135. The total amount in the pot is now $270. Joe calls Pete's $135 bet, making the pot limit $405, and raises this amount. The total amount in the pot is now $810. Mr. Mark calls the two raises by putting in $540 for a total of $1,350 in the pot. Pete calls Joe's raise of $405 and raises the pot limit, which is now $1,755, making a total of $3,510. Joe calls the $1,755 bet, making the pot total $5,265, and raises the pot limit, for a total now of $10,530 in the pot. It will cost Mr. Mark $7,020 to call Pete's and Joe's raises. Should Pete not raise and should he just call Joe's raise of $5,265, the total amount in the pot would be $22,815. The total amount lost by Mr. Mark is $7,601, and that was with only five raises. Should Pete desire to make another raise of pot limit, it would cost Mr. Mark $22,815 more to call the hand. So a player must not only watch the dealer to prevent himself from being cheated, but must also keep his eyes on his own deck while he is offering the pack to be cut.

Don't think that cold decks are used only in steer joints. The fact is, they may be switched into any Poker game in which the sharper believes he can get away with them. I once witnessed a private Draw Poker game among "friends" in which a card mechanic switched in five cold decks in a three-hour session. But as a rule, cold decks are reserved for specific high rollers.

Most sharpers have developed their own cold-deck switches. However, here are just three of these cold-deck switches that I have spotted over the years. (1) The cheat leaves the shuffled and cut deck on the edge of the table just as the waiter confederate arrives with a previously ordered tray of sandwiches or drinks. The waiter cheat holds the cold deck beneath the tray which he rests on the table for a moment above the honest deck in play. When he leaves, the cold deck remains behind and the honest deck goes with him. (2) The waiter cheat's tray simply covers the honest deck for a moment as the player cheat makes the switch under it. (3) A player cheat, after having picked up the honest, cut deck, purposely lets fall several chips from the table. The cheat then makes the switch from his lap (which holds the cold deck) while stooping down to retrieve the fallen chips.

There are countless other ways that cheats introduce cold decks into a game, but because of space limitations, the above-described methods will have to suffice.

The best protection against the cold deck is to insist that your opponents make use of the Scarne Cut (see page 257).

How to Spot Palming

A Poker cheat who specializes in palming cards is referred to in the trade as a "hand mucker" or "holdout man." Holding out cards by palming them is probably the most easily detectable cheating method used at Poker. It's next to impossible for the sharp to get away with palming among seasoned gamblers. Like sex, it can be learned by almost anyone, but doing it well enough to get by even with half-smart Poker players requires some native talent and assiduous practice.

A good many hand muckers, however, have perfected the art to such an extent that they can palm and switch the first two downcards in Seven Card Stud successfully under the sharp eyes of some seasoned Las Vegas Poker players.

When the sharper at Draw Poker does not have a confederate to work with, then he has to work lone hand. He often resorts to holding out a palmed card or cards out of a succession of previously dealt bad hands. These stolen cards he secretes about his person until the right matching cards are dealt to him. Then he switches the held-out cards back again to make a winning hand.

Naturally, the main job then is to get rid of the extra cards once the held-out cards are switched back in the hand. For example, the sharper has been holding out three aces under the crook of his knee. He is dealt a fourth ace and his big moment has come. Quickly he palms the three held-out aces from under his knee and into his hand. Now he holds four aces all right, but he also has eight cards, an embarrassing number to be caught with in a Five Card Draw game. The cheat does with his three valueless cards what he did with the three held-out aces, only in reverse. He palms them out of his hand and hides them under the crook of his armpit. Hard? Yes, but it's done all the time by hand muckers.

The best way of detecting the kind of cheating described here is to watch the players. Pay particular attention to the nervous guy who frequently hitches his chair up to the table. He's possibly holding out in the crook of his knee. Watch also for hold-outs when playing high spades at Draw Poker. It's easy to hold out a single card, and an ace of spades is all you need to win the spade bet.

By the same token, the fellow who reaches into his pocket for a handkerchief may be holding out under the arm or in a pocket.

Always keep your eyes open for any funny business. If you see something suspicious, pull out of the game. If you don't see anything, keep watching anyway.

Signaling—Poker's Least Detected Cheating Practice

Poker, like Bridge, is vulnerable to an illegal cheating practice that is next to impossible to eradicate. It involves two or more Poker-playing confederates who make use of illegal signal codes. Amateur, semiprofessional and professional cheats are all guilty of this practice. More money is lost to teams of signal cheats by all kinds of Poker players than by all the Poker cheating methods described in this chapter combined. No single Poker player, whether average, good or expert, has a ghost of a chance against a two-player team of signal cheats.

Many an otherwise honest Poker player thinks nothing of signaling a player friend to drop out of the pot when he holds a good hand. That is often done by secretly signaling the other player to drop out. Should the cheating friend have dropped out of the pot, it is common for him to turn to an adjacent active player to look at his hand, and should that active player hold a good or bad hand, the amateur cheat will use a signal to convey the necessary information to his accomplice.

Women Poker cheats who work in teams of two are prone to signaling. Poker is the game where the women signal cheat has come into her own. The beauty of a signal code between two women player confederates is that they can get away with countless gestures such as fooling with their hair, getting makeup out of a handbag, settling their dresses, etc., all under cover of these apparently normal feminine movements. One movement may mean "Raise," another, "Drop out," and still another "I hold a full house," etc. Signal codes such as the above are used successfully by many a two-woman Poker-playing team of cheats in many supposedly friendly weekly games, and if suspected, an accusation is next to impossible to prove.

Back in the late forties, when Draw Poker was at its height of popularity, almost every other fair-sized Poker game had a pair of signal cheats working. Nearly all these cheats made use of the same finger code. These signals became so common among cheats that they soon were known as the "international signs," and became known to sharps the world over.

During my World War II gambling investigations for the War Department I spotted hundreds of signal cheats who hailed from various sections of the country, all employing the international signs. A brief description of this signal code follows. One finger extended from a closed fist on the table means one pair; two fingers extended, two pairs; three fingers extended, three of a kind; hand flat on table, fingers touching, full house; hand flat on table with fingers spread out, four of a kind, etc. The signal to a partner to raise is given by putting the clenched fist down on the table and raising the thumb up and down. These signals are given for a split second only.

Finger and hand signaling is also used at Stud Poker. In addition the signaling is done with the hole card or cards, and the first upcard. When the upcard covers one or both of the hole cards completely, it usually indicates the upcard is paired with the hole card. If in Seven Card Stud or Hold Em the first two dealt hole cards are squared perfectly on the table, it indicates they are paired, and so on.

Modern signaling codes between expert Poker cheats have improved considerably in the past few decades, so much so, in fact, that I have seen them used in Las Vegas and California legalized Poker rooms against top Poker professionals.

Unhappily, the detection of signaling between two unknown player confederates, if suspected, is rarely if ever proven. To avoid detection, expert signal cheats make use of two or more signal codes and often switch from one to the other during play.

The best advice I can give to protect yourself against signal cheats is to look out for the player or players who are constantly shifting around unnecessarily, touching chips, cards, ties, constantly changing their finger positions or constantly asking questions. Chances are that these motions and actions may include a few signals. If you suspect two players of signaling, just pack the game in, because even if you are right, you can never prove signaling.

MARKED-CARD CHEATS AT WORK

My latest national Poker game survey results show that on the average of three out of every hundred Poker games played annually in the United States, the cheat makes use of marked cards. These marked cards are doctored at some time or other so that some or all of the 52 cards can be read from the back. Gamblers call marked cards "readers." Cheats refer to them as "paper," and to the average player's bankroll they are poison. They are the most widely used mechanical cheating device and are used by amateurs, semiprofessionals and top-notch pros because they require no manipulative skill, are surefire money winners and are almost never detected by the average easygoing, unsuspicious card player.

The legalized Nevada casino Poker rooms protect their customers against the menace of cheats switching in marked decks or the marking of cards during play by having the house dealer "burn" (discard) the top card of the deck prior to the dealing of each new round of cards. This discard rule is a precaution against marked-card cheats; 80% of the advantage gained by the use of marked cards is eliminated by this burn, or discard, rule.

Some time ago I invited six card-playing couples to my home and tried an experiment. I gave them a dozen decks of cards still sealed in their original wrappers. "You have all been playing cards for the past twenty years," I said. "Some of you have lost considerable sums of money at cards on your winter vacations in Florida. These packs—four Bridge, four Poker and four Pinochle—were made by twelve different manufacturers, and each has a different back design. One deck is marked and can be read from the back. I'll bet that in an hour's examination none of you can find it."

This was a challenge they couldn't resist and they went to work to prove that they could spot marked cards when they saw them. They even examined the card cases before opening the decks, looking for signs of tampering with the card-case sticker. After taking the decks from the cases, they did the same with the glassine paper in which the decks were wrapped. They found nothing. Then they began examining the backs of the cards. It was an arduous task but they stuck to it for a full hour; none of them wanted to admit that they couldn't spot a marked deck even after having been told the marks were there.

"Okay," one of them said finally. "We give up. Which one is it?"

"I have a confession to make," I said then. "I lied when I told you that one deck is marked."

One man, deck in hand, nearly threw it at me. "That," he growled, "is a dirty trick if I ever saw one. We spend an hour looking for something that isn't there. Is this supposed to be funny or something?"

"Well," I said, "it proves something. As a matter of fact, all twelve decks are marked."

Since I had lied once, they wanted proof of this statement. I spent the next half hour reading the backs of cards from all twelve decks before my friends were completely convinced. They all agreed then that they would be smart to stay out of any big-money card games until they had learned how to spot marked cards.

Like millions and millions of players who play regularly and who often lose more than they can afford, all my friends had heard of marked cards but hadn't the slightest notion of what to look for or how to examine a deck properly.

Marked cards are commonplace because they are easy to obtain. Anyone can purchase marked card decks from gambling-supply houses located in most cities of the United States. These marked decks and those obtained at many trick and novelty stores are supposedly sold "for magician purposes only."

There are a great many antigambling laws in the United States but there are none that prohibit the manufacture or sale of marked cards. Thousands of decks of marked cards are sold each week, and the only penalty is that the user may occasionally get his ears pinned back or his nose pushed in when a knowledgeable player rumbles the gaff.

It's even possible that you might buy a marked deck without knowing it from a retailer whom you know and trust because some cheat has slipped him a few bucks. On one occasion, some years ago, during the racing season at Saratoga, it was difficult to buy anything else. A card mob had jimmied its way into a warehouse and substituted a whole case of marked cards for a case that had been shipped in by a legitimate distributor. As soon as the cards were jobbed and retailed the mob went to work. Nearly every game in town had a marked deck in it, and the chumps were cheated with cards they had purchased themselves. The mob, naturally, made a tidy profit on this wholesale switching operation.

The average player has several misconceptions about marked cards. He believes, for instance, that the markings show both rank and suit. This is true only of Bridge and Pinochle decks, where the suit is important. Usually only the numerical value is indicated; but that is all the cheat needs. If he can identify the value of each card as it comes off the top of the deck or always know what the values of his opponents' hole cards are in Stud Poker, the chumps might just well be playing with their cards face up. That isn't a card game; it's a swindle.

The ordinary player also thinks the cards are marked when they are printed. They aren't; reputable card manufacturers are not on the side of the cheats. But their cards do get marked later. The gambling-supply house or the cheat himself buys honest decks of standard brands. They heat and soften the adhesive and remove both the box sticker and glassine wrapping. Then the cards are marked by hand with a special marking ink. Finally the glassine wrapper is replaced and neatly repasted, the deck reinserted in its case, and the box sticker glued on again.

Markings may be "light work" or "strong work," that is, marked with fine lines or with easier-to-see heavier lines. Light work is used by professional cheats against smart or alert opponents; against the chumps the strong work goes in because it is easier to read during play. Amateur cheats use strong work, which can often be read from across the table five or six feet away. Cards are marked near both ends so that they can be read no matter which end is exposed to the Poker cheat.

Although individual marking systems vary, all card markings fall into eight kinds of work.

Edge Work: On cards having white margins on the backs, the line between the margin and back design is thickened slightly at certain points. A mark high up indicates an ace; a little lower down, a king, etc.

Line Work: Additional small spots, curlicues or lines are added to the back design.

Cutout: A chemical preparation bleaches out or a sharp knife scrapes off a minute area of ink from the design, thus adding white areas that weren't there originally.

Blockout: Parts of the design are blocked out with white ink, or some configuration in the design is exaggerated slightly. This is especially useful on cards whose back designs are claimed to be markproof—those with overall designs and no white border. An example of this is the Bee card, whose back design is a simple overall pattern of diamond shapes. Certain diamonds are made smaller or larger by blocking out.

Shading: White areas of the card are delicately shaded with a dilute solution of the marking ink. A good marked-card man can read it from across the table.

Trims: A marking method used on cards whose back designs have white margins. The shark removes the cards he wants to be able to recognize (say the high cards) and trims a thin 1/32-inch slice off *one* side edge of the card so that the margin is narrower than on the opposite edge. So that the remaining cards in the deck will be the same size and the margins will remain equal, he then trims 1/64-inch off *both* side edges. The net effect is that the back design on some cards seems to have been misprinted slightly off center. This can also be done on some cards which have overall back designs. Again the pattern is off center and does not run off the edge of the card in the same way on both sides. The simplest detection method is to place a suspected card on an honest card from another deck. The trimmed card will be smaller.

Pictures: A good rule to paste in your hat is never to play for money with "one-way" cards, that is, cards whose backs bear pictures or designs that are not symmetrical from top to bottom. During play, a cheat can arrange such a deck so that high cards are right side up, low cards upside down. I know it sounds obvious, but card cheats know from experience that the obvious device is sometimes the one least likely to be suspected. Most players dismiss this idea, if it does occur to them, as too obvious and primitive a device to be used. Therefore the cheat, well aware of this, sometimes uses it; and a quick shuffle, after turning half the pack end for end, will destroy the arrangement and the evidence if anyone shows any sign of suspicion.

Luminous Readers: I put this one in mainly because it shows how little trust you or anyone should put in gambling-supply-house catalog copy. Some of the gimmicks they list, which the amateur cheat buys because he knows no better, are strictly sucker items. When the would-be cheat orders a deck of luminous readers at $25 to $50 per deck, he receives by express (these boys avoid using the mails) a red-backed deck of cards whose backs bear large numerals lightly marked in with green pencil. You also get a cheap pair of glasses with red-tinted lenses or a red-tinted, transparent eyeshade. When the card is viewed in red light the red back design fades out and the green markings turn dark and become visible for you alone. If you suspect this gimmick, simply ask to borrow the glasses or eyeshade for a moment. The cheater, if that is what he is, will probably be out the door and halfway down the stairs before you finish asking, because one look at the cards will convict him. Professional cheaters wouldn't be caught dead with such junk because they know that if they were caught with it they might end up dead.

The latest wrinkle in this department is a pair of tinted contact lenses made to your prescription. There is a nice profit on this sucker item; the charge is $300 per pair and up.

There are many items listed in the catalog which no smart cheat has used in years and for which many amateur cheats have paid good money only to get the horselaugh or a beating in the first halfway smart game they sit in on. The punch line here is that I know of one crooked-gambling-equipment manufacturer who retired wealthy after years of selling crooked devices (much of it junk) to cheaters and would-be cheaters. Then, with nothing to do and money in the bank, he began gambling, became an addict and went broke. And some of his bankroll went to the professional cheats who used something you can't order from any catalog—sleight-of-hand moves.

Marking Cards During Play

When the skilled cheat has no good opportunity to switch a marked deck into play, he uses a type of mark that can be applied during the game. The markings are more easily detected by a smart player, and the cheat takes more risk, but it is a mighty common practice in high-stakes games where knowing the value of one or two cards is highly important.

Nailing: The cheat digs his thumbnail into the side edge of the card and leaves a small identifying indentation which, like all markings, even expert ones, can be seen at some distance when you know what to look for. The mark is placed on both side edges so that it can be spotted no matter which way the card is held, and turning the card end for end does not change the mark's location in relation to the end of the card.

In Stud Poker, for example, only high cards are marked, the others being less important. A nail mark near the upper end of the card indicates an ace, a quarter of the way down it signals a king, halfway down it means queen, and so on.

Waving: Essentially the same gaff, except the cheat places one finger on one side of the card at the edge, two underneath, and applies pressure. This puts a bend or wave in the card's edge and the location (top, middle or bottom) supplies the needed information. Detection: Square the pack and examine edges. Nail marks, sanding and waving will stand out like a well-stacked blonde.

Daubing: A gaff similar to shading, except that the mark can be applied during play. The cheat carries a small flat container of a waxy paste called daub. Pressing the tip of a finger on this and then on the card leaves a light smudge, usually a yellowish brown, which can be mistaken for a nicotine stain. Its location on the card back supplies the information.

Pegging: A very old marking method which is sometimes still used. Here the cheater uses the principle of Braille and is able to feel rather than see the marks. When he pegs, the sharper shows up at the game with a Band-Aid on his thumb or finger. This hides a sharpened thumbtack whose point penetrates the bandage and with which the cheat pricks the cards, usually only aces and kings, in the right places. A prick applied to the face of a card raises a small bump on the card's back. When the cheat deals, the thumb of the hand holding the deck feels the bump and he second-deals, retaining the high card for himself or a confederate. Your tactile sense is just as sensitive; run a finger over the card backs now and then to satisfy yourself that the cards aren't pegged; when any player has a bandaged finger, be sure to do it.

Sanding: Another method of edge marking, also requiring a bandage. There is a slit in the bandage and beneath it a piece of fine sandpaper. The cheat pulls the card's edge along the slit. Card edges become grayed with use, and the sandpaper cleans the dirt off, supplying a white edge that stands out clearly.

How to Spot a Marked-Card Poker Cheat

Suspect a player who concentrates too much on the backs of the cards in your hand, the backs of the players' hole cards, the backs of the community cards resting in the center of the table, the back of the first card to be dealt on each round of play or the important card in any Poker game. There's nothing wrong with a natural healthy interest in the cards, but an undue interest in their back designs may be your tip to take a scholarly interest in the deck yourself.

The Scarne Riffle to Detect Marked Cards

To detect marked cards, use the Scarne Riffle Test. It is a marked-card detection method based on the principle of the animated-cartoon books with which you may have played when you were a child. When you held such a book firmly in one hand and riffled the pages rapidly with the fingers of the other hand, the figures printed on the pages seemed to move. It's the principle on which the motion picture is based. Try it on the cards you suspect may be marked. Hold the cards in your left hand face downward. Hold your left thumb firmly over the center of the back of the top card. Now pull back the narrow edge of the deck furthermost from your body with the fingers of your right hand and riffle them rapidly, keeping your eyes on the back of the design. An honest design will stand utterly still. If the cards are marked, a shifting of lines will appear on the backs. When this occurs, note the exact spot where the shift took place and compare it with the like spot on other cards. If they vary, the cards are marked.

After you have convinced yourself that you have been playing with a marked deck—then what? That's hard to answer because you can't pick out the culprit who put the marked deck into the game. In fact, he may not even be playing in the game at this time. Therefore, it's possible all your present opponents may be intended marked-card victims the same as you are.

My advice, as in all other cheating incidents, is to forget all about it and find yourself another Poker game, because as I have learned over the years, cheating is difficult to prove. Furthermore, any cheat caught red-handed (or simply accused) is dangerous—so move with caution.

THE SCARNE POKER SHUFFLE

At least 50% of nonprofessional Poker players make this mistake after a shuffle: They take the pack up into their hands to square it before offering it for the cut. Why, after taking such fastidious pains to conceal that bottom card, must they expose it thus to their opponents? Make no mistake about it—at least one hawk-eyed opponent will take advantage of that card. He'll know where it is after the cut. He can cut the pack in such a way as to force it into the deal (placing it high in the pack) or keep it out. In either case, a significant percentage swings in his favor. Square the cards flat against the table.

It must be a matter of record that I'm a card manipulator by trade. I know how to shuffle, and I'm going to take the liberty of assuming you'd like to be taught by a professional. Nothing fancy about it; it won't take much time; and, while I don't guarantee to transform you into a card manipulator, I think that the next five minutes we spend together will insure you against ever being embarrassed by shuffling badly.

First, place the deck flat on the table directly in front of you. Grab the deck on the extreme ends with both hands, thumbs and fingers opposite each other, tips resting on the table. Pull about half the cards (about a 26-card packet) off the top of the deck with your right hand while holding the bottom half with your left hand. Then place the top half flat on the table end to end with the bottom half.

Second, let go of both packets and shift your left and right hand grips to the packet ends nearest each other and riffle (interlace) the packets together by running your thumbs up the sides of each packet.

Third, after the cards have been riffled together, release your hold and with the palm of each hand slide (push) them into a single block by bringing your palms toward each other. Never take the cards off the table either for the shuffle or in the act of squaring the deck.

Fourth, get into the habit of cutting the deck just for insurance at least once during the shuffle by pulling out the bottom half and slapping it onto the top between riffles—good protection against locaters who keep track of certain cards during the shuffle.

The GIs used to call this the "Scarne Shuffle." It's foolproof, crookproof and tidy as a con man's mustache . . . and it'll save you money if you never play anything but Solitaire. It also saves wear and tear on a pack of playing cards.

Glossary

The modern glossary that follows includes not only the Poker argot, technical terms and idioms that appear in the preceding pages but also a great many other colloquial expressions in common use today among the Poker fraternity. A Poker vocabulary based on the games discussed in this book plus the glossary that follows will get you respectful attention in any Poker club from Maine to Florida, from New York City to Seattle. I have permission to say the same on behalf of the legalized casino Poker rooms in Nevada and the legal Draw Poker clubs found in California. And I'm sure I can say as much for the untold thousands of Poker clubs that flourish in all parts of the world wherever English is spoken.

ABC. A Las Vegas term used to describe the first three dealt cards in Seven Card Stud and its variants when they are ace, deuce and trey.

According to Scarne. The once universal term "According to Hoyle" has been replaced by millions of game players throughout the world with the phrase "According to Scarne," which simply means "correctly played" or played according to today's universally accepted rules.

Ace. The one-spot in a deck of cards. The highest- and lowest-ranking card in various five-card Poker hands.

Ace High. A five-card Poker hand less than a pair but with an ace.

Ace-Kicker. A three-card hand in Draw Poker, a pair plus an ace in a two-card draw.

Aces Up. A five-card hand comprised of two pairs including a pair of aces.

Action. The betting. "The action is good."

Active Player. A player still in the competition for the pot, one who has not thrown in his hand.

Advertise. To bluff a worthless hand with the intention of having the bluff seen by opponents in an attempt to get them to call a future bet that is not a bluff.

Agent. An illegal partner who resorts to cheating in a Poker game.

Ahead. Winning in the game. "I'm ahead fifty dollars."

All Black, All Red. An announcement by a player on the showdown that he holds a flush, designating respectively a flush in spades or clubs, or in diamonds or hearts.

All In. To bet all the money you have left on the table.

Angle. (1) An idea. (2) A cheating scheme.

Angling. Proposing to another player an agreement, private and outside the rules, that the pot be split evenly regardless of which player wins it, or that players refrain from raising against each other.

Ante. A stake put into the pot by each player before any cards are dealt; *see also* Edge.

Ante Up. A directive to all players to put their ante in the pot.

Anything Opens. A Draw Poker game where a specific pair of openers is not required and a player can open the pot with any hand he holds.

Ax (The). When a game operator extracts a cut (charge) from a Poker pot, a player may say, "There goes the ax."

Baby. A term used in Las Vegas Poker rooms to describe a five-spot or less.

Back to Back. Said of the first two hole cards or the hole card and the first upcard when they are paired or "wired."

Back Door. When a player on the draw makes an unexpected good hand.

Backer. Someone behind the scenes who supplies a Poker player with his bankroll.

Back In. To bet after having previously checked.

Baggage. An observer of a Poker game who is broke and does not play.

Bait. A check or small bet designed to induce opponents to stay, bet and/or raise the pot.

Bang Up. To close up a Poker game voluntarily.

Bank. The box or container of the Poker chips representing the money in the game.

Banker. The player or houseman responsible for selling chips to players and settling accounts at the game's end.

Beat the Board. To possess a hand that can beat any exposed card or cards that are exposed in any player's upcards around the table.

Beef. (1) A complaint. (2) To complain.

Belly-Buster Straight. A card drawn that fills in an inside straight.

Bet. Any wager made in Poker.

Bet Blind. To bet without looking at one's hand.

Bet Into. To bet ahead of an opponent whose face-up cards, bets or draw indicate that his hand may be better.

Bet the Limit. To bet the maximum amount permitted by the rules.

Bet the Pot. To bet the total amount of money or chips in the pot in a pot limit.

Betting Handle. This is not the amount of money won or lost by Poker players at the end of a game session. It is the total amount of money in all the pots played in that session. Most of the money won or lost at the end of a Poker session has been bet and rebet many times in many pots before it is actually won or lost. *Note:* My latest national Poker survey revealed that the yearly Poker betting handle in the United States totaled $100 billion.

Betting Interval. The round in which each active player has the opportunity of folding, checking, betting, raising or reraising.

Bicycle. The lowest possible hand in Ace to Five Lowball, A-2-3-4-5, is called a Bicycle. In Deuce to Seven Lowball a Bicycle is 2-3-4-5-7.

Big Blind. The second or third blind bet permitted in a game that possesses multiple blind bets that are made without looking at one's hand.

Big Dog. A big underdog to win the pot. Opposite of favorite.

Big Hand. A hand such as full house, four of a kind, or better.

Big Nickel. Professional Poker players' term for $500.

Bit. A jail term. "He did a year bit."

Bite. A request for a loan. "I put the bite on him for fifty bucks."

Blind. A compulsory bet made before a player is dealt his cards or looks at his hand.

Blind Opening. Compulsory opening of the pot by a blind bet as in any form of Stud and Draw Poker, provided it has been agreed to by mutual consent at the start of the game.

Blind Raise. A forced raise, usually double the amount of the blind opener's bet—made before a player has been dealt cards or has looked at his hand.

Block-Out Work. A method of marking cards in which part of the design is blocked out with white ink, or some configuration in the design is slightly exaggerated.

Blood Money. Money that is hard to get, that one has worked hard to earn.

Blow. (1) To lose. "He blew five hundred dollars." (2) To leave. "The cops are expected to raid the Poker game so we'll have to blow."

Bluff. To bet an inferior hand in such a way that opponents will think it is a strong hand and retire from the pot.

Board. The cards that are face up in a Stud game are referred to as a "player's board," as are the community cards resting in the center of the table for various forms of Poker.

Bonus or Royalty. A predetermined sum to be paid by the other players to any player holding a royal flush, straight flush or four of a kind. Bonus agreement must be made by unanimous agreement at the start of the game.

Bottom Dealer. A card cheat who deals from the bottom of the deck while pretending to deal off the top. Also known as a "base dealer" or "subway dealer."

Boys. Racketeers. "The boys financed this Poker game."

Break. To draw a card instead of standing pat in Lowball. A player who has a pat nine discards the nine to draw one card to try to improve his hand.

Buck. To persist in Stud Poker in playing against an opponent's hand whose upcards indicate it is the superior hand. Also known as "chasing."

Bug. A joker that can only be used as an ace or to fill in a straight or flush.

Build-up. The act put on by the operators of a Poker room and/or their employees to arouse the player's betting spirit.

Bull. (1) An ace. (2) A detective in plain clothes.

Bump. To raise the pot.

Bum Rap. A false accusation of wrongdoing or crime.

Bum Steer. Wrong information.

Bundle. A player's large bankroll.

Buried Card. A card placed among the discards and usually so disposed of as a result of an irregularity.

Burn. To remove a card from the top of the deck and put it aside out of play or to place it face up on the bottom of the deck; the card itself is the "burnt card."

Burn and Turn. To burn the top card of the deck prior to dealing the next round of cards. Popular in Las Vegas Poker rooms to minimize the use of marked cards.

Busted Flush. A four flush that didn't fill in.

Button. When there is a house dealer (as in Las Vegas) a small circular disc called a "button" is placed in front of a player to indicate that he is the theoretical dealer and he is to receive the last dealt cards. After each deal the button is passed to each player in clockwise fashion.

Buy-in. The minimum amount of money to secure a seat in a particular Poker game.

By Me. A phrase used when passing, checking, dropping out or standing pat.

Call; Call a Bet. To put into the pot an amount equaling the highest bet made by an opposing player on the current round of betting. Also called "seeing a bet."

Call Bet. To make a bet without putting money in the pot. To pay later.

Calling a Hand. Equaling a final bet in order to look at the active players' hands at the showdown. Best hand wins the pot.

Calling Station. A Western term used to describe a weak or bad Poker player who's next to impossible to bluff and who'll call most every bet made prior to the showdown.

Card Mechanic. A person who expertly manipulates cards for cheating purposes.

Card Mob. Two or more Poker players working as a team to cheat the other players.

Card Sense. Said of a card player who has natural card-playing ability.

Card Shark. A slang expression for a professional card cheater.

Cards Speak. A form of High-Low Poker in which there are no consecutive or simultaneous declarations as to whether the player wants to call his hand for high, low, or both. That is, the cards speak for themselves on the showdown.

Case Card. (1) The one remaining card in the deck that will improve a Poker player's hand. "He caught the case king." (2) The last card of a suit or denomination still in the deck. (3) The last one of anything, as "case note"—one's last dollar.

Case the Deck. Ability to remember most of the played upcards in Stud Poker or its variants.

Cash Out. Quit a game, converting the chips or checks to money.

Chase. To play against a better Stud hand when exposed. "You have to go broke if you keep chasing."

Check. To signify, as commonly used at Stud, Draw, and their variants, that the player doesn't want to bet in that turn of play, but does propose to remain an active player, reserving the right in his next turn of play to bet, call, raise, reraise or drop out. A player cannot check his bet if a bet has been made earlier in that round. Also known as "pass."

Check, Chip. A circular plastic token having various denominations, used in place of cash, which is redeemed for cash by the banker at quitting time.

Check Cop. An adhesive paste that a cheat places on his palm. When he helps push the pot toward the winning player several chips or coins adhere to his palm and he steals them.

Check and Raise. To sandbag (rules permitting); to check a possible winning hand with the expectation of raising any subsequent bet in the same round.

Chill. To lose interest.

Chippy. (1) A sucker. (2) An inexpert Poker player.

Chips (In the). Said of a Poker player who has a lot of money.

Chiseler. (1) A Poker player who claims another player's ante or bet. (2) A gambler who borrows money in a private Poker game and doesn't repay it.

Chump. An inexperienced Poker player. A sucker. Also a mark, mooch, monkey, pheasant, bird, canary, greenie, rabbit.

Cinch Hand. A hand that absolutely cannot be beaten (or which the player is convinced cannot be beaten); at Draw Poker, for instance, a royal flush; at Stud Poker, a combination of cards which, regardless of one's opponents' hole card or cards, cannot be beaten by any combination the opponents may draw or organize.

Clean. (1) Said of a person who does not possess a police record. (2) To win all the money from one or more opponents in a Poker session. The unlucky one is "cleaned" or "taken to the cleaner's."

Close to the Belly or Vest. Cautiously. A Stud player who bets only on a wired pair or when he has the best hand showing is playing close to the vest.

Closed Poker. Said of a Poker game in which all the cards are concealed. Also known as Draw Poker.

Coffeehouse. To try to mislead the opponents through excessive and exaggerated speech and manner. In London's Poker rooms, coffeehousing is considered an irregularity and the player so doing forfeits his hand.

Cold Caller. Said of a player who has no money invested in the pot except a possible ante, who then calls a raise and a reraise.

Cold Deck. A deck of cards which has secretly been arranged by a Poker cheat in a number of strong Poker hands for the purpose of switching later for the deck in play and taking the opposition to the cleaner's. Also called "cooler." The latest term for a cold deck among professional cheats is "package."

Cold Player. Poker player on a losing streak. "My cards are as cold as ice."

Combination. Underworld or gambling term for a syndicate.

Come (The). Staying in a pot with hope of catching the desired card. Sometimes indicating the next card to be dealt.

Community or Common Card(s). A card or cards resting in the center of the table and considered as each player's cards to help form his hand.

Confederate. *See* Agent.

Consecutive Declaration. The procedure in High-Low Poker in which each player in turn verbally declares his intention of going for low, high, or both.

Cooler. *See* Cold Deck.

Counter. A token used instead of a Poker check or chip to represent a unit of value.

Court Card. A picture or face card—jack, queen or king.

Cowboy. (1) A reckless and fast gambler. (2) A slang term for each of the four kings in a Poker deck.

Crimp. (1) To bend one or more cards in the deck in such a way that the cheat or his confederate can cut the deck at a certain place or so that a player will unknowingly cut at the place desired by the cheat. (2) The bend itself.

Crossroader. A card cheat who travels over the country seeking Poker games in which he can ply his trade.

Crumb Bun. *See* Chiseler.

Cut, Cut the Cards. After the dealer has finished shuffling the deck, the player to the dealer's right removes the top part of the deck and places it to the right alongside the bottom part of the deck. Then the dealer carries the cut by putting the bottom portion of the deck on top of the other portion and squares the deck prior to the start of the deal.

Cutout Card Markings. To mark cards this way, a minute area of ink on the card's back design is chemically bleached or scraped off with a knife, adding a white area that wasn't there originally.

Cut the Pot. To abstract a sum from the pot to defray the expenses of the Poker room; *see also* Kitty.

Cutter. A Poker-room employee (usually the dealer) who takes a money charge (called a "cut") out of the pot for supplying the Poker facilities.

Cutthroat Poker. No-holds-barred play designed to destroy the opposition by any legal means.

Cutting Out. Said of two people who have formed a partnership when one player sits on the sidelines, or when at some point one of these two people decides to terminate the partnership. That person is "cutting out."

Cut Up Big Wins (To). To reminisce, to talk over old-time Poker winnings.

Cut Up Jackpots. To boast about one's previous Poker winnings.

Cut Up the Score. To divide the loot. To share the Poker winnings.

Daub. A paste or fluid secretly applied to a fingertip, used to mark cards during play.

Dead Card. A card that has already been in play or one that has been declared out of play due to an irregularity. The opposite of "live card."

Dead Hand. A hand that is not playable, due to an irregularity.

Dead Man's Hand. Said of a hand made up of two black pairs, aces and eights. So called because it is supposed to have been the Poker hand held by Wild Bill Hickok in Deadwood, Dakota territory, when he was shot to death in a saloon by Jack McCall on August 2, 1876.

Dead in the Pot. When there is no possibility for a player to win, he's said to be "dead in the pot."

Deadwood. The discard pile, hands and cards folded and thrown in by the players or discarded prior to the draw.

Deal (The). The shuffle, cut, distribution of the cards to the players, the betting intervals and the showdown are known as the deal.

Dealer. A houseman or player who distributes the cards to the players is called the dealer.

Dealer's Choice. Poker as played often in social and home games where the deal rotates from player to player and the player dealer at his turn to deal may designate the form of Poker to be played during his deal and what cards, if any, are wild.

Dean (The). *See* Professor.

Deuce. A common term for the lowly two-spot.

Deuces Wild. A Poker variant in which each of the four deuces may be designated as being any card the player desires.

Discard. A card or cards no longer wanted by the players and disposed of into the deadwood or discard pile.

Dog. Another word for underdog. The player who hasn't got much of a chance to win the pot. Opposite of favorite.

Door Card. The first dealt face-up card in a Stud game.

Downcards. The card or cards dealt face down in Stud. Also known as "hole cards."

Draw. Cards dealt from the stock after the first betting interval in Draw Poker; to discard and receive replacements in various Stud games.

Drawing Dead. Drawing a card or cards to a hand that can't possibly win the pot, regardless of the card or cards drawn. Also known as "dead in the pot."

Draw Out. To improve one's hand on the draw and beat an opponent who possessed a better hand prior to the draw. The improvement itself is known as a "drawout."

Draw Poker. A game in which a player may discard and receive replacement cards after the first betting interval. Also known as "closed Poker."

Driver's Seat (In the). Said of the player who holds what appears to be the best hand. He is known as being "in the driver's seat."

Drop. To throw in one's hand rather than put a certain amount of money or chips in the pot to play. To withdraw from the current round or deal. Also known as "fold."

Ear. A bent corner put on a card to identify it or locate it. "He put the ear on the aces."

Ear Bender. A talkative person.

Early, Middle, and Late Positions. The early positions in a nine-handed Stud game are the first three players to act on their hands; the middle positions are the following three; and the late positions are the last three.

Easy Money Guy. Anyone who gambles big at Poker and spends winnings freely.

Edge. (1) An advantage enjoyed by one gambler over another. (2) An ante put in the pot by the dealer only.

End. A share. "What's my end?"

End Betting. The last bet prior to the showdown.

Even-Up, Even Up Proposition. (1) A bet or proposition that gives each player an equal chance to win. (2) A bet at correct odds. (3) A 50-50 bet.

Exit. To get out of the game. "I'm exiting this Poker game."

Exposed Card. A face-up card, or upcard, in Stud and in community cards resting in the center of the table.

Exposed Pair. A face-up, or open, pair in Stud and in community cards.

Face. To expose the face value of a card. "Deal me a card face up."

Face Card. King, queen, jack are called face cards. Also known as "court cards," "paints" and "picture cards."

False Cut. A crooked cut that leaves the deck or part of the deck in its original position.

False Opening. One in which the pot is opened with less than the required rank hand and is therefore dead.

False Shuffle. A crooked shuffle that appears to be an honest shuffle, but in fact does not mix the cards at all, especially when executed by a skilled card mechanic.

Family Pot. A pot in which most of the players are in at the showdown.

Fast Company. Seasoned or smart gamblers.

Fast Game. The speed at which the action betting is progressing. A fast action game would be one in which most of the players are betting, raising, and reraising. Conversely, a slow game would be one where there is little betting, raising or reraising.

Fat. Said of a player with plenty of money. "He's fat." Same as "loaded."

Fatten. To increase the money or chips in the pot.

Favorite (The). The Poker player with the best chance of winning the most money or pots during a Poker session. The opposite of "dog."

Feed. To put money or chips into the pot or kitty.

Fever. The Poker habit. "She has the fever, she can't stay away from the Poker tables."

Fifth Street. The fifth card dealt each player in Stud Poker.

Fill In. To draw or buy one or more cards that will make a complete hand such as a straight, flush, full house or better.

Flat Call. Same as call. The "flat" denotes that the player did not raise.

Flat Limit. A betting limit that is constant, say a $2 maximum on each bet, raise, or reraise in each round of play.

Floorman. A Poker-room employee who oversees and supervises the action in the Poker room.

Flush. A hand consisting of five cards in the same suit not in sequence.

Fold. To drop out of the pot.

Foul, Irregular, or Dead Hand. A hand that has forfeited all right and chance of winning the pot and must be thrown into the discards, such as a hand having more or fewer cards than are permitted under the rules of the game.

Four-Card Straight. A hand consisting of four cards in sequence not of the same suit, such as 3,4,5,6, or 10,J,Q,K.

Four Flush. A hand consisting of four cards in the same suit not in sequence.

Four of a Kind. A hand comprised of four cards of the same rank and one odd card. "Wow, I win the pot with my four queens."

Free Card. A card drawn or dealt without the player's having put any money or chips into the pot.

Free Ride. A round of cards in Stud or Draw in which no player makes a bet; each therefore gets his next card or cards free. The opening round in Draw, in which no player makes a bet—each player therefore draws cards free.

Free Roll. When a player in High-Low Poker has one half of the pot cinched and is competing for the other half.

Freeze-out. A game in which a player has lost his original buy-in and is out of the game. Some such games permit the player to add additional money to his original buy-in.

Front Money. A player's winnings.

Full House. A hand consisting of three of a kind and a pair. "I have a full house—three aces and a pair of tens."

Full Seat. The first player to act on his hand. In Draw Poker, it's usually the leader.

Full Table. Table at which no seat is available and there is no more room.

Fuzz. A policeman or peace officer.

Fuzzing (the Deck). Mixing the cards by drawing two cards simultaneously from the top and bottom of the deck in order to premix a fresh deck prior to shuffling.

Gaff, G, or Gimmick. Any secret device or method that accomplishes or aids in cheating. "His gaff is marked cards."

Gallery. The nonplayers who are spectators and kibitzers.

Gambler. When this word is applied to a Poker player, it means that he is a highly skilled player.

Game. Any form of Poker played, be it Draw, Stud, or any of their variants described in this book. "What kind of Poker shall we play? Let it be Five Card Draw Deuces Wild."

Get Behind It. To back or try to shield a crooked move in Poker.

Get Out. To regain one's losses. "I got out of the Poker game even."

Get To. To bribe a police officer or politician to avoid a Poker raid. "We're O.K. I got to the police chief."

Get Your Feet Wet. An invitation to a spectator to get into the Poker game.

Girls. The four queens in a deck of cards, also known as ladies, hookers, babes, dames and chicks.

Give Him a Card. To let your opponent get a free draw.

G-Note. A $1,000 bill.

Go for the Money. To cheat. "That mob at Duke's Poker game is going for the money."

Good Man. (1) A skilled Poker cheat. (2) A good Poker player. (3) A good Poker-room operator or dealer.

Good Thing. A good bet or a good hand.

Gorilla. A bouncer or muscle man in a Poker room.

Go South with It. (1) To put money in one's pocket during a Poker session. (2) To palm a card or cards from the deck secretly. "He went South with a couple of aces."

Grand or G. $1,000.

Grind. A low-limit Poker game that requires a good many players and good action in order for the operators to make a profit.

Gyp. A Poker crook or cheat.

Half-Pot Limit. A fixed betting limit that permits a player to bet, raise or reraise no more than an amount equal to half the size of the pot.

Half a Yard. $50.

Hand. (1) The cards dealt to, drawn or bought by a player. A Poker hand must be comprised of five cards on the showdown. (2) The period of time between the dealing of the cards and the winning of the pot.

Handle. *See* Betting Handle.

Hand Mucker. A card cheat who specializes in palming, holding out of play and reintroducing valuable cards into a game.

Hard Rock. A tight player. "He's a hard rock. The only time he plays is when he has a pair back to back."

Has a Sign on His Back. Said of a Poker cheat who is widely known as a crook.

Hay. Money, chips, dough, sugar, cabbage, lettuce.

Heart. Courage. "He has plenty of heart. He always bets his hand up."

Heavy. A big-time mobster.

Hedge. To bet against a Poker situation already bet in favor of, in order to be sure of a possible profit, or to cut down or limit a possible loss.

Heel. (1) A cheap Poker player. (2) Anyone who is not good.

Heist. To hold up or rob someone.

Hidden Percentage. This is determined by calculating the chances of making the winning hand and comparing the result with the amount the pot will pay you if you do make your hand.

High. (1) The player who has the high hand at any betting interval or on the showdown. (2) High card face up bets first at Stud Poker.

High Roller. Big-time gambler or Poker player.

High Spade Bet. A side bet usually made in Draw Poker in which the hand containing the highest spade card wins.

Hit. To win money at Poker.

Hold Check. A postdated check.

Holdout Artist. A gambler or cheat who when calculating the score or dividing the amount of winnings with his partner or partners says that his winnings are less than they are and pockets the rest.

Hold Over. To hold the best hand continuously against a certain player.

Hole Cards. The face-down cards dealt to a player in any form of Stud Poker. Also known as "pockets."

Hook. A word occasionally used to describe a jack.

Hop or Crooked Shift. A secret sleight-of-hand move made after the cut, which replaces the cards in their original positions.

Hot. Said of a player on a winning streak. "That guy's so hot he can't lose a pot."

House. The operator or operators of a Poker game that provide the space, equipment and the dealers for the game, etc. In turn they charge a fee for the service by taking a cut of each pot or an hourly charge.

Hoyle (According to). An incorrect term for any set of modern rules. In reference to Poker, Edmund Hoyle died in 1769 and Poker was first heard of in 1834, 65 years after his death, so Poker cannot be played "according to Hoyle."

Hoyle, Edmund. An English barrister and codifier of game rules who wrote a book on only three card games—Piquet, Whist and Quadrille—which are now obsolete.

Hush Money. (1) A bribe paid to a policeman or politician to permit the operation of an illegal Poker game. (2) A bribe paid to someone to keep him from talking.

Hustler. A top professional Poker player who makes the rounds of various Poker games. Also known as a "rounder."

Ice. The money paid to police and politicians for permitting an illegal Poker game to operate in their locality. So called because it takes the heat off. Also called "fix money."

Immortal Hand. A Poker hand that is sure to win the pot. Also known as a "cinch hand" or a "lock."

Imperfect Deck. A deck minus one or more cards; a deck with one or more cards whose backs are marked, mutilated, or a different back design from the rest of the deck.

Improve. To draw cards that better one's hand.

In. Having called the highest betting opponent, active in the pot.

In the Bag. Said of a Poker pot that is crooked. "The pot's in the bag for the dealer."

Indices. Number designs or letters printed in the top left-hand and bottom right-hand corner of a playing card.

In the Hole. *See* In the Pocket.

In the Middle. To be the player (caller) sandwiched between two players who are raising and reraising. Also known as "whipsaw."

In the Mouth. Said of the first player to act, who is also known as the "leader."

In the Pocket. Hole or face-down cards are "in the pocket."

Inside Man. An employee of a Poker room who handles the bookkeeping and the finances.

Inside Straight. Four cards of a broken sequence needing a card of an inside rank to form a straight, such as 3, 4, 6, 7.

Insurance Bet. A side bet (common in the yearly Las Vegas World Series Poker Tournament) between two players participating in the tournament, or between one of the participants and a nonplayer, or between two non-players, or between a player and a bookmaker (professional gambler) who will accept bets from anyone, present or not, on the outcome of the tournament.

Interval of Betting. Period of deal in which players open, check, raise, re-raise and call. Also known as "betting round."

Iron Duke. A hand that is sure to take the pot, or a hand played as though it were a certain winner.

Irregularity. Any departure from the Poker rules, an inadvertent error—not a cheating or intentional misdeed.

Jackpots. A form of Five Card Draw in which the holding of a pair of jacks or better is required to open the first round of betting.

Jacks Back. A hand of Draw in which, if the pot is not opened, the hand becomes Lowball.

Jam Pot. One in which a number of players are raising and reraising each other.

Jerk. *See* Lob.

Joker. An extra card added to a 52-card deck and used as a wild card to represent any card the holder desires.

Joker Wild. Any Poker game in which the joker is used as a wild card.

Juice. The charge extracted by the house. Same as "cut," "rake-off" and "vigorish."

Kibitzer. A non-player who stands behind the players to watch the game and pass comments about the action or type of play.

Kick. To raise.

Kicker. An unmatched card held with a pair or three of a kind held in the hand when drawing partly for deceptive purposes.

Kitty. A special fund belonging to all the players built up by taking a fixed sum out of extra-large pots. Used to help defray expenses or for some other purpose.

Knave. Jack of any suit.

Knock It. A rap on the table signifying to check, pass, or waive the cutting of the deck.

Ku Klux Klan. A Southern name for three kings.

Ladies. Queens.

Lam. *See* Runout Powder.

Lame (To Come Up). To be unable to pay lost wagers or borrowed money. "Jack came up lame and took a powder."

Lay Down. For each active player to expose his hand by placing it face up on the showdown.

Lay Off. Not to play. "I'm laying off playing Poker for Lent."

Leg. One game of a series of Poker pots.

Legging a Hand. Continually checking the pot with a strong hand. Also known as "limping."

Legit Game. An honest game.

Legit Guy. A person who has no underworld connections. This does not necessarily imply that he is an honest man.

Light. A term denoting that the player owes chips to the pot. The amount owed is indicated by drawing an equal amount from the pot and placing it a little outside the pot facing the player who is short. "I'm light five dollars."

Light Work. Doctored cards marked with very fine lines. "I had to put light work in the game because the players were smart."

Limit. The fixed, agreed-upon ante, the maximum amount to open, to raise, and the number of raises permitted.

Line-up. The players in a Poker game.

Line Work. Adding small spots, curlicues or lines to the back design of playing cards so that they can be read from the back by the cheat.

Live Card. A hidden card in an opponent's hand or in the remaining part of the undealt deck. A card that is not dead because it has not yet been played.

Live Hand. A Poker hand held by an active player.

Live One. A rich Poker sucker.

Lob. A hanger-on around gambling joints who runs errands for players. Also called "jerk."

Lock. An unbeatable hand in a particular situation, also known as a "cinch hand."

Long Run (The). An indefinite time period in which the theory of probability is supposed to give each player the same number of good and bad hands.

Look. To call the final bet just before the showdown.

Looking for Action. Said of a Poker player who is trying to find a game.

Lookout. A Poker-room employee who sees that everything runs smoothly and is on the constant alert for crookedness by both players and Poker-room personnel.

Loose Player. A player who gets involved in most pots regardless of whether he holds a weak or a strong hand.

Lugger. A person who transports players to a game. Not to be confused with a "steerer."

Luminous Readers. Marked cards that can be read only through tinted glasses. The most dangerous and amateurish method of cheating. "The sucker wore tinted glasses and caught Joe cheating with his luminous readers."

Make. To recognize a cheat.

Make Good. To satisfy a pot shortage by adding cash or chips. Also, to satisfy the amount of a verbal side bet.

Map. A check. "Don't take that guy's map. He's a paperhanger."

Mark. A sucker.

Marker. (1) An IOU. (2) A numbered chip or plaque used at Poker and casino games to keep track of money owed the bank.

Mechanic (Card). A skilled card cheat who resorts to sleight of hand to accomplish his crooked work. "The card mechanic got caught dealing a card off the bottom of the deck."

Mechanic's Grip. A method of holding a deck of cards (in either the left or right hand) with three fingers curled around the long edge of the deck and the index finger at the narrow upper edge, away from the body.

Mess. Said of a draw or buy that failed to improve a hand.

Mexican Standoff. Act of quitting a Poker game when one is even, or is a very small winner or loser. "I played a Mexican standoff."

Michigan Bankroll. A large bankroll consisting mostly of one-dollar bills with a bill of large denomination on the outside as a wrapper.

Milk (the Deck). To simultaneously draw the top and bottom cards (of a fresh deck) prior to the first shuffle.

Misdeal. An illegal deal after which the cards must forthwith be reshuffled, cut and dealt again by the same dealer.

Mitt. A hand of cards.

Money Management. (1) The proper handling of your Poker bankroll as a professional. (2) The proper amount of money necessary to enter a particular game. (3) How to handle your money during various betting hands.

Mortal Nuts. (1) A cinch hand. (2) The winning hand at a specific betting interval.

Move. Sleight of hand. "That's when he made the crooked move."

Move In. To bet all your money on the table either in a high-limit or table-stakes game.

Mug. (1) A low character. (2) A sucker or chump.

Murder. Hard to beat. "That game's murder."

Muscle Man. A tough guy or bouncer who keeps order in an illegal Poker room.

Nailed. Caught cheating in a Poker game. "He was nailed red-handed switching the deck."

Natural. A winning five-card Poker hand (deuces wild) containing no wild cards on the showdown. "I have a beautiful natural straight flush."

No Limit. An erroneous statement. In all Poker games the player can only bet the amount in front of him, as in Table Stakes, or the maximum betting limit agreed on beforehand.

Number Two Man. A card mechanic expert at dealing seconds. *See* Seconds.

Nut. A gambler or gambling enterprise's overhead expenses. "The nut's too high."

Nut Flush. An ace-high flush.

Nut Player. A player who tends to play only excellent hands at the start.

Nuts. The best possible winning hand at a particular betting interval. "It's tough to beat that character since he won't bet unless he has the nuts."

Odds. Correct odds are the ratio of the unfavorable chances to the favorable chances; *see also* "Payoff Odds."

Odds On. Odds at less than fifty-fifty.

Office. *See* Signal.

Okay. Protection furnished by politicians and police enabling an illegal Poker game to operate.

Old Bill. A word or hand signal (open palm on chest or table) which is a cheater's international sign. "Is there any other cheater in the game?"

On the Come. To bet a hand with possibilities of filling in on the draw or with the next dealt cards in Stud as opposed to betting on a hand that is already complete. "Joe's on the come, drawing one card to a four-card possible flush."

On-the-Cuff Bet. A free bet for the player.

One Big One. Gambler's term for $1,000.

One-Carder. Said of a one-card draw in Draw Poker.

One-Ender. A possible one-card straight with only one end open; four cards of different suits in sequence such as A-2-3-4 and A-K-Q-J.

One-Way Action. When two players are involved in a Poker pot or game.

One-Way Cards. Cards whose backs bear pictures or designs that are not symmetrical top to bottom.

On Tilt. Said of a player who's playing exceptionally badly after losing a big pot. "He's betting those hands as if he was on tilt."

Open-Ended Straight. A holding of four cards in different suits with both ends open such as 5,6,7,8 or 10,J,Q,K.

Openers. The cards required to open the pot in regular Draw Poker.

Open Game. Similar to games in Nevada Poker rooms, where anyone may occupy any vacant seat at the Poker table.

Open Pair. In Stud Poker, a pair among a player's upcards. "Your bet, sir. You show (high hand) a pair of kings."

Open Poker. Any form of Stud or other form of Poker involving community cards where one or more cards are dealt face up.

Open Seat. An unoccupied seat at the Poker table.

Open Up. (1) To start a Poker game. (2) To give information. "He opened up to the law."

Ordinary Pass and Out. A pass-out game in which each player must ante an equal sum.

Out Draw. *See* Draw Out.

Outfit. *See* Combination.

Out in Front. To be ahead money at the Poker tables.

Outs. Playing an inferior hand with the hope of outdrawing your opponents.

Out of Turn. Betting or receiving a card or cards in some other player's turn of play; not in natural or legal sequence.

Over Cards. In various forms of Stud Poker, a higher pair which must bet over a lower pair.

Overhand Shuffle. The old-fashioned shuffle, now obsolete in most Poker games, which the dealer executes by holding the deck in one hand above the other and pulling off a continuous series of cards from the deck and letting them fall into the bottom hand.

Overhead (To Go). To be unable to make good on gambling debts; *see also* Nut.

Overlays. Cards in Stud that are higher in rank than any opponents'.

Overs. Should a player ante or put into the pot an amount larger than required and thereafter should another player make a bet, the overage (overs) cannot be taken out of the pot.

Pack. A 52-card deck.

Packet. A part of the deck, less than the whole.

Pad. Payroll. "Everybody's on the pad including the cop on the beat."

Paint. A jack, queen, or king—also known as a face card, court card and picture card. "There are six paints left in the deck."

Pair. Two cards of the same denomination.

Pair Poker. Describing a Draw Poker player's game when he seldom draws cards to fill in straights or flushes. "Murray is playing Pair Poker this hand."

Paper. Marked cards. "I laid down paper in the Poker game."

Paperhanger. A passer of bad checks. *See* Map.

Partners. Two or more players forming a team in a sophisticated Poker game to cheat the other players with prearranged signals.

Pat Hand. In Draw Poker, a five-card holding that a player does not try to improve by a draw, such as a straight, flush, etc.

Pass. Check, play.

Payoff. The collection of a bet.

Payoff Odds. The odds at which a bet is paid off, usually less than the correct odds except for honest proposition bets.

Peek (The). A cheating maneuver of a second dealer to look at the top card of the deck secretly. If it helps his hand, he'll deal seconds to his opponents and save the top card for himself.

Peg. To mark cards during play with the sharp point of a pin or thumbtack concealed in a bandage on a finger or thumb.

Pencil (The). The privilege of signing drink or food checks for players. "He has the power of the pencil."

Penny Ante. A game in which the ante (if any) and the bets such as the opening bet, raise or reraise in each round of play are literally a penny or some other small sum. "The whole family is playing penny ante Poker."

Percent. A percent sign stands for "over hundred." Thus 15% equals $15/100$ or .15.

Percentage (P.C.). An advantage obtained by offering less than the true odds. "The percentage should have given Joe 46 to 1 odds instead of 36 to 1 on drawing the king of spades to make his spade royal flush."

Philistines. Loan sharks.

Phony. (1) A person who pretends to be something he isn't. (2) A crooked deck of cards.

Picked Off. To get caught bluffing.

Pile. The amount of money or chips the player has on the table before him for betting.

Pips. The markings on non-picture cards indicating their rank and value. Ace possesses one pip, deuce has two, trey possesses three, etc.

Play. (1) Opening bet, call, see, and stay in. (2) Betting in general.

Play Back. To reraise a raise or reraise.

Player. Anyone who sits at a table and gambles his money at Poker.

Pony Up. To ante into the pot.

Position. Not where you are seated in the game, but where you are in relation to the opener in Draw, or to the first bettor in Stud in any particular hand.

Pot (The). An area somewhere near the center of the table that contains the total cash or chips bet on any single round or hand of play. "The pot you just won was the biggest of the night."

Pot Limit. A betting limit that permits a player to bet the total of the pot as a single bet.

Pot Odds. The calculated odds the money in the pot represents in ratio to the money it will cost you to play and the chances of winning the pot.

Private Game. Any game that has no houseman or banker and in which no charge is extracted for the privilege of playing. Also known as a social or home game.

Professor. A smart old-time Poker player who can calculate odds and percentages. Also called "The Dean."

Proposition Hustler. A bettor who offers betting propositions which appear at first glance to be fair or in favor of his opponent, but which actually give the hustler a big advantage. "The proposition hustler laid Pete 15 to 1 that he would not be dealt a four-card flush in his first five cards, when the correct odds are 22 to 1."

Proposition Player. A paid house player whose duties are somewhat like those of a shill except that he does not gamble with house money but rather with his own money. He keeps his winnings and pays his losses.

Public Game. A Poker game that's open to all, such as the legal Poker rooms in Nevada's casinos and the legal Poker clubs in California.

Pull Down. To take down or pocket part or all of the cash or chips resting in front of you for playing purposes.

Pull Through. A crooked table riffle shuffle which appears to be an honest shuffle. After the riffle takes place, the cheat does not push the two interlaced packets of the deck together. Instead he expertly pushes one packet through the other and slaps it on top of that packet, leaving the deck in its original position.

Punk. (1) A small-time character or chiseler. (2) A young man, a novice who hangs around Poker games.

Quack. A noisy and complaining player when losing.

Quadruplets. Four of a kind.

Quart. A four-card straight flush.

Quarter Chip. A Poker room or casino chip with a $25 value.

Queer. Counterfeit money.

Quint. A straight flush.

Quit (the Game). (1) To pocket your cash or cash in your chips and leave the game. (2) Also, to fold up a hand.

Quitter. Said of a Poker player who can't stand the pressure and leaves the game after losing a big pot.

Quitting Time. An agreed-upon time to end a Poker game.

Quorum. The minimum agreed number of players needed to start a Poker game.

Rabbit. (1) A timid person. (2) A sucker or inexperienced Poker player or gambler. "If I had a couple more rabbits like him, I'd never work again."

Rack. A box to hold chips or checks.

Rail. The velvet rope separating Poker players (Las Vegas style) from spectators in some Poker rooms.

Raise. To bet a larger sum than the previous high bettor, which must be met by all players if they wish to remain active in the pot.

Raise (Freezer). A special optional call bet created by me that is made after three or more successive raises have been made in one betting interval. At this period a player has the option of freezing (stopping) the raises by placing an equal amount into the pot as the previous player—and calling, "Freeze." This announcement prevents any further raising during that betting interval.

Rake-off. The house cut of the pot.

Rangdoodle. *See* Pot Limit.

Rank. The ordinal position of a card in its suit.

Rap Pot. To refuse to draw cards in Draw Poker.

Rat. An informer.

Read. To try to figure out an opponent's hand. "The way he bet, I read him for a full house."

Readers. Marked cards.

Ready Up. To get ready to make a crooked move in Poker.

Red (in the). (1) Owing money. (2) Unprofitable. "The expenses to run this Poker game are so big that it has put me in the red."

Redeal. A new deal by the same dealer after an irregularity in the previous deal.

Renege. To refuse to honor a lost wager or debt; to welsh.

Reraise. To bet a larger amount than the previous raiser. "He reraised the raiser."

Riffle Shuffle. A shuffle executed on the table by separating the deck into two packets and interlacing both packets together while riffling them with the thumbs and finally pushing both packets together.

Rig. To gaff or make crooked. "The game is rigged."

River Card. Said of the last or seventh card dealt face down in Seven Card Stud or its variants.

Rock. A player who won't lend any money.

Roll (to). To legally turn a face-down card in a player's Stud hand.

Roscoe. A revolver or pistol.

Rotation. The clockwise order in which Poker hands and cards are dealt and in which legal play proceeds.

Rough It Up. To bet heavily, thus enlivening the tempo of a Poker game.

Round. To deal a round is to deal each player a complete hand. To bet a round is to afford each player, in order, his choice of whether to check, bet, call, raise or reraise.

Royal Flush. An ace-high royal flush is the highest possible hand without wild cards.

Royalties. Payments paid to the holder of a predetermined Poker hand such as four of a kind, a straight flush or a royal flush by each participant in the game, whether an active or nonactive player in that particular hand.

Run-out Powder. A gambler who leaves town without paying off his debts is said to have taken a "run-out powder" or to be "on the lam."

Sand. To edge-mark cards with sandpaper.

Sandbag. To check the probable best hand in an attempt to lull your opponent into a false sense of security by an earlier indication of weakness, and when your opponent bets, to raise. "Watch that character when he checks because he's an expert at sandbagging."

Sandwiched (In Between). To be in between two players who are betting the limit and raising each other.

Scarne Cut (The World-Famous). A defense against card cheats. To execute, pull a group of cards from the center of the deck and place them on top of the deck. Then simply cut the deck in the usual manner by cutting a packet of cards off the top of the deck.

Scarne Riffle to Detect Marked Cards. To execute, the deck is held in the left hand lengthwise with fingers on the bottom and thumb on top. The fingers of the right hand bend the upper part of the deck backwards and riffle them rapidly. If the back design of the cards has been altered, no matter how minutely, the onlooker will see dots jumping back and forth, and the chances are 99 to 1 that the deck is marked.

Scooping. To declare for both high and low in a High-Low Poker game. Also called "swinging."

Score. (1) To win at gambling. (2) To succeed in any enterprise. (3) To win by cheating. (4) The money won by cheating.

Score a Big Touch. To fleece a player or players for a large amount of money.

Scratch. Money.

Screen Out. To cover up or misdirect attention away from a crooked Poker move.

Second Dealer. A Poker cheat who deals the second card from the deck when he appears to be dealing the top card.

See. To call in the last betting round.

Send It In. To keep raising the limit in limit games or betting all the money or chips in front of you in a table-stakes game.

Shading. A method of marking cards. The backs of cards are delicately shaded with a dilute solution of marking ink the same color as that already printed on the backs.

Shark, Sharp. A card cheater. *See also* Mechanic.

Shift the Cut. To return secretly the halves of a cut deck to their original positions.

Shill. An employee of the house who is used as a Poker game starter.

Shiner. A small mirror that secretly reflects the top card of the deck as it is dealt. Usually concealed in rings, cigarette cases, match boxes, etc. A dangerous and amateurish method of cheating.

Short Money. Said of a player who does not have the cash for a buy-in in a particular game.

Show. To face or expose a player's entire hand on the showdown.

Showdown. The act of decision. After the last bet has been called by all the active players on the final round of betting, each active player, starting with the player who is being called, and moving clockwise, exposes his full hand for all to see, announcing the rank of his hand at the same time.

Shuffle. To mix the cards together preparatory to the cut and deal.

Shy. Same as "light." A player out of chips plays on credit for the balance of the hand. He designates the amount he is shy by taking an identical sum from the pot and moving it several inches outside the pot facing him.

Side Bet. A bet between players made privately and put aside separate from the pot.

Simultaneous Declaration. In forms of High-Low Poker with declaration, the method of declaring whereby each player reveals his declaration at the same time.

Sit In. To become a player in a Poker game.

Sixth Street. The sixth card dealt to each active player in Seven Card Stud Poker.

Skimming. Secretly taking money from a gross handle of any gambling venture.

Sleeper. Money left on the table by a player either in collecting a pot or in making change, and picked up by another player.

Slough or Slough Up. To close up. "We sloughed the game." "The police sloughed the town."

Slow Play. To check or bet a small amount with a good hand.

Smooth. Describing a good hand.

Spade Bet. A bet by two or more players (generally at Draw Poker) as to who will be dealt the highest-ranking spade among his first five cards.

Spit. A community card turned face up by the dealer in the center, which may be used by all active players.

Splitting Openers. To discard one or more cards of your opening requirement in various forms of Draw Poker.

Spot Card. Any card ranked from ace to ten.

Squeeze. To look at your cards by spreading them apart as slowly as possible so that the indices will be revealed only to you.

Stack. The chips belonging to a player. Also "stack the deck," to arrange cards in a cheating manner during the shuffle.

Stake. The money with which a player enters a Poker game.

Standard Deck. 52 cards, 13 of each suit, clubs, diamonds, hearts, and spades in each suit (A-2-3-4-5-6-7-8-9-10-J-Q-K). Also called a "regular pack." *Note:* Each of the four suits has the same value.

Stand-off. When two or more identical high hands appear on the showdown and players divide the pot equally. Also called a "tie."

Stand Pat. In Draw Poker, to refuse to draw cards, and to choose to play one's original dealt hand.

Stay. To remain as an active player by putting up an amount of cash or chips equal to the biggest bet made during a betting interval.

Steal a Pot. To win a pot by bluffing or by failure of another player to press his advantage with a higher-ranking hand.

Steerer. An individual who secretly works for a crooked Poker establishment and brings customers to the game to be fleeced.

Stiff. (1) An unlucky player. (2) A non-player.

Straddle. The second or possibly the third and biggest blind bet that permits multiple blind bets.

Straight. Five cards in sequence of mixed suits such as 5,6,7,8,9.

Straight Flush. Five cards of the same suit in sequence.

Streak. A run of good or bad luck.

String Bet. A method of betting that's considered illegal in most high-stakes Poker games. It's a bet in which the amount of the bet is placed into the pot piecemeal. The player places a part of the bet into the pot, then hesitates, and then completes the remainder of the bet. It's considered to be illegal because during the hesitation the player making the string bet can observe the reaction of the other active players.

Stripped Deck. A deck with certain cards removed, such as the 40-card Italian deck in which the eights, nines and tens have been removed from the deck.

Strippers. Crooked decks in which high cards are trimmed narrow, low cards wide in the middle. The cheat uses them to cut when betting on high card. Otherwise rarely used to cheat at Poker.

Stud. The large family of Poker games in which some cards are dealt face up and others face down.

Substitution. An exchange of cards. The player discards one or more cards and is dealt a like number of cards from the deck to replace them, or in some Poker variations, players exchange one or more cards.

Suits. The four sets of 13 cards each found in a standard Poker deck—clubs, diamonds, hearts, spades.

Swing. To declare high and low.

Table. The playing surface. Also a group of players.

Table Stakes. A betting limit in which the maximum bet is the amount of money or chips in front of the bettor. The bettor cannot bet more than the amount before him on the same round. After that amount is depleted, the player may bring out more money or chips, in between hands.

Table Talk. Idle chatter during play short of coffeehousing.

Tail. To follow someone.

Take a Bath. To lose heavily or go broke.

Tap-out. An expression used in Table Stakes which means "I'm betting all the remaining money or chips I have in front of me."

Telegraph. To give away unknowingly the fact that a cheating move is about to be made, usually by some clumsy preparatory action or by a change in attitude.

Tell. A giveaway trait of players. This can be physical, psychological or intuitive. "Joe's 'tell' is lighting up a cigarette whenever he's trying a bluff."

Third Street. The third card dealt to each player in various forms of Stud Poker.

Tie. Two or more winning hands of the same value requiring the pot to be split.

Tight Player. A player who seldom bets unless he holds a strong hand.

Toke (or Token). A slang expression for the word "tip."

Top (Off the). The gross handle of a game or gambling scheme. "Take the expenses off the top."

Total Ante. The total amount anted by all the Poker players.

Touch. (1) A loan. (2) To borrow money. (3) A Score.

Trap. A bet that is not what it appears to be.

Trey. Any three-spot card.

Trim. To fleece, gyp, clip, beat, etc.

Trims. Crooked cards gaffed by trimming some cards one way and the others another way.

Trips. Three of a kind. Also called "triplets."

Turn. A player's proper time to drop out, check, raise, reraise or call.

Turn Down. To fold or drop out.

Two Pairs. A hand containing two pairs of different rank and a fifth card.

Two-Way Call. A declaration of both high and low in any variation of High-Low Poker, rules permitting.

Two-Way Hand. A Poker hand that has a possibility of winning both the high and the low in a pot.

Underbet. To make as small a bet as the rules permit. This is done when a player holds a poor hand and he's hoping to better it on the draw. Often done when holding a good hand to entice an opponent to raise.

Underdog. Said of a player who has little chance to win at Poker. "He's a 40 to 1 underdog to win this year's Las Vegas World Series Hold Em Championship."

Under the Gun. The position of the first player to act in a Poker game.

Unlimited Poker. Most Poker authors describe Unlimited Poker as a game in which no betting limits exist and a player can bet any amount he desires.

This is strictly poppycock. There is no such Poker game. In fact, there is no casino or gambling venture anywhere that permits unlimited bets.

Unpaid Shill. Poker-room operators' term describing a Poker player who is the first to open the game and the last to quit.

Up. (1) The act of anteing. (2) The higher of two pairs such as "aces up."

Upcard (or Cards). The face-up card or cards legally dealt in Stud and its variants. Also called "open cards."

Uphill. *See* Chase.

Velvet. Money that has been won.

Vigorish, Viggerish or Vig. A percentage extracted from the pot or an hourly charge taken by the Poker game operator to enable the house to make a profit on the game. Also known as a "rake-off" or "cut." "I wouldn't play Poker in that joint because the vigorish is so high it breaks all the players."

Wave. (1) To bend the edge of a card during play for identification purposes. "I caught that card cheater waving the corner of the ace." (2) The bend itself.

Way Off. Imperfect or incorrect. "You're way off when you say that big pot last night held $15,000 in cash."

Welsher. One who does not honor his gambling debts.

Wheel. *See* Bicycle.

Whipsawed. Sandwiched in between two players (possibly confederates) who are reraising each other back and forth.

Wild Card. A card that the holder can use to represent any card; *see also* Bug.

Wild Game. Any form of Poker in which one or more cards are wild.

Window. The card that the player purposely or inadvertently exposes at the end of his Draw Poker hand.

Window's Open (the). The cheating is being done ineptly.

Wired. When the hole card and the first upcard in Five Card Stud or a variant are of the same rank, they are said to be "wired" or "back to back."

Work. (1) Crooked cards. (2) The gaff itself.

X (the). The control of all the illegally operated Poker clubs in town. "The Irish mob has the X on the Poker games."

Yard. $100.

Zinger. A stare at a player in an attempt to put a so-called hex on him, causing him to throw his winning hand into the discard pile prior to the showdown. My friend Ben "Evil Eye" Finkle (the inventor of the Zinger) once hit a Poker-playing opponent with the Zinger and won the pot with a pair of deuces after his opponent threw in his four aces.

Zing It In. To bet heavily.

Zombie. An expert Poker player who shows no emotion either when winning or losing big money. "You can't spot any of his giveaways. He plays like a zombie."

Index